Camila's Story

MIRROR BOOKS

1

Published in Great Britain and Ireland in 2025 by
Mirror Books, a Reach PLC business,
5 St Paul's Square, Liverpool, L3 9SJ.

www.mirrorbooks.co.uk
@TheMirrorBooks

Print ISBN 9781917439442
eBook ISBN 9781917439459

Design and production by Mirror Books.

Printed and bound in Great Britain by
CPI Group (UK) Ltd, Croydon, CR0 4YY

Cover image: Adobe Stock
(Posed by model)

This book was printed using
FSC approved materials.

MIX
Paper | Supporting
responsible forestry
FSC® C013604
FSC
www.fsc.org

THROWN AWAY **CHILDREN**

Camila's Story

Louise Allen

with Theresa McEvoy

MIRROR BOOKS

Acknowledgements

Catherine Lloyd, Alex Plowman and Karen Furse are always the first readers of the manuscript, and I'm grateful for all their suggestions.

The cases I reveal in my books are all based on true experiences, but I have changed names and some details to protect their identities as they go on to build new lives and families of their own.

PART ONE

I

Gabby

'Smile!'

Robbie slings his arm around Gabriella's shoulders. The happy couple pose obligingly outside the campervan – an engagement gift from her parents. Marjory clicks away with her iPhone, taking photographs from every possible angle.

'Right, move sideways so we can see the front of it,' Marjory directs.

It's not just any old campervan. The cream-coloured Volkswagen has the classic split-screen so beloved of enthusiasts and has been immaculately restored; it's an Instagrammer's dream, especially in this sunshine, parked at an angle by the corner of the grand steps leading up to the house, with Marjory's peonies just coming into bloom behind to complete the picture.

More poses, more smiles.

'Now open up the side door so we can see all the gear in the interior.'

Inside the van, nestled next to a portable BBQ and supply of coal, is a brand-new wicker hamper, filled to the brim with organic food from the farm shop, plus the bottle of Champagne that was gifted by Robbie's mum, snug inside a cute little cooling jacket that Marjory has lent to them. Though she spotted it when they were packing, Gabby has chosen to ignore the old-school stash tin wedged beneath the fresh asparagus, which she knows contains Robbie's bit of weed for the trip. The cupboards are filled with more goodies and the little fridge is well-stocked with beer and French rosé, plus plenty of tonic to go with the gin, Gabby's preferred tipple.

One cupboard is full of shoes: mostly Gabby's.

They climb aboard, close the doors and wave goodbye to Gabriella's parents.

'Don't do anything we wouldn't do,' John calls out, with a wink.

Gabby wonders if there's an age at which dads stop embarrassing their daughters. She's 22 and he's been doing it for as long as she can remember, so probably not.

She winds down the window and sticks her tongue out at him, as if she is still the cheeky 10-year-old who sat on his lap.

He makes a mock-horror face, playing the same game.

'Bye, Dad! Bye, Mum! Love you!'

Gabby waves as Robbie begins to pull away down the drive. Then she flips down the sun visor to check her hair in the mirror, smoothing down the fringe-trimmed fabric of her cream dress at the same time. She is nailing the boho look and is the height of 'festival chic', at least according to the glossy images in the fashion magazines. While Robbie looks the epitome of the laid-back surfer dude in his *Rip Curl* shorts and *Patagonia* shirt, a perfect sartorial match for the two surfboards strapped to the top of the van. As well as the surfboards on the roof, two mountain bikes are attached to the rear of the camper. Almost all of it is new. Her parents have been most generous, as they always are.

They have everything they could possibly need for their adventure to Cornwall. The drive will take about six hours in their little van, which they've named Nir-van-a. Gabby's choice, but a nod to Robbie's musical tastes and a pun that all their friends appreciate.

'This is the life, eh?' Robbie reaches over and puts his hand on her knee.

She smiles back at him. Her fiancé still looks exactly as he did when they were first at school together: clean-cut and baby-faced. She likes to think of Robbie as a bit of a 'bad boy', although he has never put a foot wrong in either her or her parents' company. But he's always seemed cool because of his love of skateboarding and his occasional dabbles with graffiti art.

Robbie gives a final beep-beep of the horn as they pass through the electric gates at the top of the drive, before the gates begin to close automatically behind them.

And they are away.

Maybe she thinks of Robbie as edgy because his upbringing has been so different to hers. While they haven't always enjoyed the kind of wealth they do now, her parents have always made a point of giving Gabby the very best they can afford. Robbie's childhood couldn't have been more different. He grew up in a council house, where his parents drank a lot and neglected him. Then, when his dad died, Robbie's mum started a 12-step programme and seems to have sorted herself out a bit, but she still relies on benefits. They joke that he was 'dragged up' while she was nurtured and indulged. It's probably why they get on so well – because they are such opposites.

'You sure you don't mind me driving?' Robbie says. 'I mean, I feel like it's really your van, coming from your parents.'

'It's *our* van. It's a gift to both of us. And I'm more than happy for you to drive. I'm not too sure about manoeuvering it around. It's bigger than my Audi! And anyway, it gives me a chance to put my feet up and relax.'

Gabby does indeed have her feet on the dashboard, having already kicked off her Birkenstocks into the footwell. Her recently-pedicured pink toenails match the pale pink of the suede sandals, and are also the same shade as her fingernails.

'Lucky us. Isn't this just perfect?' Gabby sighs.

Her weather app confirms that the good weather is set to stay for at least the next few days. Perfect for sun, sea, surf and sex.

Even better, they won't have to spend all their time living in the campervan, fabulous though it undoubtedly is. Marjory has booked them into a couple of bijoux hotels and some interesting Airbnb places for a few nights to break up the trip.

Her mother knows her so well! Gabby is very excited by all the camping adventures, but will definitely want a comfy bed, a warm bath and a hair wash every few days. They've planned their route carefully so that they can stop off at different beaches on the way.

'Time for some tunes. Listen to this!' Robbie fires up

something loud with incomprehensible lyrics. Gabby smiles and nods along, although the beats do nothing much for her. She much prefers vintage Take That, who she went to see with her mum in London last year, or Taylor Swift. But she doesn't say so, knowing that Robbie's musical tastes are far more sophisticated than hers.

After they've been driving for an hour or so, Gabby brings the conversation gently round to their relationship.

'This really is an opportunity for us to just, like, spend some quality time one-on-one. We don't often have that, you know?'

Robbie is leaning into the steering wheel like a trucker. 'Yeah, babe. I'm looking forward to that, too. Can't wait to get to the first campsite and get cooking up the sausages your mum got from that farm shop. They are totally boss.'

She hates it when he talks so 'street', and he looks like he's only half-listening to her. Gabby wants to talk about them as a couple, the next steps in their relationship, begin planning in earnest for the wedding. Not the bloody sausages in the cool box.

'We'll have time to think about the wedding. How to make it perfect. We should, you know, set an actual date.'

'And we could also just enjoy being engaged for five minutes!'

There is a lull in the conversation. Gabby soon fills it.

'I wonder if Taz and Zoe will ever get engaged. Do you think they're serious enough?'

Taz is Robbie's best mate. He's a permanent fixture. Taz has been the one solid thing in Robbie's life from the moment the two of them first met at nursery. Partners in crime. Robbie's mum let them roam free, or wasn't sober enough to notice what they were up to. The way Robbie tells it, she was happy for Taz to stay round as often as he liked, or for Robbie to disappear to Taz's house. The boys are more like brothers than best friends, which gets to her sometimes, even though she doesn't really like to admit to herself how much their closeness and longer shared history bother her. The 'boy-stuff'. They skateboarded together in regional competitions, did stunt-biking, surfing and inline skating. Things that Gabby has *zero*-interest in. But she's going to give this surfing malarkey her best shot. As far as she knows, Taz doesn't surf. Although no doubt he'd be excellent at it if he did; he's good at all sports.

Gabby tells herself to stop thinking about Taz. After all, she has Robbie all to herself for two whole weeks as they travel through Devon and down to Cornwall. It will be bliss.

'I don't know if I mentioned it, but I reckon that Cornwall is going to be the place to get my tattoo.'

Gabby flinches at this, just as she did the other day when he first brought up the subject of tattoos. They aren't really her bag. Her job as a junior accountant in the insurance firm where she did her apprenticeship has only reinforced her conservative attitudes. She lives up to her workplace nickname of 'Little Miss Sensible', has embraced it, even, and can't quite get her head around her fiancé having a tattoo.

'We could get matching ones, if you're up for it.'

'Maybe.'

'That's my girl!'

It's not a totally ridiculous idea. It would be a real statement of their love. Gabby begins to soften. 'I don't really know where I'd put a tattoo, though.'

She begins to survey her body to see where the most discreet location for a partner-tattoo might be. She decides that her ankle might be a good place. Robbie sings along to the music some more while Gabby flicks through her phone, googling 'small sexy tattoos'.

Generally, areas with more fat and muscle tissue, like the upper arm, forearm, thigh, and back, are considered less painful for tattoos.

Hmm. She doesn't like the sound of that. Perhaps she should go for the thigh. It can't be her arms, as they are often on show at work in the summer, especially as she does upper-body at the gym. She's quite proud of the tone she's managed to achieve there. More than Zoe, anyway. Zoe dropped out of university and now works in *Fat Face* which, in Gabby's opinion, doesn't really count as a 'proper' job. Taz is besotted with Zoe, which means that they see quite a lot of her. If Gabby's completely honest with herself, her arms are probably bigger than Zoe's, but definitely, definitely more toned, and she knows which she prefers.

'Rob, do you find Zoe attractive? Be honest.'

'Hmmm?'

'Zoe. Do you think she's fit?'

'Gabs, my love, you know I think you are the most beautiful woman in the entire universe. I haven't ever thought about Zoe that way. She's just Taz's girl. I don't ever think about other women. Why would I?'

Gabby raises her eyebrows at him in a pouty 'I don't believe you' face.

Robbie ups his declaration. 'Babe. Why are you even asking me this? You are, without doubt, the sexiest, most beautiful woman I have ever met and I am so fucking lucky to have you.'

This is exactly what Gabby needs to hear. She nods, satisfied. For a short time, at least.

The long road stretches ahead.

As they drive through little towns with strange names, Gabby enters into one of her favourite daydreams: imagining the wedding and her future. A perfect future with Robbie. It has only ever been Robbie. She hasn't been with anyone else before.

But Robbie has, and she hates that he wasn't a virgin when they met. It seems unequal, when she has given herself to him. She tries to bat the thoughts away, but sometimes, like today, they refuse to go. She will always have to live with the fact that her man has been with someone before her. She knows who it was, another girl at school. Thankfully, She-Who-Will-Not-Be-Named moved away from the area years ago and got married very young.

And she already has children.

Something Gabby wants more than anything.

II

Gabby

They are four days into Gabby and Robbie's #SouthWestTour, as Gabby is enjoying tagging it on all her social media channels, when Robbie receives a text message from Taz.

'Fucking A!'

Gabby doesn't need him to say another word; she can guess what it is from the way that he can't contain his excitement.

'Listen to this! *Mate, we're in Newquay, Fistral beach until Sunday, fucking great, eh? Surf and beers up!*'

Gabby sighs. Robbie beams like a schoolboy getting ready to go out to play.

'Did you know Taz was coming down this way before we arranged our trip?'

Gabby knows the answer. It's *because* of their trip. Taz will have had the idea of joining them and then they will have hatched a plan between them, no doubt about it.

'Oh, Gabs. Let's meet up with the crew on Friday night, camp out and surf till Sunday, yeah?'

Friday is one of the hotel nights that her mum has pre-booked for them, and it looks to be one of the nicest ones, right on the beachfront with a restaurant that opens out onto the water. And anyway, Gabby doesn't want to spend the weekend with Taz and the twats. This is supposed to be their special time; time for her and Robbie alone. She wants a romantic weekend with her fiancé. Maybe one which involves them finally setting an actual date for their marriage, a conversation that Robbie continues to manage to dodge.

She reminds Robbie about the booking, leaving out the part about the magical, romantic setting. Her bottom lip wobbles and a few tears leak out. She doesn't want them to, but she has worked so hard to make this engagement trip perfect. Robbie spends loads of time with Taz when they're home, why does he have to come and gatecrash this, too?

Robbie leans over to her and kisses her on the forehead. 'You don't have to come, baby. You have a nice, relaxing night at the hotel. I'll see the boys then catch you after.'

This is not the response Gabby expected. Nor is it anywhere close to what she wants. It would be *awful* to sit in a restaurant all by herself. It would be lonely and embarrassing. Why doesn't he understand that? The whole point is to be there *as a couple*. Why is he being so insensitive?

But she doesn't want to ruin the mood of their trip, and she doesn't want to be a nag. Robbie is so clearly thrilled at the prospect of meeting up with Taz that she decides to control herself, to not explode. It's one night, after all. No reason to fly off the handle and potentially drive Robbie away.

That is not the way a good wife would behave, and she wants so much to be that.

She wants a loving marriage, she wants to be a parent, she

wants stability. She has it all planned out. In her perfect vision of the future she wants to live no more than a mile or two from her parents. Soon enough she will have Robbie all to herself, so she can put up with him having a night or two with his mates in the meantime. She doesn't want to be the killjoy, the nagging bride-to-be. So, she pulls herself together and, with fake cool, smiles at him.

'Yeah, you're right. That will be fun. It will be great to see them all. Let's go together.'

Besides, there is no way she is going to give Robbie any opportunity to spend time with Zoe, who will almost certainly be there and is so much better at 'being one of the boys' than Gabby is.

She calls the hotel. There is enough time to arrange a cancellation without a fee. Her mum will understand. Anyway, she is busy with her own plans and making the most of the time while Gabby and Robbie are away. She and her dad are in Spain, looking at buying a second home out there.

Gabby reminds herself that she needs to be kind. She is the lucky one with a supportive family. Robbie hasn't had all the life opportunities that she has. This is his holiday, too. As an only child and the apple of her parents' eyes, she knows she has lived like a princess. She has wanted for nothing. But she has always tried to be aware of that privilege, make sure that she doesn't take it for granted. She knows only too well that not every little girl gets to have a pony.

Besides, her parents have also worked hard to make sure that she is grounded. Gabby went to the local secondary school, a bog-standard comprehensive. When they were first looking at choosing schools, her parents didn't have the money to send her to a private school. But even if they had, it wouldn't have been their first choice. Both Gabby's parents are themselves from down-to-earth families who worked hard for their successes.

They were never badly off when Gabby was little, but the real money came later, when her father, a builder, took the plunge and went into business on his own. They could never have predicted the meteoric rise of his construction company, which builds quality homes on small plots of land, four or five units at a time. Now he is a real contender in the building market. He isn't competing with the big boys like Barratt or Taylor Wimpey homes. They're not quite in that league. Her dad is just a good businessman who knows his market and has had some lucky breaks over the years. These days he buys up big back gardens or small fields and builds hamlets. Nice houses. Proper homes. He's well known and well-respected in the area for doing good work. The firm has a good reputation.

Marjory is also no stranger to hard work. Her mum used to work in retail before Gabby was born. Then, when Gabby was old enough to go to school, her mum helped to run the family construction business. They have always worked hard and are now enjoying the fruits of their labours, living a good life. Gabby has had everything she could ever have wanted, including lots of love from both sides of her family.

All the things that Robbie hasn't.

Anyway, there are still a few more days of the trip to go whilst it's still just the two of them. Gabby makes sure that the days are lazy and carefree, fun and full of great sex. If she is a sexual goddess, the supplier of orgasms, Robbie will always be good to her. He won't be so keen to go running off to Taz...

Lying on their sunloungers, she walks her fingers down Robbie's hot, tanned back.

'Mmmm,' she murmurs. 'Again. I want it again.'

Robbie obliges. He is a very considerate lover.

Sunshine and a bit of a tan is definitely making Gabby feel sexier, and the close proximity of vanlife together has brought them even closer emotionally as well as physically. How could it not? Gabby convinces herself that their love is growing stronger by the day. She is trying really hard to be adventurous, joining Robbie on cycle rides and long walks, even though she'd prefer to lie in the sun and top up her tan.

By Friday morning, the day they are due to meet up with Taz, Gabby is beginning to feel a little less concerned about the fact that he is gatecrashing their romantic getaway. They pack up the camper, a task which is becoming easier as they grow more familiar with the routine. They both have their little jobs to do. Robbie sorts out all the electrics and packs away the equipment, she makes sure all the washing up is done and everything is packed inside the van ready for the off.

They park the camper in a car park right near the beach that Taz has suggested. They can see Taz's car parked a little way away.

'Excellent! Taz is already here,' Robbie says, taking the key from the ignition.

'Excellent,' Gabby echoes, though less enthusiastically than her fiancé.

She recognises a few more of their friends' cars. Perhaps it would be more honest to say they are Robbie's friends. Gabby has a couple of associates at work that she goes out with occasionally, but otherwise their social life revolves entirely around Robbie's scene. It's always been that way. His friends are just cooler than hers. She laces her fingers through his as they walk onto the beach together, to a chorus of 'wassups' from the gathered group. Tins of lager and cider are already strewn on the sand, and there are large sharing packets of crisps opened out on a flattish rock.

Gabby watches Robbie and Taz hug and knows that she has done the right thing. They are genuinely so pleased to see each other. He will have a great night. She can put up with it all for a few hours. The other men welcome Robbie with pats on the back and thrust a can of cider into his hands.

Gabby stands awkwardly. You don't need to be Sherlock Holmes to work out that she is the only woman at this exclusive beach gathering. There's no sign of Zoe, or any other girlfriends. Just her. No one for her to talk to. Why didn't he mention that? Perhaps she should have stayed out of the way at the hotel after all. Still, at least she can be here to look after Robbie later, when he's had too much to drink and smoke.

She sits down on a towel that's crusty with dried salt water and sweeps away the sand from her legs.

'Get your laughing gear round that,' one of the men says, tearing a tin of lager from its plastic six-pack ring and handing it to her. She recognises him from a few BBQs and house parties back at home, but can't remember his name.

'Great, thanks.' She smiles and just in time manages to prevent herself from asking if there's a glass – to stop her looking like an idiot. She contemplates going to get a glass from the campervan, but then decides to just get over herself and does indeed 'get her laughing gear' around the can.

The men sit facing the sea and begin impenetrable

conversations. They plan their surfing, laugh at things that aren't funny, talk about girls, skim stones into the waves.

Gabby scrolls through her phone, grinning and bearing it while sulking on the inside. She is surplus to requirements here. It's hard not to revert to a six-year-old version of herself, but she will control herself, for her fiancé's sake.

III

Gabby

When the fortnight is up and Nir-van-a is trundling up the driveway back to her house with Robbie at the wheel, Gabby suddenly feels blue. It's great to reach home and she is very much looking forward to her own bed, but her parents are away and it also feels like the adventure is over. She wants to keep the holiday going and, remembering how much Robbie enjoyed his beach night with Taz and the boys, suggests having some friends over to her parents' house.

'We should make the most of having the house to ourselves while they're still in Spain.'

Robbie practically lives at Gabby's house these days. Neither set of parents minds this arrangement. Robbie's younger brother and sister are still at home, so it's one less to clean up after as far as Robbie's mother is concerned. John and Marjory are generous hosts, delighted to see their daughter settled and content and very happy to welcome Robbie into their family home.

'Great idea, babe.'

It's totally the house for entertaining. Her parents have a heated pool and jacuzzi with a purpose-built party area. Her father has put his building skills to good use and also installed an outdoor bar and kitchen. A huge white sail awning keeps the rain off, but the weather is still set fair, so it won't even be needed.

Robbie is still nodding enthusiastically. 'It'll be nice to see some of the guys again. It's been intense, just the two of us.'

'Intense? What do you mean *intense?*' Gabby has enjoyed the second week of the holiday much more, once the encounter with Taz and 'the lads' was behind them and she and Robbie could concentrate on each other. They still haven't set a wedding date, which somehow makes her feel less 'engaged', in spite of the ring on her finger.

'I mean *good* intense. You know I can't get enough of you to myself. But it'd be nice to have a crowd over now we're back. You're right. As always.' He nuzzles her neck and pulls her down to sit on his lap.

They make a little guest list together. As always, it's mostly made up of Robbie's friends, and Taz and Zoe are top of the list. Then a few more of the couples in their crowd. Ten people in total.

Gabby sends Robbie to the village butcher to collect a pile of steaks and burgers, then to the farm shop to pick up salad vegetables from the list she has made.

'Take my car, if you like.'

Gabby's white Audi is parked on the drive next to the campervan. Robbie's blue transit van that he uses for work is parked alongside.

'Actually, I'll take mine,' Robbie says, grabbing the keys.

'Good job. I'll unpack those,' she says, when he returns. 'I've got another list for you.'

'We can feed the five thousand from this lot! What else do we need?'

Booze, snacks and nibbles, it turns out.

'You'll be able to get it all in Waitrose.'

'I don't know why I can't just go to Lidl. It's the same stuff and much cheaper. Half the price, probably. Who'll know when we've tipped it all into bowls?'

'I will.'

The first part of the evening goes very well, oiled with plenty of prosecco for the girls and beer for the boys.

Robbie is ably assisted at the BBQ by Taz, and after everyone has eaten their fill, the pair make a little production line of spliffs to pass around. Gabby shakes her head gently when one reaches her, though she's the only one to pass; everyone else has a hit. She doesn't need it, she learnt a long time ago that it only makes her feel tired. Still, everyone else seems to enjoy it, so she tries to be tolerant. They all become super-mellow, then start laughing. Gabby doesn't understand the joke, but they seem to be having a good time and she is the host, after all, so she goes with the flow and joins in with the laughter.

Taz turns up the music. 'Time for some dancing!'

Gabby doesn't particularly like dancing, either. She'd rather turn the tunes down a bit and talk quietly to some of the people there; not that many of them are capable of talking after smoking all the weed, but she smiles and joins in. It wouldn't do for the host to kill the party vibe.

Robbie takes off his shorts and shirt and, stripped down to his underpants, jumps into the pool with a loud whoop. This starts a lemming-like procession of bodies behind him. Gabby is the only one to stay dry. There is no novelty for her in jumping into a pool that is there all the time, and certainly not at this time of the evening when it's almost dark.

'Someone's got to fetch the towels,' she jokes, good-naturedly, heading off to grab a pile from her parents' airing cupboard.

When she comes back, she can't help noticing that Zoe is dressed in pristine white underwear that looks even better than a bikini on her slender body. She glances at Robbie. How can he *not* notice this goddess dripping next to him? She does her best to ignore the little stab of jealousy and thrusts a towel at Zoe.

'Here. You must be freezing.'

When they are all dry again, it's more prosecco and more beer.

The garden looks beautiful, lit up with the discreet solar LED lantern system that John has designed, augmented by the light from dozens of candle flames reflected in their glass cloches which Gabby has been lighting while their guests were still in the pool. Everyone looks relaxed and happy. There is singing and laughter and Gabby knows that the little gathering is a perfect success.

Taz turns down the music, grabs an empty prosecco glass to tap his keys against, and clears his throat.

'I've got an announcement to make.'

Nine heads turn towards him.

He leans forward in his chair and holds Zoe's hand.

'I'm delighted to say that this beautiful woman has agreed to be my wife!'

There are woohoos and cheers of joy and support. Gabby

joins in with the well-wishing and congratulations, even though she feels a little empty inside, for reasons that she can't explain, even to herself. 'Wow, that's – wonderful.'

The words sound hollow, even to her own ears.

Robbie shoots a look at her. 'You okay, Gabby?'

'Fine!' she says firmly, with a smile. 'It's wonderful news. I'm so happy for you both.'

How easy it is to lie. And why can't she just be happy for them?

Gabby ensures that her smile stays firmly fixed in place as Zoe tells the story of how Taz went down on one knee while they were in a restaurant. It was all planned beforehand. The staff were already in on it.

'So they were on standby with the Champagne!' Taz can't help himself as he joins in with her story. Their excitement is evident as they overlap each other in the telling.

'All the diners clapped! I felt like I was in a movie.'

Zoe shows off her ring to the assembled company. It's beautiful. A sapphire that matches Zoe's blue eyes, with a little ring of diamonds around it. It glints in the moonlight. Gabby wonders how she didn't notice it before.

'It's an antique,' Zoe says, proudly.

'Which is a way of saying that it was cheaper than buying a brand new one,' Taz jokes, and everyone laughs.

Gabby stares down at her own engagement ring. Zoe's could only have cost a couple of hundred pounds at best. Robbie dutifully spent a month's wages on hers. Somehow that knowledge isn't enough to console her or compensate for the fact that Zoe has stolen the limelight at Gabby's party. Gabby and Robbie don't have a similar 'fun' story to tell about their engagement, with everyone clapping at the moment she said yes. Because they have been together forever and it was always a matter of when, not if, for them, they just kind of slid into 'being' engaged, egged on by her parents.

'Great party, Rob!' Everyone congratulates Robbie on the way out, as if she hasn't spent hours decorating the place and making sure that everyone is happy. The lack of appreciation only makes Gabby feel worse.

When everyone has gone, she goes into the house to fetch a bin liner for the empties, while Robbie crashes out on a sunlounger. Why does everything good turn out so badly? Why does she feel so rubbish after what should have been a lovely party? Gabby takes her frustration out on the empties as she gathers them all up in bin bags. The noise of breaking glass as empty bottles are hurled against one another drowns out the sound of Robbie's snoring.

IV

Robbie

'How was the trip, then?'

Robbie looks at his mother, at the pile of dirty dishes swimming in greasy water in the sink, and at their tired kitchen with its broken units, grubby cupboard doors hanging off their hinges. It's only walking back in like this after a few weeks away that he really notices it all with fresh eyes. It's a world away from the inch-perfection of John and Marjory's place. He wishes he could give his mum a fraction of what Gabby's family have.

'Yeah, Mum. It was great. Sand, sea, surf.'

'And another word beginning with 's', I expect,' she says with a knowing raised eyebrow. 'So the wedding's still on, is it?'

Robbie has been with Gabby for years. From time to time, part of him wonders if they may not be right for each other, and comments like this one from his mum don't help, but whenever he feels worried about their relationship, he reminds himself that it's been seven years since they first got together, and that's what they say, isn't it? The seven-year-itch.

He makes a mental note to try to fix the kitchen up a

bit when he has time. Robbie trained as a carpenter after he left school at 16. He was lucky and walked straight into an apprenticeship. His mum went through a really low point when his dad died in a car accident shortly before Robbie met Gabby. His mum had always enjoyed a drink, but in her grief it became a crutch until she sorted herself out. It was a tough few years for Robbie and his brother and sister. The house fell apart a bit for a while. Robbie spent as much time away from the house as he could, hanging out with Taz, because that was easier than seeing his mum fall apart or being roped into taking care of his siblings.

But he could do something about the house now. Help his mum to fix it up a bit. He's got the tools as well as the skills. And he probably has his father to thank for that.

His dad had been an electrician and made no secret of the fact that he believed in trade over higher education.

'You'll never be poor if you've got a trade,' he'd told Robbie, despite what New Labour were banging on about at the time. He can still hear his dad's voice in his head, beginning a political rant, even though he's been dead a decade.

'That Tony Blair's a con man. Education, Education, Education, my arse. Debt, Debt, Debt is what that really means. And where are all these jobs for hundreds of forensic scientists and events managers?'

It's funny how he can't shake off the values of his parents, even though Robbie moves in a very different orbit now with Gabby.

His dad was adamant that not everyone was meant for university. It was the privilege of only a few. 'And who keeps the country going while all the media graduates are working in

McDonald's? Getting that many students into university to do crap courses is a way of brainwashing them into debt.'

Gabby didn't go to university either. She went straight into the world of work after A-Levels, even though she was smart enough to go.

He wonders if his dad would have liked Gabby more than his mum does. Robbie misses his dad. He could do with his advice about what to do about the next stage of his life. Lately he's been thinking a lot about the future. He earns decent money and loves his work, but sometimes he worries that he's losing touch with his roots.

He loves Gabby, adores her, even. But he worries that they might just be too young to be settling down. At 23, Robbie feels as if the world should be his oyster. He's always dreamed of travelling, ever since he and Taz started skateboarding and doing the competitions years ago. They'd have sleepovers, eat pizza and watch *The Big Wednesday;* dream about surfing and living that laidback life. The time away with Gabby has kind of reignited some of that. Sleeping in Nir-van-a, falling out of bed onto the beach, getting the buzz for surfing. It's all been great. But Gabby didn't love the campervan experience as much as he did. She needed the little hotel breaks in between. It would have been more fun to go with Taz, but that's a ridiculous thought to have. It's time to be grown up about these things. It's not Gabby's fault that she doesn't love surfing and biking as much as he does. She tries.

He worries that marriage will mean losing his freedom. But growing up means responsibility. That's the sacrifice he will have to make. It's the sacrifice everyone makes.

He envies Taz and Zoe and the way they are about each

other. Taz seems so much more relaxed about getting married, but then Zoe is more chilled and probably has less lavish tastes than Gabby. Zoe's background is closer to Robbie's. When he first knew Gabby, at 16, he believed she was out of his league. They were in the same year at school, so he'd been aware of her for a few years, but their paths had never crossed properly. She was one of the rich kids. You could tell because she had that long, perfectly straight hair, and the kind of confidence that only comes with money. But he got to know her at a house party in the village. Robbie remembers that he had been keen on a different girl then, a girl called Lottie who dressed like Pink and was totally different to Gabby.

But Gabby, whom he'd never really taken seriously because she was so straight, was into him. She made a play and he couldn't believe his luck. Taz told him he was punching above his weight. So he regularly reminds himself how lucky he is to have Gabby.

'You staying here tonight?' his mum asks, interrupting his thoughts.

Robbie nods.

He needs a night at home. The truth is that things haven't been great with Gabby since the party. She's been very upset and has made his life difficult over the last few days. She's sad that Robbie has never actually *asked* her to marry him. They are engaged, technically, but there was no drama to it. They just sort of decided that getting married was the next step and suddenly there were campervans and congratulations and bottles of Champagne and trips away. Robbie can kind of see Gabby's point. Taz and Zoe's version of things sounded much cooler.

And the key thing is that Taz had *surprised* Zoe with the proposal. It's that element of surprise and romance that's missing from his and Gabby's version. Gabby wanted a better 'origin story'. And she deserved one. Robbie feels like he's let her down, and he needs to put it right.

The first stage is to approach John and 'ask' him, properly, for her hand in marriage. Underneath it all, Gabby is very traditional, and she would like things to be done the traditional way. Of course she would.

Then he needs to make some sort of romantic proposal. Ideally in a place that is nice and public so that there's an audience for their special moment. It isn't just a contract or a formalisation of their relationship. It needs to be the real deal. He's had a few ideas about how he could do it, and has taken the first step by organising a rendezvous with John, freshly returned from Spain, at the pub.

'Yes, I'm staying. But I'm going out for an hour or so first,' he tells his mum.

His mum raises a questioning eyebrow. 'You've only just got here!'

'And I'll be back. I've just got to pop and see a man about a dog.'

'Oh, yes?'

He doesn't tell his mum that he needs to go through the business of asking Gabby's father, formally, if he can marry his daughter. She wouldn't understand. Especially given that the old man already bought them a campervan as an engagement present. Nor will she think that buying a second engagement ring was a good idea. But Gabby has shown Robbie some links to the kind of ring that she'd really like to have. At an eye-watering sum.

The kind of money Robbie hadn't even known it was possible to spend on jewellery. But Gabby deserves the best.

His mum might understand the romance bit, though. He tries to explain about making a proper proposal and outlines his idea. He wants to do it in London, after watching a show.

'I've booked tickets for *Mamma Mia!* at the weekend. Not my thing, obviously, but Gabby'll love it. She loves the film.'

His mum purses her lips and then lets out a low whistle. 'Bet those tickets cost a pretty penny on a Saturday afternoon in London!'

Robbie smiles thinly. It's true that he's now down to using credit cards to pay for everything. His salary just doesn't come anywhere near to covering his outgoings at the moment. He spent a fortune on stuff for the party which has come at the end of an expensive trip.

'Yeah, well. It doesn't matter what it costs. I want it to be perfect.'

'You'll always be broke as long as you're with that one – you know that, don't you?'

'Can't you just be happy for me, Mum?'

'I'll be happy when you are,' she replies, pausing just long enough to let that comment sink in before she carries on. 'So, tell me, what was the last engagement all about, then? Haven't you just come back from your engagement trip? Or am I missing something?'

'That was just to become engaged. We made a formal commitment to each other to stay together, sort of thing. This is to actually get married. Set a date and that.'

She shakes her head. 'If you say so, but it's beyond me. That's normal is it? To have two engagements?'

'It is if you're Gabby.'

As he is saying the words he knows it sounds as stupid as it actually is. But, somehow, Robbie knows it's the right thing to do to make sure that his beloved Gabby is happy.

'Hmmm. And am I expected to buy another gift? Because if I am, whatever it is, it won't be able to compete with a campervan.'

'Don't be daft.'

'I could say the same to you.'

In the pub with Gabby's father, Robbie orders the drinks. A pint of ale for John and a cider for himself. He wants to pay his way. He never wants John to think that he's freeloading. They stand at the bar while the drinks are being poured and chat about their respective holidays. John must be in his 50s, but he looks well on it, especially after the Spanish sunshine.

He is casually dressed in denim jeans and a white t-shirt. At first glance there is nothing remarkable about his clothes, just what must pass for standard fare on a building site beneath overalls or, as now, in the pub. But a second look reveals the sculpting cut of both, that leads the eye towards the discreet embroidered designer logos.

Robbie knows that John doesn't just wear it well. He buys it well. It would be nice to afford the best of everything one day, as John does.

When they are settled at a table, Robbie explains why he's asked to meet.

'Son, I'm over the moon, you know that. I can't think of anyone better for our girl. Cheers!'

They each take a sip of their drinks and there is a pause

before John continues. 'I have to say, though, I did think you'd already popped the question.'

'Well, not technically. We *became* engaged, if you know what I mean.'

'What Gabby wants, Gabby gets,' John says, with a wink.

'But I am going to do things the traditional way and propose properly. I've been thinking about how to do it and to make it perfect. So you mustn't say anything to her about this conversation until afterwards.'

'My lips are sealed,' John says, solemnly, taking another swig of his pint.

Robbie has picked out a spot on the Southbank of the River Thames, a place they went to years ago to look at the skateboarders. Back when Gabby was as enthusiastic about his dreams as he was. Robbie pushes that thought aside before it's allowed to take root. 'I think it will be perfect.'

'Well done, son. Sounds wonderful. She's lucky to have you. You've got my blessing. Of course.'

Robbie explains about the new ring.

John raises an eyebrow at the price. 'She's got expensive tastes that girl of mine. I tell you what, I don't mind putting a bit towards it to help you out. We don't want the young couple starting out married life in debt, do we?' Robbie begins to protest, but John slaps him on the back. 'I'll not hear a word more about it. I remember my roots, and I remember what life was like before my business took off. Now, my round!'

Robbie is a little embarrassed about the offer of financial help, but at the same time, he's grateful for it. His finances really have taken a battering lately and the second ring is *very* pricey.

He enjoys the second pint much more than the first.

It's Marjory who drops them at the station ready to catch the train for London at the weekend. She gives Robbie a little wink as she waves them off. Robbie is mortified.

In spite of himself, Robbie enjoys the show.

Gabby loves it, too, though she still prefers the film. 'And I'd love to go to Skiathos one day, where it was filmed!'

'Then, babe, I shall take you there!'

Robbie promises to start looking for a hotel in Skiathos. He hopes it won't be too expensive. But he can see how happy it will make Gabby. They go to Giraffe for dinner and afterwards, as they stroll the promenade along the riverbank, the evening is exactly how he pictured it. The weather is perfect, and there is a beautiful sunset. He can time this beautifully. There is just a slight chill in the air as the sun starts to go down, meaning that Gabby wants to wear his jacket. He drapes it over her shoulders. She loves that sort of chivalrous gesture. He takes that as his cue to go down on one knee, just outside the Royal Festival Hall.

It's bustling with tourists who begin to nudge one another and gather round in a circle. Suddenly they are centre-stage in a small crowd. Robbie swallows. He takes her hand and clears his throat.

'Gabriella, love of my life, would you do me the honour of becoming my wife?'

Gabby screams and cries – with what he hopes is happiness. He loves seeing her happy.

The onlookers clap and cheer and take photographs. One of them has videoed the proposal and shares the video with the happy couple.

Robbie is off the hook. Gabby has her origin story.

V

Robbie

Robbie gets out of the shower and steps onto a threadbare, greying bathmat that must have been white once. He puts on a clean shirt and trousers and heads over to Gabby's house. As he parks in the front drive, John steps out ready to welcome him in. He is smoking a Spanish cigar that he brought back duty-free. Robbie shakes his head when John offers him one.

The home of his soon-to-be-in-laws is looking more and more like a Spanish villa that's been transported from the Costa del Sol.

'Just trying to bring a taste of that sunshine back here!' John says, when Robbie comments on it.

It's no secret that they are super-keen to return to Spain at the earliest possible opportunity, 'Get away from all the grey weather as we head into autumn.'

But this late-September weekend has been fine and warm, and both John and Marjory are on good form.

'Our little girl is getting married!' Marjory repeats from time to time, clapping her hands together as if she is remembering it

31

afresh each time. 'That was a lovely touch, Robbie, you asking her father for her hand. Top marks!'

Gabby is wearing a long summer dress and is still tanned from their Cornish trip. She looks radiant. Robbie walks up to her and kisses her on the cheek. She holds out her hands, the first engagement ring is on the fourth finger of her right hand and the new one sits beautifully on her left.

Gabby's mum sighs and smiles at Robbie. 'Look at the sparkle on that rock. That's a good diamond, that is.'

It wants to be, for what it cost. Robbie is still smarting from having to part with such an absurd sum for something so small, even with John's very generous contribution to its purchase. Still, Gabby is pleased, and that's what matters.

Champagne is poured and glasses clink as toasts to the happy couple are made. When Marjory announces that supper is ready, they sit down at the table in the dining room with the bi-folds open. Although it's a fine night, there is a breeze that warrants inside-eating.

'You can just tell that the season's on the turn, can't you?' Marjory says, with a shiver. 'Not like in Spain.'

They tuck into the huge paella that Gabby's mum has made.

'This is excellent, Marjory,' Robbie says.

'I got the recipe from the chef at this restaurant we love over there. So it's authentic.' Marjory smiles. 'Always the charmer, aren't you, Robbie!'

Then Gabby's dad clears his throat and explains that he'd like to make a little announcement. 'So, Robbie, as you know, we are really happy that you are going to be the husband of our precious girl. We already love you as if you're our own son, and we know that you are the right man for her, Robbie. So, with that in mind, I want you to join my firm, work for me. I think you'll find my rates will be better than the ones you're currently on.'

He looks at Gabby. Did she know this was coming? She could have warned him.

'That's very kind of you, John,' Robbie says. He wants to explain how much he actually rather enjoys his job, but realises that his acceptance is taken as a done-deal when Gabby's mum follows up with, 'But there's more news. I'll just come out with it. We want to buy you both a house. We want you to have a good start in your married life together. We've got the money to do it now, and there's no point in it just sitting there in the bank. We might as well put it to good use. It'll be a bit of security for you both as you start a family. We're very much looking forward to becoming grandparents.'

Wow. They aren't even married yet and his future in-laws are already talking about babies.

'Give us a chance!' Robbie splutters, having just picked that moment to take a gulp of wine.

Their generosity is overwhelming. But only if he lets it become overwhelming. He listens to John explaining how delighted they are to be able to give them a helping hand up life's ladder. At the same time as panicking about the grown-upness of it all, he realises precisely what an opportunity is being offered to him. He'll never have to struggle again. He will have all the things that everyone seems to want in life: a wife, a new home – mortgage-free, and a solid career. Everything is being handed to him on a plate. That makes him a very lucky boy indeed.

Yes, it's responsibility. Of course it is. But it's also security, like Marjory says. And for someone who has grown up the way Robbie has, there's a lot which makes that attractive. He couldn't say no, even if he wanted to. John and Marjory are almost as much his family as his own mum is. He doesn't say no, because this is a dream come true: no mortgage, good pay, an adoring wife and good in-laws. Perhaps this is *the* dream, or at least it should be his new dream. The surfing and skateboarding were childish nonsense. Now he is really going to have it all. Robbie holds his Champagne glass up, joins in with another toast and smiles.

'Thank you. I'm so happy to be part of this family.'

Once the plates have been cleared, Gabby and her mum start looking in earnest at venues online. Everything is so expensive. Robbie tries not to notice the cost. He doesn't have to, after all. He won't have anything to do with that bit.

'It's traditional that the bride's family pays for the wedding,' John reassures him.

Robbie has never particularly been one for tradition, but for once he is glad of it! He can just see his mum's face if she was expected to contribute to these prices.

'So, do the happy couple have a date in mind?' John asks.

Robbie is just about to answer, 'No, not really,' when Gabby jumps in.

'Yes, we do. March.'

That's less than six months away, Robbie realises with a lurch. Is that long enough to plan a wedding? Don't they take, like, a year to organise?

'A spring wedding is perfect,' Marjory agrees.

He's about to suggest they leave it a little longer but then it dawns on him why Gabby might have picked the spring. Taz and Zoe have planned an early summer wedding and he'd put money on Gabby wanting to be first. Robbie breathes out slowly, but it must draw attention because John notices and puts his hand on Robbie's shoulder.

'You'll get used to it, son.'

John is right, he decides. And the path of least resistance is always the best way with Gabby. She has a way of getting what she wants, so he might as well go along with it rather than putting obstacles in the way.

Gabby pores over images of castles and country estates, while Gabby's dad gives Robbie another drink.

'And what do your family think of the forthcoming nuptials, Robbie?'

He wonders why John has to speak like that. Like he's a character in Shakespeare or something. 'Forthcoming nuptials.' Robbie can just imagine the snort of derision his mother would give to that. The truth is, his family aren't that impressed with the whole thing. They are so down on Gabby. They always have been. It makes him feel more protective of her. He doesn't understand why they seem so opposed to Gabby and her family. Robbie's younger sister, Jenny, sneered when she heard the news that they were actually getting married.

'Because, really, Robbie, you're worlds apart. It'll never last. She looks down on you. How many times has Princess Gabby been here in the last six years?'

'Don't call her that! And of course she doesn't look down on me.'

Robbie hasn't actually given Gabby's visits to his home that much thought until Jenny asked the question, but when he looks back he realises that Gabby hasn't set foot in his family home for a good three years or so now. But there's a very good reason for that. It makes sense that they stay at her folks' place, after all, they have much more room there and everything is much nicer. It's true that Gabby always finds an excuse to sit in the car and wait for him to come out rather than go inside but, given the reception his family give her, who can blame her?

But these are all things he doesn't really want to think about. Meanwhile, he can hardly say to Gabby's parents that his own family aren't keen on the union. It would sound rude.

'Oh, Mum's delighted,' Robbie says. A white lie. 'And I reckon my sister is jealous. I'll be the first one in the family to leave and get married. I think she thought it would be her first.'

'I was thinking, Robbie, knowing that your brother is also in the building trade, whether he might consider coming over to the family firm, as well? It could be good, two brothers working together. Keep it in the family!'

'Oh, thank you. I don't know. That's a generous invitation. I could ask him.'

It's another little white lie. Robbie does know; Simon would never consider working for John. He's already said as much.

'I wouldn't want to work for the squire. I wouldn't want to be in his pocket. You got to be your own man.'

'I'll let you know what he says.'

Marjory and Gabby decide that they've found the perfect place for the reception. It looks like a castle and is connected to some literary figure.

'So romantic!'

'And you'll have a church wedding, of course?'

It sounds like a question, but Robbie understands that it isn't. It feels as if big, important decisions are already being made without any input from him. John must see the look of panic on his face.

'Let the women have their way, Robbie. All the little details are important to them. What matters is that you're getting married. Another toast to the happy couple,' John says.

Robbie raises his glass automatically.

Things seem to be moving very fast.

VI

Gabby

It turns out that Gabby need not have been so hasty in choosing her wedding date after all.

Taz and Zoe announce that she is pregnant, so their wedding is being put back for now.

'We can't afford a wedding *and* a baby,' Taz explains, with a shrug. 'And we want to give our baby the best start we can. The wedding can wait for a while. It will give us longer to plan, anyway.'

Once again, congratulations flow for the happy couple.

Their news both pleases and frustrates Gabby.

On the one hand, all eyes will be on Gabby for the first wedding among their friendship group. She will be the only bride. The competition is gone.

On the other hand, Zoe seems to be garnering more attention as a mother-to-be than Gabby does as a mere bride-to-be.

Zoe already has a neat little bump on display. Gabby finds it bizarrely antagonising. Especially when she watches Taz hold his hand over the bump or stroke it gently, almost absent-mindedly, when he is seated next to her. They look so happy and comfortable together. And baby talk seems to have taken over from wedding talk. Everyone wants to know how Zoe is feeling, whether she's having any morning sickness, what kind of a birth she is planning, whether they've started on the nursery yet.

At each gathering where she is on the sidelines, Gabby feels more and more resentment towards Zoe for being pregnant first. It doesn't matter that she knows her feelings are totally irrational, there's nothing she can do about them. She can't control the way she feels. She tries to console herself with the knowledge that, unlike Zoe, she is doing things the right way round, the traditional way. Her child, when it comes, won't be illegitimate. In the eyes of God and the law, that makes Gabby the better woman.

But Zoe seems to be taking to pregnancy like some sort of earth mother. She positively glows with it.

Gabby has always wanted a child in theory, and now she begins contemplating motherhood in earnest. What would it actually be like to carry a child for nine months and give birth? It looks wonderful on Zoe. What will it be like to look after the baby once it's born? She doesn't doubt that it will be hard, but if Zoe can manage it, then she can too. She'll certainly be able to give her future child much more, materially, than Zoe ever will.

The more she thinks about it, the more Gabby realises that she doesn't want to wait any time at all for a baby after she marries Robbie. They've talked about it and she knows that Robbie would like to wait a bit longer. He's talked about wanting to enjoy each other first rather than rushing into parenthood.

She needs to convince him that they should start having children straight away. He's always looked up to Taz, so she talks about Taz a lot, and how well-suited he seems to fatherhood, knowing how similar the two boys are. How wonderful it will be when they have children growing up together.

At the same time she puts a great deal of effort into continuing the 'insatiable sexual goddess' routine she cultivated for herself while they were in Cornwall.

While they wait for the house purchase to go through, which looks like it will happen in time for the wedding so they will be able to move in straight from their honeymoon, they have her parents' house to themselves more and more. Gabby's parents are making increasingly frequent trips to Spain as they deal with the various stages of buying their property out there. There always seems to be something to handle: builders, utilities, estate agents.

'Do you really both have to go?' Gabby asks. 'Can't Dad deal with it?'

'Of course he can. But I like going with him,' Marjory explains.

Selfishly, Gabby would like to have her mother around more to help with the practicalities of the wedding: there are decisions to be made over the catering, and the flowers, and the wedding favours, and hair and make-up, and bridesmaids, not to mention the all-important choice of the dress itself. Every day is a wedding-planning day. The list is endless. But they have reached a good compromise.

'But because I'm away a lot, I thought it would be a good idea to organise a wedding planner to take care of some of it. I've been looking into it.'

Initially, Gabby isn't sure. 'Do we need one? I've got lots of ideas of my own!'

'I know you have, darling, but as you're already discovering, it's a lot of work. With a wedding planner, you carry on having ideas and then it's their job to make them happen. You'll still have all the creative input.'

'It will add to the expense.'

'Yes, it will, but I think it'll be worth it. It will also make me feel better that everything is in hand when I'm backwards and forwards to Spain.'

Gabby agrees. Because actually, all the booking and checking and organising is the boring bit. Her mum is right. It will be good to leave all that to someone else. The wedding planner is called Felicity and she is as enthusiastic as Gabby about all the details that Gabby wants to include.

'It's your special day. It has to be *exactly* how you want it.'

The costs are already escalating away from the original budget by several thousand pounds, especially with the appointment of Felicity, but Gabby knows her father doesn't mind. John is pragmatic.

'Don't worry, my darling. I only have one daughter, and it's one day in your lifetime.'

'So, can I talk to you about the designer I've been thinking about for the dress, Daddy?'

'Ouch!' John says, when Gabby shows him. 'Actually, it's a very good job that I only have the one daughter, if that's the kind of money we're talking about. But, if that's what my princess wants, then, of course, that is what she'll have.'

There's also no denying that, while her folks are away, having the freedom of the whole house to themselves is a bonus.

Robbie would never smoke weed when her parents are around, but without them there, he has free reign. And, while Gabby doesn't partake herself, she knows that Robbie likes it. She encourages him to get stoned because he has less inclination to go out when he's relaxed after a spliff or two in the evenings.

She also knows that it makes her seem less uptight. Taz has talked about cutting back on that kind of stuff, because it isn't fair on Zoe while she's pregnant, and Gabby likes being seen as cool about that kind of thing.

As well as a wedding to organise, there is a new house purchase to complete. The house that they have found and put an offer in on is less than a mile from Gabby's parents. To be fair, Robbie wanted to move a little further away so that they had their independence, but Gabby has convinced him of the practical necessity once they start a family. Her parents also suggested moving directly into town, rather than near them on the outskirts, where the two of them might better enjoy the lifestyle of restaurants and cafes and things to do, but Gabby disagrees. They will want that close proximity so that Marjory and John can help out with childcare and be on hand in an emergency, and a family home is easier to find out here.

She had a very clear picture in her mind when they started house-hunting: a five-bedroom property with a garden and garages for their cars. They wouldn't be able to get anything like that if they were right in town. The one she has managed to find is set right back from the road and in a smart, new cul-de-sac. Much safer for a toddler when the time comes. Absolutely perfect.

Now that all the paperwork for the purchase appears to be going through, Gabby has begun looking for furnishings. It will be wonderful to move in there straight after the wedding. Perfect timing for starting out on their own.

On Friday night, when Robbie comes home from work, he mentions that Taz has invited him out for a beer.

'Just Taz?'

'I don't know who else will be in the pub. Maybe a few of the lads will be about. It's just a drink.'

'Can't I come?'

'I don't know if that's a great idea. I think it's just us boys. Zoe isn't going. You'll only be bored. To be honest, I think Taz just needs a mate to talk to. Things have happened pretty fast for them with the pregnancy coming unexpectedly.'

Didn't Gabby just know it. 'Okay. Which pub are you going to?'

'I don't know. The one by the river, I think. You don't mind, do you? I've hardly seen him lately.'

'But I was going to cook a Thai green curry for us tonight.'

'That sounds lovely. Eat without me. I'll have it when I get back. Promise I'll only have a couple. I won't be too late.'

There's the sound of a horn outside. She watches him glance out of the window.

'That's Taz now. Love you.' He plants a kiss on her cheek and grabs his jacket from the chair.

And then he is gone. Just like that.

Gabby suddenly feels lonely. If she'd known he was going to go out she could have organised to do something else. And he seemed so keen to get away. She wonders why he still needs to go out with Taz. Why she isn't enough for him. It seems that, no matter how hard she tries, in bed and around the home, she's never quite good enough. She gives him the freedom to get as stoned as he likes. Most girlfriends – or fiancées – wouldn't be that tolerant. Why does he need anything – or anyone – else?

It feels somehow as if she's losing control over Robbie. Maybe he doesn't love her as much as he once did.

The wedding is still a couple of months away, but there's only one sure-fire way she can think of to make sure that she is the centre of his universe, just as Zoe is the centre of Taz's world.

She needs to get pregnant.

VII

Robbie

'Timing was impeccable, mate,' Robbie says, as he jumps in Taz's car.

'Where are we headed? A quick one in the Riverside Arms?'

'Why not? Drive on, Jeeves!'

'I'm not your chauffeur. Just because you work for the squire and you're marrying money, don't think you can boss me around.' Taz gives him a playful punch.

'Oh, fuck off! Just because you're about to become a father doesn't mean you're the big man here.'

They both burst into laughter as Taz hands him a spliff.

'Thanks, mate. I tell you what, getting a night out at short notice went more smoothly than it might have done.'

'She didn't kick up a fuss, then?'

'Nah, seemed fine with it. We're not joined at the hip, you know.' Robbie is pleased with how he has managed to engineer a night out without a row. Gabby does seem to have become more clingy lately.

He thinks he gets it, though. There's a lot going on with

wedding plans and house stuff. A lot to organise. But, if he's honest with himself, it's feeling very samey, night after night stuck in Gabby's house. It's starting to feel a little bit claustrophobic. Robbie has already seen a drop in invitations from his mates to go off and do stuff. A few went away last weekend to Amsterdam and he wasn't even asked. He used to do all this stuff with his mates, go away and get stoned, but now, with this engagement, he has marked himself out as the grown-up, the one with the responsibilities. He misses his mates, and he needs this night out.

Gabby doesn't have much time for his friends. She makes no secret of the fact that she thinks they're all a bunch of losers and, to be fair, she's got a point in some ways. None of them have made much of their lives so far – if you measure lives in terms of careers and money. Most of them are just the same useless layabouts they were when they were all at school. But they'll all have to grow up at some point, just as he is. He finds the word 'responsibility' a bit frightening, so he substitutes 'responsibility' for 'safe future' in his mind. He's the one lucky enough to be getting married, not them. He'll be the first of his siblings and friends to do so *and* he'll be the one going to live in a five-bedroom house with a massive garden, so they can all back off with their negativity.

'She's got you under the thumb a bit, and you're not even married yet.'

Robbie laughs Taz's comments off. He can't complain because he is having tons of good sex and Gabby doesn't mind if he's smoking a bit of weed.

Life is good. And after the wedding they'll move into a fuck-off house and live a great life. So what if he becomes a dad

46

sooner rather than later? Her parents will only be a 10-minute walk away and will help with babies anyway, like Gabby says.

When the two men are in the pub, and Robbie is only a third of the way into his pint, his phone goes.

Hey babe just checking you got to the pub ok. Miss you. Xxx

'Hang on a minute, mate, just let me reply to this,' Robbie says, interrupting Taz's analysis of Liverpool's performance in the match the previous weekend.

He tries to be reassuring, but the messages continue through the evening, every 15 or 20 minutes or so. To the point where it gets a bit embarrassing.

'She's checking up on you,' Taz says.

'She's just got a lot on, with the wedding and that,' Robbie defends her.

But Robbie notes that Zoe doesn't message Taz once. She's sound as a pound, Zoe. Not for the first time, Robbie thinks that his mate has done well for himself hooking up with Zoe.

'We should get the girls together more,' Robbie says, taking a sip of his third pint. Part of him thinks that if Gabby spent more time with Taz's fiancé, some of Zoe's chilled-outness might rub off on her.

'Actually, Zoe's had some thoughts about organising a hen night for Gabby,' Taz says.

'Oh, good.' Robbie hasn't thought much about his stag night yet, and says so.

'Don't worry, that's my job to sort. It's all in hand,' Taz says, tapping the side of his nose.

'How's the house-buying going?' he asks, changing the subject.

'Yeah, almost there, I think.'

'Mate, you must be stoked. You're a jammy bugger. I wish we had that kind of start to family life. We're looking for a bigger place to rent, now. We need a second bedroom. For the nursery. And that means more moolah. Which means I need to do a bit more overtime.'

'Yeah, I know, it's a touch. We're very lucky.' Robbie takes another sip. The house isn't *really* what he would have chosen if it had been left up to him. Certainly not the location. But it's way beyond anything they would have been able to afford by themselves. So he keeps reminding himself how lucky he is. His siblings keep taking the piss out of him for becoming a boring old man. His sister, Jackie, regularly checks the back of his head, 'looking for the bald patch'.

Robbie's mum has also begun to ask him if this is 'really' what he wants. Marriage, a big house, fatherhood. 'You'll be a dad soon, if you aren't careful,' she warned him just the other day. Robbie isn't quite ready for fatherhood, and it won't happen before the wedding, but it seems to be sitting well with Taz, whose face breaks into a soppy grin every time he talks about the impending arrival of the baby.

With pint number four, they move to wedding chat. Taz is nervous about his speech as best man.

'Mate, it's easy. You crack a few jokes, tell some stories about the mischief we used to get up to, big up Gabby and wish us well for the future.'

'Yeah, but it's a big responsibility. And there'll be more of Gabby's family there then our mates. It's just not my kind of audience. And in that venue, too. Not my natural habitat.'

'No, but then your natural habitat is a filthy pit. About time you had a bit of refinement in your life!'

Robbie carries on the banter that he knows is expected of him.

'I don't want to let you down. But I'm not gonna lie, I'll just be glad when it's all over.'

'Yeah, me too.' The words slip out before he has a chance to stop them. The lager is loosening his lips. He wishes he could open up properly to Taz, but that would be a betrayal of Gabby. As the wedding draws closer, she is becoming a total hormonal bridezilla.

'You should see the size of the file for the wedding,' Robbie says. 'She keeps asking for my opinion on this or that flower, this or that colour. I just nod and tell her it's all lovely, beautiful, wonderful. Where am I supposed to get an opinion on fucking gerberas, or whatever?' Robbie laughs.

'You're one up on me, mate. I don't even know what a fucking gerbera is!'

'As far as I can tell, it's just a great big daisy. With an even bigger price-tag. Thank fuck her folks are paying.'

They laugh some more.

'Cheers to the fucking gerberas!' they toast with the next pint.

The conversation moves on. It turns out that the only thing that Robbie does have a strong opinion about is the choice of wedding car. He wants something that reflects the younger them. Or at least the younger him. He wants a yellow Hummer.

Taz nods enthusiastically. 'Yeah, man. Like the one in Bad Boys II!'

It's a movie they used to watch together way before they were old enough to have seen it according to the age-rating.

'Is Gabby cool with that?'

'She doesn't really know about cars. I haven't mentioned it yet.'

'Well, it's your day as much as it's hers. Do it. Book the Hummer! Tell her that's what you want. It'll be wild!'

After a sixth pint, Taz convinces him to book the car. He should have a choice over at least one aspect of the day, shouldn't he?

VIII

Gabby

What Gabby wants, Gabby gets. Everyone says so. Including Gabby. So it is no surprise to her when the second little line turns blue on the pregnancy test. Robbie has already left for work, so she tells her mum first, hoping that isn't some kind of betrayal.

'Oh!' There is a little pause before Marjory says, 'Congratulations!' It lasts just long enough for Gabby to notice.

'What's the matter? Aren't you pleased for me?'

'Of course, darling! It's fantastic news.'

'And aren't you happy to be a grandparent? It will be so lovely, being so close, having you around to help.'

'Ye-es. It's wonderful. Absolutely. But don't forget, we won't be here *all* the time. We'll be spending some of the year in Spain.'

She is impatient all day while Robbie is at work, planning how to deliver the news over dinner. But when he arrives home, she's too excited to wait any longer.

'I've got a surprise,' she says as soon as he walks through

the door. Gabby is practically exploding with excitement, but Robbie doesn't share her enthusiasm at the announcement.

'What's wrong? Taz was over the moon to find out he was becoming a father.'

'And I am, too. I am. I just didn't expect it to happen before the wedding. I thought we'd have some time together on our own first.'

'And we will. We'll have the months of the pregnancy.'

'You know what I mean. Everything's happening so fast.'

'It's perfect. I'll still only be 10 weeks by the wedding day, so it won't even really show.'

The hen night that Zoe has organised is happening a month before the wedding, at Gabby's request.

'Shouldn't it be the weekend before?' Zoe asks, doubtfully, when they book the date in.

But Gabby and Robbie are having their little trip to Skiathos just before the wedding and, as Robbie said, everything is happening fast.

'Isn't the honeymoon supposed to come *after* the wedding?' Zoe jokes.

Gabby explains that Skiathos isn't actually a honeymoon. It's a little holiday before the wedding so that she can top up her tan. And it's romantic, because they're going to where *Mamma Mia!* was filmed. Which, Zoe should remember, was actually the show they saw on the night they got engaged.

Because both the bride-to-be and the bridesmaid are pregnant, Zoe organises with the rest of the group, including Marjory, to go and spend an evening where they make jewellery. In reality, this means threading beads onto wire in an 'artful' way. Some of the girls drink prosecco while they are doing it. The girls try to egg Gabby on to go out clubbing afterwards.

'Oh, no. In my condition, that's the last thing I want to do.'

But the hen party is insistent.

'You must, darling. It's your hen night,' her mum persuades her. 'You're only young once!'

So Gabby relents, against her better judgement. The club is banging and Zoe dances all night long with a bottle of water in her hand. She's moving into the final trimester now and blooming.

The other guests have a blast, while Gabby sulks in a corner, astonished at how irresponsible Zoe can be, wantonly putting her foetus in danger by throwing shapes on the dancefloor.

'There's no harm,' Marjory says. 'When I was pregnant with you I was out most weekends with my friends having a laugh. Relax! It's good for the baby.'

'The midwife told me to listen to my body. And being in a heaving nightclub is not what my body is telling me to do. I feel sick. This is supposed to be my hen night and nobody cares what I want to do or how I'm feeling! I'm going home!'

Gabby is shocked when her mother, and at least one of her so-called 'friends', doesn't try to stop her from leaving.

And nothing is going right with the wedding, either. Even though there is this wedding planner, Gabby still seems to be having to do most of the checking herself. She seems to be on the phone to Felicity multiple times a day. Sometimes Felicity doesn't take her calls, which infuriates Gabby further. 'I mean, what are we actually paying her for?'

The car hire has become a real sticking point. Robbie has got some bizarre idea that he wants something called a

Hummer. And in yellow. Which doesn't go with the colour scheme at all and will be a nightmare to get in and out of in her dress. Gabby wants something sophisticated, elegant. Whatever car it was that William and Kate had at their wedding. A lovely old Aston Martin. Something like that. Or, even better, a horse and carriage. Something really traditional and fairytale. Not the beast of a thing that Robbie has suggested. It's ridiculous.

When they are at dinner the next day, Gabby brings up the subject.

'Look, Taz agrees it would be cool. And you've chosen every detail of the wedding. I want this one thing!'

Gabby can't understand his insistence. He's barely picked a thing for the wedding. Why does this matter so much? The tears come more easily these days, perhaps because of the pregnancy.

'Why do you want to ruin everything by picking something so ugly for our beautiful day?'

Robbie gives in. As she knew he would. But not before she's told him a few home truths about Taz and his mates and the whole thing blows up into a huge row at the restaurant.

'Where are you going?' Gabby asks in disbelief as Robbie gets up from the table.

He doesn't answer.

Robbie is gone for four days.

Gabby's messages go unanswered. She tracks his phone and sees that he has gone back to his mum's.

She wonders if she has finally pushed him too far. Her messages are increasingly apologetic. She also sexts him a few times. He's never been able to resist that.

It does the job, and he is contrite on his return. To her relief, he agrees to the horse and carriage.

'Well, actually, two white horses with bows that will match the fabric of the bridesmaid's dresses,' she says, showing him a picture.

The wedding is back on, and the make-up sex is sensational.

With three weeks to go until the big day, Zoe has organised a night out for the four of them. A final run-through of all the wedding plans. It's a good idea, but Zoe manages to be supportive and hurtful in almost the same breath.

'A chance to relax and catch up properly. Taz and I have noticed all the tension. I mean, Robbie's not been himself lately. This will be a chance to all enjoy ourselves together before the wedding.'

Who does Zoe actually think she is? As though all of a sudden she's the relationship guru as well as the pregnancy expert.

In the restaurant, both Taz and Robbie order a beer before the food.

'But you're driving,' Gabby says, sharply to her husband-to-be.

'It's only one,' Robbie counters.

'Why is Robbie driving if you can't drink anyway? I'm driving us,' Zoe says. 'It seems silly to stop Taz having a beer given that I'm pregnant and teetotal.'

Oh, yes. Bloody perfect Zoe. But Gabby hates driving at night and Robbie said he was happy to drive. Why does everyone always make her out to be the bad guy?

Gabby orders a mineral water and asks for a straw.

Zoe looks at her strangely, but she can't be bothered to

explain. She wanted her teeth whitened in time for the wedding but was refused because of the pregnancy. She has been using very expensive teeth whiteners and toothpaste instead, and needs to drink through a straw as much as possible so as not to undo all the hard work.

They get onto the subject of the wedding itself, beginning with the bridesmaids' dresses. Which are beautiful. 'The colours are meant to represent a wildflower bouquet, as if they have been gathered up from the meadow,' Gabby explains, dreamily.

Zoe starts to say that most English meadows are a mixture of red poppies, blue love-in-a-mist and white daisies, but soon shuts up when Gabby shoots her a warning look.

'Whatever. These subtle pastel shades are exactly what I want,' Gabby says. 'And they'll work perfectly with *my* dress.'

Gabby's dress is top secret. It's being made especially for her by a designer in Bath. Her dad accidentally let the cat out of the bag the other night by revealing that the dress is costing 10 grand.

'I know it's going to be amazing,' Zoe says, which makes Gabby feel a bit better.

'So, how's your best man speech going?' Gabby asks Taz.

Taz laughs. 'Oh, I don't really know. I haven't actually written it yet.'

'What do you mean, you haven't written it yet? I need to know it's done and I need to know what's going to be in it. Can you email it to me by Wednesday?'

She reaches down into her handbag for a notebook and tears a piece of paper from it to jot down her email address.

What is Taz thinking? That he can just turn up and waffle

on about the good old days with no preparation? He's even more of an idiot than she thought he was.

The conversation tails off after that. As soon as the main courses have been eaten Taz says that they should get going soon. 'Work in the morning.'

It suits Gabby to cut short the evening. They need to pack for Skiathos anyway. And she doesn't want to spend any more time than she has to with Zoe and Taz. Once the wedding is out of the way, she won't have to.

IX

Gabby

The dress is collected from the designer's studio following the final fitting.

It is even more beautiful and breathtaking beneath her fingers than she remembers from the multiple fittings. It is a work of art.

Gabby hangs it in her room, from the top of her curtain rail, since it is too long to fit inside her wardrobe. It couldn't be more perfect. There are so many things about it which are special. It has been crafted from rare corded Lyon lace – woven on looms that are over 150 years old. It's those layers of tradition that Gabby loves. It has also been designed with so many magical details, including hand-cut floral appliqués that go over the bodice and single shoulder.

Yes, it's extravagant. Yes, she knows she'll be judged for spending that much money on a dress that can only be worn once, but how many times do you get married? Her father can afford it, and she knows she'll look a million dollars in it in the morning. Every penny of the £10,000 price tag will have been worth it. Her favourite part is the chiffon-panelled train that trails behind as she walks. It has a delicate charmeuse slip beneath the gown, but the internal boning of the bodice gives a kind of structure to her shape that she's never known in an item of clothing before. And she needs it.

There's not actually any sign of a baby-bump yet; Gabby checks every day and is torn between wanting it to show and wanting to have a flat tummy for the wedding day. Instead of a bump, though, Gabby just feels as though she has got bigger everywhere, as if she is retaining more fluid since the pregnancy started. She has been weighing herself every day and has kept a record in another spreadsheet, this one private to her. The measurements matter. It doesn't look as if she has put on weight in real terms, but she definitely feels bigger.

And one little spanner in the works is that, even though it was meant to be guaranteed sunshine in Skiathos, the weather on the Greek island was overcast. As a result, Gabby doesn't have the tan she expected for the wedding. She looks pale against the fabric of the dress. Having spent all that money on it, she needs to carry it off and do it justice.

'I'm going to need some fake tan,' she frowns.

So Marjory pays over-the-odds for a mobile spray tan lady to come to their home on the eve of the wedding, in order that Gabby can have a fresh spray of colour.

'I suppose we might as well join you,' her mum says, 'since the tanning lady's coming here. The colour from Spain fades so quickly.'

So Marjory and John also have a spray tan.

'No expense spared for my little girl,' John says. 'We all want tomorrow to be as perfect as it can be.'

Even Gabby thinks that her father might have overdone it when he seems to be a vibrant shade of orange, rather than brown, as he emerges from the treatment.

Gabby adds the mobile tan to the spreadsheet she has been working on for the last few months, detailing all of the costs of the wedding. She has shared it with her father to show how all the money is being spent, given that he is funding it. She is happy with this practical task, feeling more in control of things when she can see where the cash is going, even though very little of it is her own money. Thank goodness for the generous Bank of Mum and Dad.

Doing the spreadsheet is a bit like what she does at work. In the last few weeks before Skiathos, it has felt almost therapeutic to be at work, away from the stress of caterers and florists and dress-fittings and bloody Felicity. Work is the only place she has really felt herself. At work she can complete spreadsheets and boxes to her heart's content and people appreciate her. At home, it seems the harder she tries, the more trouble she causes.

'It's all very well keeping track of where the money's being spent,' John mutters. 'It doesn't seem to have done anything to rein in the rising costs.'

'I thought you said that no expense was to be spared!'

'Absolutely, darling, absolutely.'

In spite of a facemask and her scented candles, Gabby struggles to sleep on the eve of her wedding day. Tomorrow she and Robbie will finally tie the knot and make everything perfect for the arrival of their little one. She is so excited for her special day and the tiniest little things circle round her head, so she has to keep getting up and checking them. Bizarrely, she dreams that the train of the dress has got caught up in the ride-on lawnmower her father uses, and has to get up at one point in the middle of the night to check that it hasn't actually happened. The more she worries about not getting to sleep, the further away sleep gets. Eventually, she drops off in the small hours of the morning. Her alarm is set for 7am, giving her an hour alone before the reportage photographer arrives at 8am to begin recording all the details of the day.

It is here. It is finally here. The photoshoot begins with close-up shots of the dress embellishments while it is hanging up, and then again while it is laid out ready to wear.

The hairdresser and make-up artist are primed and ready, and work in tandem. Once the beautifications are complete, Marjory helps Gabby into the dress, lacing up all the buttons at the back.

'My little girl. Beautiful!'

Her mother has a tear in her eye.

Gabby can't ignore the fact that 12 hours overnight has done nothing to tone down her father's fake tan. She pushes away the thought that he looks a bit like Donald Trump once he's dressed in his morning suit. John double-checks all the locks as they prepare to leave the property, any wrong-uns in the vicinity will be well aware that they will all be out for the day. He carries his top hat in his hand. The horses and trap are outside in good time and Gabby is delighted to see that neighbours are gathered there with their cameras to take pictures and watch the event.

John helps her up into the carriage and she gives them a queenly wave as she takes her seat. They give her a little cheer as the horses are commanded into action and the carriage wheels begin to turn. She really feels like the fairytale princess in a storybook. Here it is. It is finally really happening. She sits holding her bouquet in one hand, while her dad takes the other and holds it. She feels every inch the princess as they ride the short distance through the village to the church.

Though there are still things to worry about. Have they left too early? Too late? Is Robbie already in position at the church? What if the carriage has to circle the church because he is late? He wouldn't do that to her. He wouldn't.

Things have been so strained between them lately. Even in Skiathos they didn't manage to rekindle their former love. She puts it down to the baby. Robbie doesn't seem to find her as attractive now that she's pregnant as he once did.

What if he has a change of heart?

X

Robbie

Robbie pulls nervously at his cuffs. He feels horribly restricted inside his suit. It's a beautiful day, so all these layers that he isn't used to wearing are making him feel uncomfortably warm. Gabby has insisted on cravats which make him feel trussed up like a turkey. The only consolation is that Taz looks just as ridiculous, and just as hot. He's sure there will be a film of sweat across his brow, but he doesn't want to wipe it away, aware that all eyes are on him.

The church is full. There are so many people; there isn't an empty pew as far as he can tell. It's astonishing that all these people are here to see him and Gabby marry. There are familiar faces in the crowd: his own family, a few mates. But most of them are strangers, from Gabby's side. It's overwhelming. But everyone is smiling. Apart from Jenny, who sticks her tongue out at him when she turns and catches his eye. His siblings, especially his little sister, have not been kind in the run-up to today. They have nicknamed his bride 'Princess Gabby' and joke that she has a footman (him) to take care of every whim.

Why can't they just be happy for him instead of trying to suggest that he's making the wrong decision?

His mum's smile looks fixed in place. Last night she asked him if he was still sure he wanted to 'go through with this charade'. She urged him to reconsider, told him that there was still time to opt out. It wasn't too late. Nobody would think any worse of him. But whatever anxieties he has, he's just had to put them to one side. He couldn't do that to Gabby, love of his life, mother of his child.

Taz puts a reassuring arm on top of his. Steadying him. His best friend, by his side. Robbie gives Taz an appreciative nod in return and swallows. His mouth is dry as they wait. He can't remember it ever feeling this dry before, even waking up after the worst benders. He wonders if he'll be able to say his vows without his tongue sticking to the roof of his mouth.

And all of a sudden, the church door is open and sunlight is flooding in and there she is.

The ceremony goes by in a blur.

After, he feels almost like royalty as the cameras snap away and confetti is tossed into the air.

Cars are lined up along the avenue ready to transport guests to the reception venue a couple of miles away. To Robbie's absolute delight and amazement, parked outside the church is a huge yellow Hummer to take him and his new bride.

She did it!

The one thing he wanted and she did it for him.

Sod the naysayers! In a second, all the doubters, especially his family, can be dismissed. With that one gesture all is well. His own doubts are banished. She loves him, as he loves her.

The rest of the day is full of joy and fun. The first of the wedding speeches comes from the father of the bride. John talks about how proud he is of his daughter and her new husband. How delighted he is to welcome Robbie into the family firm. He makes a joke about becoming a grandfather more quickly than he expected to, and explains how the arrival of their first grandchild is interfering with their move to Spain.

'Obviously, we want to be here to support our daughter through this next step of her life,' he adds, hastily.

He makes another joke. 'If you know Gabby well, you know how demanding she can be. It's no small relief to be handing her over to Robbie!'

Everyone laughs, good-naturedly. Robbie checks to see how Gabby has taken her father's comments. She's still smiling. How could she not be? Everything is perfect.

Robbie keeps his own speech short and full of thanks. He's not really one for public speaking.

Then Taz gives his speech and it's a good one. Good old Taz. The first part is very funny. Gabby allowed a moderate level of lads' talk and memories and silly stories, and then she helped Taz script the latter part of the speech, telling the story of their love. How meeting Gabby changed everything and Robbie was the luckiest and happiest man in the world.

Taz meets him round the back of the wedding barn for a quick inhale of a spliff after.

'Well done, mate. The deed is done!'

Gabby's dad, having paid for the wedding, has used the event as an opportunity to entertain some American clients who are investing in a few construction projects.

It seems strange to Robbie that at his own wedding, the main two tables in front of the top table are full of Americans that he has never met. But, to be fair, he has never met half the people in the room, and the fact is, they could never have pulled this off without John's financial backing. He can't begrudge him a few of his own guests.

Part of the entertainment is Morris dancers. Typical 'English village', and Gabby loves a traditional touch. But they also go down very well with the wealthy American clients, who lap up the display of 'merrie olde England' and start to join in with the dancing.

John sips at his Champagne and gives Robbie a wink. Robbie can't help but admire his father-in-law's business acumen. John has used his own daughter's wedding to yield a good return on his investments.

One day, that will be Robbie, too.

Robbie's mum is less impressed.

'I can see right through him, that father-in-law of yours. How dare he use your wedding to conduct business!'

'It's not exactly like that.'

'Don't be a fool. Of course it's like that. Those American guests are being treated like royalty at your wedding. The Morris dancing wasn't for Gabby. My foot. It was for them. He knows what he's doing. I bet it means that his accountant can write off some of the cost of all of this.'

'So what? He's spent a fortune on the wedding. Why shouldn't he claim some of it back if he can? He's building a golf course and he's never done that before. He needs the yanks' investment to do it. It's a big deal.'

'Oh yeah, some kind of vanity project that is. A golf course! What have you done, Robbie? What on earth have you done?'

'Jesus, Mum. *One* day. Can't you just let it rest for *one day?*

Tell me how beautiful my bride is. Tell me how well I've done for myself. Tell me how happy you hope I'll be. Wish me all the best for my future.'

Suddenly, his mum's eyes fill with tears.

'You're right, son. I do only wish you the best. Just remember that money isn't everything.'

But as the Champagne flows and John and Marjory present them with another surprise wedding gift: a honeymoon in an exclusive resort in the Maldives, and Gabby has never looked so glowing and beautiful in her amazing designer dress (which he can't wait to remove later), it's hard not to think that money goes an awfully long way.

XI

Gabby

Gabby knew this day would come eventually, her parents have dropped enough hints. She just didn't realise it would be quite so soon after the wedding.

She is nearing the end of the second trimester of her pregnancy when her parents announce they are making the move to Spain, permanently. Not only that, but their departure is almost immediate. They have spent months putting their affairs in order. The big house is on the market, their possessions packed up and transported abroad, and the flights are booked. John isn't retiring, exactly. He has decided he can manage the business remotely, leaving a team in the UK whom he trusts.

Gabby can't believe that her parents are going to leave her, in this great big house that she only chose because of its proximity to her family home, when she is just about to have a baby. It seems callous.

'But what are you going to do over there, Mum?'

'I've got myself a little job out there, too, darling. It's only back in retail, a small shop.'

'Why though? You don't need to do that. You don't need the money!'

'True, but I need it for me. And it means that I'll be able to learn Spanish properly by interacting with customers. I need to speak the language if we're going to make a real go of it over there, and I don't have your willpower to study. I can't do it in a classroom.'

'But if you're working, how will you be able to fly home and help me with the baby?'

'Darling, you don't need me anymore. You're a married woman, about to become a mother. Millions of women have done this before you. You'll be fine.'

But Gabby isn't sure that she will be fine without her mother there to support her. It feels particularly cruel, as if they are running away from her. And perhaps, in a way, they are. Her dad keeps saying things like, 'It's about time you learned to stand on your own two feet' and talks about the fact that now he has set them up financially it's time they 'made their own way in the world'.

'Will you at least fly back for the birth?'

'Of course we will, darling. We can't wait to meet our new grandchild. We'll fly over for a couple of weeks when the baby is born. I'll make sure to book holiday time from work.'

It doesn't sound like much, but it will have to do.

There are a few viewings on the house, but no buyers come forward, so John and Marjory leave Gabby in charge of finding a family to rent it.

'You don't mind, do you, darling? It's good to know that you're here to take care of everything.'

It feels like everyone is deserting her. Taz and Zoe are

busy with their new baby. Zoe is always off at this or that baby group: rhyme time, baby massage, baby yoga, mothers' coffee mornings. They just don't see them anymore. Robbie has been out once or twice with Taz, but only for a couple of hours. They never see each other as a foursome. Zoe and Taz can't go out in the evenings because they can't afford a babysitter, and anyway, 'I'm just not ready to leave him yet,' Zoe says. 'You'll understand once you're a mother.'

Robbie is working long hours, too.

'Your dad's given me this opportunity and a big salary. I've got to prove I can do it and I'm worth it.'

And when he isn't working, he has enough new toys to keep him occupied. He bought himself an expensive drone with his first new pay cheque and seems to need to spend hours 'mastering' it.

Once her parents have departed, Gabby feels increasingly lonely. And bored. During the middle months of her pregnancy she was tired all the time, but as she moves into the final trimester, she finds a burst of energy. It's difficult to know where to channel it. She manages her parents' property, but has had lots of responsibility taken away from her as she heads towards maternity leave. Her nest is built, ready for the arrival of their 'little princess'. The furnishings are all complete, the nursery is kitted out.

In some ways, Gabby is a little disappointed that she isn't having a son first. Of course Zoe has had a boy first. They've called him Benjamin. Gabby would like to have given Robbie a first-born son. She suspects that Robbie feels that too, although he hasn't said.

To fill her time, she takes to cooking and baking with a kind of frenzy, partly to feel busy and partly in an attempt to fulfil the role of domestic goddess. The sexual goddess identity has waned, rather, with the pregnancy. Robbie certainly seems to have less of a sexual appetite as her body has grown with the baby. She will need to address that sooner rather than later.

She takes a large batch of cakes into work one day and all her colleagues tell her how wonderful they are, how she has been hiding her light under a bushel, how she is wasted in accounts and should set up her own baking business. Gabby wallows in the praise. It's a little lightbulb moment. Rather than putting her feet up and waiting for the baby, Gabby decides to become busier. A side gig making decorated cupcakes for businesses. Why not? By the end of the day she has set up her own bakery, come up with the name – Gabriella's Cupcakes – and a business plan, designed a logo, and ordered some flyers from the printers.

'How are you going to manage all this alongside a fulltime job and a baby?' Robbie asks, incredulous.

'Watch me,' she replies, full of the kind of entrepreneurial spirit her father has always had. 'Maternity pay isn't great. I'll be bored at home with a baby. Why should I settle for a lower income just because I'm a mother? I won't. If my dad can run a business, then I can run a business too. There's no point standing still.'

'But babe, our baby will need you.'

'And I need this. I'm destined for more than just motherhood,' Gabby says. 'I'm not going to sit back. Our daughter needs the best, just like I had. And I'm going to give it to her.'

They are sitting at home, Robbie in front of the TV, Gabby doing her business accounts, when her waters break.

It's a difficult labour, but their baby is bald and beautiful.

Gabby is dismayed that she doesn't come out with hair; she thought all babies were supposed to be born with hair, girls especially.

They settle on the name 'Camila'. None of their friends have a girl called Camila. It's unusual enough to be distinctive. Gabby only knows of one other girl with that name, and she is married to the king. 'But we'll spell it differently, just to differentiate her,' Gabby says.

People soon try to shorten Camila to 'Cammy'. Gabby tries to discourage this as much as possible. 'I just prefer it if she's called by her proper name.' Though she doesn't mind it so much when they are at home, in private.

They'd begun to drift apart a little through the pregnancy, but birth brings her closer to Robbie again. She's felt as if he's been more distant since the wedding, and the novelty of saying the word 'husband' wore off quickly. Their lives have, in a short space of time, become routine. But now Camila upsets that routine in the most delightful ways.

Their house is full of dehumidifiers, play zones and soft mats for rolling around on. If there is a gadget available, Gabby wants it for Camila.

'Our precious, beautiful girl is going to have the best start in life.'

Gabby carries her in a sling and makes sure that the skin-to-skin time the hospital said was good for babies is carried on once they are home. She lies naked with her daughter, and encourages Robbie to do the same.

'This way we create the best attachment scenarios for our girl.'

Robbie takes a whole month of paternity leave, encouraged by John.

It's a special and precious time for them. Gabby creates a cocoon of love for her little family unit. They have everything they need, apart from her parents, whose visit from Spain at the time of the birth was brief. When the month is up, Gabby employs a 'cleaner-plus', the 'plus' part meaning anything else: washing and ironing, changing the beds, cleaning the fridge and cooker, even putting the shopping away when the Ocado delivery arrives.

When Robbie suggests that this is quite an indulgence, Gabby argues that this leaves her with time to focus entirely on Camila.

Camila remains stubbornly bald, a problem that Gabby solves by finding pretty bonnets and cute bows and headbands to coordinate with the designer baby clothes she dresses her daughter in.

When Camila is three months old, Gabby decides that it's time to employ a nanny part-time, so that she can return to growing her fledgling home cake-baking business before she returns to work at her office. They have left the date of her return to the office vague – somewhere between six and eight months.

Gabby is determined to do it all. As well as getting an enormous sense of validation and satisfaction from the cakes, a successful business will be a way of making her father proud of her.

She is looking forward to the return to work, confident that she has done everything possible to prepare the ground in a way that won't harm Camila. She has read enough around the subject to affirm that it is emotionally safe to leave a very loved baby, who has attached to their parents, in the care of another adult. Sara, the nanny, is happy to increase her hours to enable Gabby to go back to work sooner.

Robbie's mum comes to visit the week before Gabby's scheduled return.

'It seems strange to spend such a lot of money paying people to look after Camila when you could do it yourself and just wait a bit longer to do your cakes.'

She has a way of making the cakes sound as if they are nothing.

'People pay a lot of money for my cakes,' Gabby defends herself.

'Businesses must have a good deal of money to spare if they can afford to fork out that much for cupcakes for their staff. The world might be a better place if they gave some of that money to charity rather than letting it go to waste.'

Gabby has to bite her tongue. How dare this woman speak to her like that in her own home? As if spending money on her cupcakes is 'waste'. Robbie's mother is nothing. A reformed alcoholic. What gives her the right to be so critical? She doesn't know anything about anything. It only makes Gabby more determined than ever to make her business work.

In a matter of weeks after her return to work, she has doubled her orders. She has exceeded the targets she set herself on the business plan by more than she could have dreamed. She invests in a huge freezer that she keeps out in one of the garages. This enables her to make cakes to order, box them frozen and then, by the time they are delivered, they have thawed ready to eat. She is very busy. Sara, the nanny, is a godsend, a kind of

Mary Poppins figure who makes it all possible. Robbie takes on more and more responsibility within the family firm, meaning that John and Marjory can gradually relinquish duties and settle down to their life in Spain. Gabby and Robbie have very little time left over for each other at the end of the day, but that's normal for a couple at their stage of life.

Life is a whirlwind of Instagram posts that present motherhood as a beautiful journey (though Sara isn't mentioned publicly) and business as always on the up. Her cakes are a work of art, and so is her daughter. Gabby is keen to present to the outside world the image of she and Robbie as the successful couple who have it all, and herself as the super-efficient career woman managing motherhood with ease. The truth is, though, she and Robbie are exhausted all the time.

And then, when Camila is only six months old, Gabby discovers that she is pregnant again.

XII

Gabby

'If I can manage one, then I can manage two,' Gabby tells herself continually as the new baby grows inside her.

She sends out invitations to all her friends to come to her second-pregnancy baby shower, mostly other mums from the different baby groups and some friends from work. She hesitates over sending one to Taz and Zoe. They've kind of drifted apart. They haven't seen them in so long; in fact, they haven't even met Camila, but Robbie will like it if his old best friend is there.

'Yes! I'd love to see Taz,' Robbie says, stroking his beard. The beard is a recent addition. Not so much to look like a hipster, although it suits him, but to give him one less thing to do every day and a little bit more time in the morning.

Marjory is flying back from Spain to attend. Gabby knows how to entertain; it will be a lavish and fun event, with lots of cakes, all made by Gabby, and a guess-the-gender game.

Because this one is a boy, so Robbie will get his son and Gabby will have managed the perfect pigeon-pair.

But, as soon as Gabby is in the same room as Zoe, she remembers why she has allowed the friendship to drift. Zoe starts explaining how she and Taz have decided to only have one child.

'Actually, we've made the decision not to have any more because we believe that another child will only contribute to the climate crisis and we want to do all that we can to reduce our carbon footprint.'

But, even if you do think that the world is about to implode because of the environmental impact of having kids, why would you *say* that to a pregnant mother at her baby shower? Zoe is as insufferable as she always was. Sanctimonious bitch.

'We also like our life just as it is. One child satisfies our human yearning to continue the genes, it's not greedy or irresponsible and we can travel and do more with one child than we could with two.'

Gabby needs her to stop talking. She feels as if she's fraying at the edges. This is *her* party and once again, Zoe is ruining it.

When Josh is born, everything seems to multiply exponentially. Two children, two babies, is definitely not the same as one. Despite having a day-nanny, and Sara really is excellent, their lives are just so busy. Gabby sometimes thinks she might be driving herself mad. Staying focussed on winning in both the business world and the domestic sphere means that she is shattered all the time.

The cake business continues to grow, so much so that Gabby can no longer run as a solo-enterprise. She takes on two staff members to help, plus a delivery driver, which also means thinking about finding other premises outside the home.

The truth is, their house no longer feels like a home. There

77

are always so many people coming and going: cake staff, the cleaner, the gardener, the nanny. Sometimes it's all too much.

As always, Robbie is there to make things right.

'We need some time just for us. Simple stuff. Days out to ourselves. We'll start with a picnic.'

It turns out, though, that Robbie doesn't actually mean 'just' them. Since the baby shower he has been back in touch with Taz. The family picnic will include Taz, Zoe and Benjamin.

And suddenly, the whole thing turns into another production.

'You don't have to do it all, Gabs. I'll get the cushions and blankets and bits you want from IKEA, and get Zoe to help with the food. She won't mind.'

Much as she hates having to make arrangements with Zoe, Gabby relents and suggests that Zoe organises some of the food: healthy dips for the toddlers, salsa, couscous and hummus, with carrots and cucumber sticks.

Gabby warms to the idea. She can make some spectacular cakes and it will be very picturesque with the babies. She can put it all on Instagram.

They rendezvous at the country park. It is a beautiful day, and Robbie and Taz are instructed to build a shade area and install the blankets and cushions. Robbie has brought with him little cotton wigwams for the children to play in, along with a BBQ and cool box.

'Blimey, Zoe and I would only take a fraction of this with us on a day out,' Taz says.

Gabby doesn't like the way Robbie laughs it off. 'Mate, I just do as I'm told.'

Gabby has her phone on a tripod ready to film some clips

throughout the day to make a reel. There are two power banks ready loaded, white light circles and other pieces of tech.

'It feels more like a film set than a day out with friends,' Zoe mutters.

Gabby displays her cupcakes on a three-tier cake stand, warning them that they are not allowed to eat them.

'Not yet, anyway. I want this to look perfect!'

Camila is dressed in a beautiful little dress, but Josh is having a colicky day and is on his third outfit already. He is a little fractious. But all the fresh air will do him good and maybe she'll finally get a decent night's sleep.

Gabby can't help noticing that there's a big difference between Benjamin and Camila developmentally, even though Ben is only a few months older than Camila. His language is coming along much better than Camila's and he's much more steady and controlled in his movements than she is. She knows that you shouldn't compare, but it's impossible not to. Gabby has always compared herself to Zoe. Now the bloody woman seems to be doing motherhood effortlessly, too.

At that moment, Camila comes careering over on her unsteady toddler legs, making a beeline for the cake stand.

'Stop her, Rob!' Gabby screams, before her carefully-curated set is destroyed. 'Get away from the bloody cakes!'

Robbie runs over to scoop up Camila before she topples the stand.

'Calm down, she's only doing what any normal child would do!' Taz says. 'Chill out!'

There's nothing Gabby hates more than being told to 'chill out'. She tries to pull herself together when she realises that everyone else has frozen and is looking at her.

Benjamin breaks the sudden stillness by moving towards his parents and sitting on Zoe's lap. Then Camila bursts into tears.

'Do something!' Gabby screams.

Robbie runs around after the children, entertaining them for a bit while Gabby gets the last picnic bits set up.

But, after they've eaten, her husband soon disappears off with Taz away from the picnic area, presumably to smoke a spliff. She knew that would happen.

As usual, Gabby is left with the kids to manage and all the clearing up to do. That isn't how she pictured her domestic set-up. She needs to bring Robbie back in line.

Thankfully, there's enough footage for Instagram and Facebook to show that the day out was idyllic and enchanting, even if it wasn't.

'But they were so judgemental, Rob. Like their parenting is better than ours.'

Gabby is sulky on the way home from the picnic. Happily, both children have fallen asleep in their car seats in the back.

'I'm sure it's not meant like that. You know how it is. New parents can be judgy of other parents. It's hard not to compare. And they've only got one kid. Zoe doesn't run her own business like you do. They can channel everything into him. They don't know what it's like.'

'Hmm.' Gabby isn't convinced. Zoe eats away at her sense of self-esteem in a way that no one else seems able to.

Robbie goes on, 'Taz was telling me that they're into gentle parenting, which means they never raise their voice to Benjamin. That's why they all reacted when you shouted at Cam.'

'I don't know how they do it. I mean, they haven't got a pot to piss in.'

'Ah, they can't help it. Taz works hard. I think they have enough money to cover the bills, not much for luxuries. And money isn't everything. Taz was telling me they've got themselves a little allotment patch by the railway station and they like to spend their summer evenings up there.'

'Very wholesome, I'm sure.'

'Yeah, they reckon Benjamin's already into gardening and nature.'

'See, that's exactly the sort of thing I'm talking about, Robbie. He's barely two years old. How can he already be into gardening and nature? Is he some sort of fucking child prodigy?'

'You know what I mean, Gabs. They just like to be out in the fresh air.'

'It's alright for some.' Gabby sits back further in her seat, wondering where it's all gone wrong. She thinks back to the campervan trip they took when they were first engaged. How free they were back then, though they didn't even realise it.

She resolves to cut Taz and Zoe out of their lives again, as much as she can. They're just very different people. And she doesn't like the way Robbie is talking, as though his friends' lives are somehow better than theirs, after she's worked so hard to carve out a perfect life for them. Their financial security gives them everything they could want. But if it's such a perfect life, then why does she feel so empty?

Gabby manages to avoid any more social engagements with them for more than a year. Fairly easy when there isn't that much time for social engagements anyway. Time moves on. The children keep growing.

Then, out of the blue one day, Robbie says, 'Oh, guess what? I had a message from Taz. I've invited them over at the weekend, if that's okay? Be great to have a catch-up and get the kids together again. Ben's going to be four soon!'

'Well, it shouldn't come as that much of a surprise,' Gabby says dryly. 'He's only a few months older than Camila.' Straight away the old hurts and comparisons rise up.

When the inevitable knock at the door comes, of course Josh, approaching terrible twos, is in the middle of a tantrum.

'For fuck's sake, Robbie, sort him out,' Gabby hisses.

But there's Zoe, standing on the doorstep looking all fresh and natural like a country yokel, with no make-up, wearing a white cheesecloth dress and a dreadful straw hat. And, Jesus, are those yellow crocs? Gabby didn't think anyone still wore those. And Benjamin, dressed in a little chequered shirt, still looking annoyingly precocious.

'Hey maaaate, it's been fucking ages.' Robbie brings Taz in for a hug.

Gabby notices that Taz looks lean and fit and tanned, while her own husband looks flabby and pale.

Zoe frowns and covers Ben's ears. 'I'd prefer it if there wasn't swearing in front of the children.'

Jesus, she's at it already with the criticisms and she hasn't even walked through the front door yet, Gabby thinks.

They head into the kitchen. Zoe has come bearing homemade gifts that she distributes from a wicker shopping basket.

'That's a –' Gabby pauses as she searches for the right word. 'An interesting bag, Zoe.'

'Oh, this? I found it in a charity shop last year. I love it. I use it every day.'

Gabby, with a collection of designer bags upstairs, struggles to hide her distaste.

Out comes a hideous corn dolly for Camila. 'I wove it myself,' Zoe says.

Zoe hands her some drooping flowers.

'From the allotment,' she gushes. There are some vegetables for Robbie. And Taz has brought a jar of pickled courgettes.

'Last year's crop,' he explains as he hands them over to Gabby. 'We had a glut. They're delicious.'

Gabby sucks on the straw of her gin. Since her most recent teeth-whitening experience she's back to drinking everything through a straw. She's going to need a lot of gin to get through this afternoon, she decides.

XIII

Zoe

If she's honest with herself, Zoe is as relieved as Gabby that they haven't seen anything of each other. Gabby isn't a good influence and she's difficult to be around.

'She's just too much,' Zoe has said, on a number of occasions. But she is doing her best to forgive and to see Gabby's behaviour in a kind way. Her controlling nature is just the way she is. And her temper is because she's so busy and stressed.

But, as they stand outside the house she's certain it's a mistake to have come when she hears Gabby swearing at Josh through the open window from upstairs. She looks at Taz first and then squeezes Benjamin's hand.

Then she kneels down and whispers in her son's ear. 'Ben, if you feel scared or uncomfortable with anyone or anything, you let Mummy and Daddy know, okay?' She kisses him on the head. 'We love you, beautiful boy.'

Robbie looks completely different. Wearing a pink polo shirt with the collar turned up and a pair of white sliders with socks he looks very preppy. Or he would, if he wasn't so much rounder than the last time they saw him. He looks seriously unfit. When Robbie swears too as he greets Taz, Zoe is not impressed at all. Is Robbie pissed? If he isn't, he's well on his way.

Gabby is dressed in an expensive-looking summer dress, but then she always did love a label. Her nails and toes are perfectly manicured and her hair is shorter, cut into a sharp bob. She looks well-maintained, but different, older. But where Robbie is definitely carrying extra timber, Gabby has become thin. Perhaps too thin. Zoe reminds herself to try to be kind and opens her arms to embrace her old friend. The hug she receives in return is stiff and cold.

Robbie is excited, reminding Zoe almost of an old person who lives on their own and doesn't want their visitors to leave. He is talking so quickly it's hard to keep up.

With little in the way of soft furnishings to soak up the sound, their feet echo as they walk across wood and then slate tiles on the floor. Zoe has to stop herself from gasping at the size of the giant island in the centre. The island itself is probably bigger than Zoe's whole kitchen.

The giant bi-folds are open. There are bowls of crisps and cold meats. Zoe has become vegetarian and prefers organic food, avoiding processed products as much as possible.

Camila is in the garden, bouncing on a trampoline that has been buried into the lawn. Wow. That must have taken some work. And the garden is so long, way bigger than their allotment. At the end is a field full of wheat.

'Looks a bit like your parents' place, back in the day,' Taz observes.

It is picturesque, no question, but Taz is right. It's the

sort of home you would get in your 40s or 50s when you had been successful. But this home was given to them. The car, the furniture and the lifestyle. It was all handed to them on a plate.

Robbie busies himself fixing drinks and seems incapable of shutting up. He leans towards Benjamin and begins to chat to him. 'Alright, Ben, how are you mate?'

Zoe isn't sure if it's ridiculous or endearing to talk to a child like that. He goes on to tell Benjamin how he and his dad have been mates since primary school. 'Almost since your age.'

It's a conversation with a child who isn't remotely interested, but perhaps it's for Robbie's own benefit as much as Ben's.

Camila and Josh come out from the garden and into the kitchen. Robbie picks Camila up and kisses her on the cheek, but she doesn't smile. He aims a high-five at Josh, who seems bewildered. Perhaps it's all for show.

'I've got some gifts for the children, too,' Zoe says.

Camila and Josh sit on the floor to unwrap their presents. Camila has a little corn doll. 'Look, Mummy!'

Gabby, sucking away on a large gin, barely seems able to acknowledge her daughter. Josh opens his present: a garden set with a little garden trowel, fork and a few packets of seeds in it.

'This one's cress, which grows really fast,' Zoe says. 'You'll be able to see the results of your hard work in a couple of days when you plant them.

'What do you say?' Robbie demands.

The children are quite sweet; meek and well behaved.

Robbie pulls a £10 note from his wallet and waves it at Ben.

'I remember doing that at home with my mum,' Robbie says. 'Dad made a big fuss at how delicious the egg and cress sandwiches were.'

Zoe remembers that Robbie's father died when he was quite young.

'I'm sorry, I didn't mean to—'

'It's fine. It's a good memory.' But Robbie looks a little sad. 'Let's head outside,' he says.

'How d'you find the gardening, mate?' Taz asks.

Robbie looks a little sheepish. 'Oh, we have a gardener.'

'You're missing out. Gardening is so therapeutic.'

'And how, exactly, is mud and pulling weeds therapeutic?' Gabby snaps.

Zoe isn't sure how to answer that. Or quite why Gabby feels the need to be so catty.

After an awkward start, the children begin to play with each other. It's instigated by Cam.

'Would you like to play with my dolls?' she asks Ben.

Zoe is pleased when Benjie does so easily, but it isn't a surprise. He has his own dolls at home. But everything about the day makes her realise how totally opposite they are as people now. Gabby and Robbie seem to thrive on material wealth. They are poles apart in terms of their respective attitudes to parenting. Gabby hardly engages with her children and barely seems interested in them. Zoe wonders if they are merely tick-list successes. They differ in their attitudes to most things, actually.

Robbie makes a crass remark about a gay couple, then apologises, evidently remembering Zoe's open bisexual interests. He looks uncomfortable when Taz, who has always supported her, explains that while he has never felt physically attracted to men himself, he understands why women would be interested in other women.

'Given how awful the male population can be.'

Gabby snorts audibly when Zoe talks about performing some of her own material at a poetry slam in a nearby town. She is drinking heavily today, never far away from a fishbowl of iced gin.

As the afternoon wears on, it's clear that Robbie and Gabby's way of doing things is a very different approach to how to live. Zoe and Taz have chosen to lead a much more low-budget, simple kind of existence. When Benji was born, they agreed to forgo material gain, especially while Benji was young and needed all their attention. Zoe knows how important the early years are, and how they can never be regained. But Gabby doesn't seem to give anything much to her children. With Gabby preoccupied with food and drinking, Zoe finds herself sitting on the lawn playing with all three of the children. Josh and Camila seem like very loving children and quickly attach themselves to Zoe, much to the consternation of Benjamin at one point, who seems a little put out.

Taz recognises this and sets up a mini football pitch, getting the children to kick a ball into the goals.

'Way to go, Cam!' Taz calls.

'Her name's Camila,' Gabby slurs.

Taz is such a natural nurturer. Zoe loves the way he cheers them all on when they score, running around the lawn as if they've won a cup final at Wembley. The children love it.

The BBQ food is nice, although it takes a long time to arrive. Robbie is slow to get everything underway, mostly because he is quite drunk, too, and it takes the intervention of Taz and Zoe to make sure it all happens.

As the day moves towards bed and bathtime, Zoe overhears

Robbie whisper to Taz, 'Fancy a line?' He puts his index finger on one nostril and sniffs.

Zoe is shocked. Why are they even contemplating doing that around the children?

'Na, mate. Thanks anyways,' Taz says.

Zoe helps clear up, although 'helps' actually means doing it all, because Gabby is really quite pissed by this point. They leave with a very tired Benjamin who is instantly asleep in his car seat. The car is a good place for a postmortem of the afternoon.

Taz is concerned about his old friend. 'He just seems a bit lost. Like he hasn't grown up. Did you see he offered me a line?'

'And they're both drinking too much given that they're around the kids. I feel like something's going on there.'

'I'm glad we're not like them.' Taz says. He is quiet after that.

Zoe is torn. On the one hand, there's a kind of relief that they've got through the afternoon, but it wasn't enjoyable in the way that it should have been. It would be easy just to walk away and not see them again. On the other hand, there are children involved, and perhaps they have a duty to be around a bit more. The state of Robbie and Gabby, who were once very good friends of theirs, is a concern.

'I think they probably need our support rather than our judgement,' Zoe observes as they reach home.

'Yeah, I think I need to be there again for Robbie,' Taz agrees.

Taz, Zoe and Benjamin are asked over more often but, despite the invitations coming back the other way, Robbie and Gabby never want to go over to Zoe and Taz's humble little house.

'It's a shame, because I think Camila, especially, would like it here,' Zoe says.

Their place has been more or less given over to Benjamin as a play zone. There is a little plastic greenhouse by the backdoor where they have encouraged Benji to grow courgettes, sunflowers and cucumbers from seed.

Each time they go, they notice that both Camila and Josh seem quieter and quieter. Zoe takes to offering to take the children out sometimes. They have days at a sunflower maze and a local farm where they are lambing.

One morning Taz and Zoe go to the house to collect Josh and Camila to take them to a petting zoo. When they arrive, Gabby is stomping about in a furious temper, cursing at every opportunity.

'Is everything okay, Gabby?' Zoe asks.

'No it fucking isn't!' Gabby throws a pile of bedding by the washing machine. 'More fucking work.'

'What's happened?'

'Bloody Camila has started wetting the bed. I don't know what's wrong with her. I've told her it's wrong, she ought to know better and she's a very bad little girl!'

All these words cut through Zoe who knows that this is the very last way you help a child to stop wetting the bed.

'Do you know why she's wetting the bed, Gabby?'

Gabby doesn't take offence at the question, thankfully, although Zoe was more than prepared to stand her ground if she did.

'I'll tell you fucking why. Because she hates me!'

Zoe doesn't believe Gabby is serious at first and waits for the good-humoured punchline. It doesn't come.

Zoe only needs to look at Taz and he is busy getting the children out of the house and into their car. They have spare car seats these days, as they seem to have been taking Camila and Josh out more often to keep them safe and away from what Zoe has come to think of as Gabby and Robbie's uselessness, but is now beginning to realise might be more damaging.

When they return the children, Gabby is out at the hairdressers, which is a relief of sorts. Zoe certainly believes that Camila is happier that only her dad is home.

Robbie looks a bit drunk, or perhaps stoned. It's hard to tell. He's watching the football and there are a load of tinnies on the big glass coffee table. Zoe hates that table. It sends shivers across her thinking that one of the children might have an accident and crash into it.

Zoe settles the children in and helps herself to their fridge, though there isn't much in there to speak of. Not the usual 'children live here' pots of yogurts, cheese triangles, grapes or hummus.

In fact, nothing in the fridge says 'children' other than a little bit of cheddar and, in the salad drawer, a small end of a cucumber. It looks like one of the ones that she has given them, with the tell-tale allotment appearance rather than supermarket perfect.

She opens the cupboard to see if there are any dry foods or tins that she can quickly throw together to make a meal for the children. There is half a packet of dried pasta shapes. Well, they can go with the cheese and cucumber. It's better than nothing.

Zoe swiftly sets about boiling the pasta and grating cheese into the steaming result. She adds a bit of cucumber as garnish, convinced that every meal must present something green or of vegetable-origin in or on it.

She sits all three children down at the kitchen island to eat, hastily washing up the pots, pans and plates as soon as they've finished. She puts everything back away again just as it was, doing her best to leave no trace.

She catches herself wondering why exactly she is behaving like a thief in the night when she is doing nothing more than feeding Gabby's children, but there is something scary about Gabby. Or perhaps not about her, but about her behaviour.

It feels as if some battlelines have been drawn. Zoe knows that she has to put the children's needs first, even if that means somehow betraying their friendship, albeit a friendship that seems to have become extremely one-sided.

It's a week later when Taz and Zoe head out for the opening night at the new Mexican-fusion restaurant in town. Zoe's mum is happily babysitting Benjamin.

The owner of the restaurant, Luc, was part of their old surf and skate crew, so it isn't a cosy little romantic date for two, but a raucous crowd from the old days, most married or with young children now. There is no sign of Robbie or Gabby.

'Anyone seen Rob lately?' someone asks.

'Yeah, two kids now,' Taz says.

It's explanation enough for why he isn't there. The conversation moves on, but when the customers begin to thin out at the end of the evening, Luc pulls Taz and Zoe to one side.

'You hear about Robbie and Gabby and the rumours about her latest business?'

'The cakes?' Zoe says. 'She's very busy with it. We have the kids quite a bit.'

'Not the cakes,' Luc says.

And what he tells them next sends them reeling.

PART TWO

I

Louise

A Decade Later...

As we say our goodbyes, Crystal fiddles with the bun that sits high on top of her head.

'You make me think of Amy Winehouse in her later days. I mean, not the tragedy part,' I say, hastily, 'but the hairstyle.'

'I think you're hilarious, Louise.'

Crystal is our about-to-depart foster placement who has been living with us for the last three months, since her abortion, and, as well as thinking that I'm hilarious, she also thinks I'm 'out there'.

I think she needs to get out more and meet more people. Which she is about to do.

The goodbye gift we've chosen for her is a kitchen starter set with everything she could need to cook with in her new flat, along with a new set of IKEA bedding that I noticed her eyeing up on a recent visit.

I hope it will help towards her new start.

She moves slowly and her arms hang awkwardly, as if she never quite knows where to put them. To me she seems like a little girl trapped inside the body of a grown woman. As she climbs into the car with the social worker, I'm struck once again by her height. She is very tall and the enormous bun makes her seem taller still. When I stand next to her, I feel pocket-sized. She already towers above Lloyd, and she's still only 17. But, without doubt, she is one of the loveliest young women I have ever met.

I suspect that has always been one of her problems. Being so much taller than all her peers makes her seem older. Teachers expected more from her because they confused her height with age and maturity. A quirk of genetics; both her parents were tall. I haven't met them, but I've heard her mum talk on the phone.

I don't like what I've heard.

I know that her parents haven't lived together since Crystal was a baby. They couldn't be in the same room together, apparently. Crystal grew up with her mum who, by all accounts, appears to have been quite selfish and even cruel at times.

Crystal used to have to sleep on a camp bed in the lounge. She didn't have her own room. Her mum would sit on the sofa with the TV blasting out, so Crystal couldn't sleep. The poor girl had to get herself up for school in the morning, tired out. Her mother wasn't careful about the men she had round either, and Crystal saw far more than she should. She also experienced abuse at the hands of some. But, if Crystal said anything to her mum, she would drag her by her ponytail around the flat, calling her a 'fucking tart'. Despite all this, all the horrors that have happened to her, Crystal is kind and softly-spoken.

Eventually she was put into a residential home. She would have been so happy in a nice foster home. During her stay at residential she was raped and made pregnant by one of the workers. It's all been hushed up. The whole thing is a concern. Who is protecting whom and why? Money and reputations, no doubt. The worker has disappeared and the police have made sure that he never contacts Crystal again. But these decisions were made without her, and made rapidly, like the one that she should have an abortion.

When I was asked to look after Crystal after the abortion, I agreed, but insisted that there was no way she should come straight here, to another strange place, traumatised by the procedure. I wanted to get to know her first. So I made sure that I did. While she was coming to the end of her time in residential – a second home, she'd been moved from the one where the assault occurred to another one, I went to see her twice a week. We hit it off straight away.

And she is thriving.

She is clear in her mind that having the abortion was the right thing to do, and I'm supportive of her decision. She knows that raising a child is not easy. She also wants to do an apprenticeship. Through Spark Sisterhood, my charity, I have found her an apprenticeship with a catering company. She is so excited and, with a bit of joined-up thinking, her social worker has found her an assisted living accommodation just 20-minutes walk away. Even better, I can drive to see Crystal in less than half an hour. So, if she needs us, I can quickly get to her.

Crystal and Lily, our long-term foster-placement, have been getting on very well, too. I hope it's a friendship that will continue. We've agreed that Lily can get the bus to visit Crystal if they want to see each other. Lily is all talk and very little action these days, but I can do my best to try to make sure they do see each other.

The boys, Jackson and Vincent, also think the world of Crystal. She is so gentle and generous and has bought everyone a little present to say goodbye. She has a big heart, this girl. And I've enjoyed having her here. The house has a new dynamic now that the family are all growing up and getting so much older, and I'm having some trouble getting used to it. My role is less 'mother' and much more 'taxi driver' these days. They are rarely all here at the same time, either, so the house doesn't feel as bustling as it used to. I miss it, but can also see the benefits: I can get more work done for a start. To be fair, I haven't noticed a decrease in the amount of housework and clearing up though. They like making meals and doing random baking – that can be rather frustrating, especially when they pile up all the pots and pans by the empty dishwasher or leave baking slime all over the sink and table and then eat all the cakes and biscuits without sharing. The joys of domesticity!

No sooner is Crystal in the social worker's car and we have waved her off, than my phone rings. It's Kendi, our supervising social worker.

'How was it, saying goodbye to Crystal?' he asks.

'It was fine. It's not goodbye, anyway. I'm popping up on Saturday with the gang to see her in her new home.'

He laughs. 'You can't let them go, can you?'

'Nope, I can't.'

'Listen, Louise. I'm sending you a referral. I want you to take a look with Lloyd and let me know what you think.'

'Surely you're going to give me a little more than that?' I ask.

He laughs again. 'I think you will be able to help her, that's all. She's called Camila and she needs experienced carers. See what you think when you've read it through, then let's talk.'

Crystal's departure has already left me feeling empty, I don't mind admitting. She is probably one of the 'easiest' children I have ever had the privilege to look after. And that includes my own children.

I head upstairs, pull back her bedding and air the room. I look out of the window and get caught up watching the cats play-fighting in the garden. They are captivating. I can see exactly why cat videos are so popular on TikTok. I could probably watch them leap about for a lot longer, but that would be procrastinating. I'm about to turn away when I realise that the cats aren't play-fighting at all. They are, in fact, traumatising a vole. I knock on the window; both cats look up as if to say *What? Me? I didn't do anything. Me neither!*

I pull open the sash from the top and head downstairs to the washing machine. I think a large beast has emptied out their entire wardrobe onto the kitchen floor, then realise, due to the colours – or rather lack of them – variations of black, that no, it is, in fact, Jackson's laundry. I start with his load, then move around the kitchen. I fuss over Dotty and Douglas and promise the two jackahuahuas a nice walk once I have finished all the jobs.

I do all that I can to ignore Kendi's message. Do we really want another child so soon? It's nice to have at least a little gap, time to reset, space to process the hole that has been left, before we offer fresh invitations to our home.

I take Hetty, the vacuum cleaner we keep upstairs, out of the cupboard, and carry on with Crystal's room, but it strikes me straight away that it's not Crystal's anymore. I know without even looking at the referral that this will soon be Camila's room.

Here we go.

It's as simple as that. I start the rapid journey of transformation from zero to Camila. I don't often hear the name Camila. It was always one of the Sloane Ranger names from the 80s and we do have our Queen Camilla. I'm imagining a rather shy young lady with a Lady Di haircut. Maybe a string of pearls?

I find myself vacuuming the entire upstairs, washing out the bathroom sinks, wiping down window ledges, and more. This is my subconscious avoidance technique. Actually, not even that subconscious, but at least it is productive. With another armful of washing, I head downstairs and apologise to the washing machine who, if it were a horse, would be rescued from this level of overwork. Another load out on the line and another load in. I head to my studio to look at my emails.

Sure enough, Kendi has sent an 'Egress' email, a procedure which I hate, although I understand the need for security. I have to wait for a code to come through and it's that waiting which messes with my head. I resent it when I'm busy. I feel that I want to shout out loud, 'Come on, come on, we haven't got all day!'

Eventually, it comes through and I'm in.

I begin to read. Wow! This is a referral and a half – yikes.

I've seen plenty of referrals over the years and my first thought with this one is *don't do it*. But that's partly because I have been living with blissful Crystal, who should really be the poster girl for fostering.

Camila is a different proposition altogether.

She needs help, lots of help. There are things in this referral – well, perhaps one specific thing – that would have many people, even experienced foster carers, running a mile in the opposite direction. Do I have the space, time and bandwidth to give this? I try to think about it rationally. I'm working on not one, but two books at the moment, one of which is for a new series, *Slave Girls*. There are deadlines looming. With Camila's level of need, I suspect it could easily be me who could become the Slave Girl – or at the very least, the Tired Old Girl.

Time for a second opinion. I knock on Lloyd's studio door, even though it's partially open and I can hear that he isn't on the phone or in an online meeting. My husband laughs at me.

'Louise, why do you knock?'

That's a good question. I think I know the answer: ingrained behaviour from childhood, born out of pathological fear that I must get all courtesy and manners absolutely right or I will die. Well, that's what it felt like at the time.

I sit down with my laptop, moving his nuts and raisins and polyfoam crackers out of the way to make space for it on the desk. He is successfully losing weight by making different snack choices after his GP suggested that he could do with losing a few pounds.

I read out the referral, explaining first that Camila, or 'C' as she is in the referral, also has a younger brother in care, but that the siblings have been separated for many years.

'C has struggled to regulate for the last two years. Her carers are exhausted after a year of continuous battle with C, who seems locked in destructive behaviour, such as–' I pause. 'Brace yourself – banging her head against the walls.'

'Ouch, that doesn't sound good.'

'And smearing her own excrement and blood on walls, furniture and herself.'

Lloyd puts his polyfoam cracker down and makes a face of incredulity. 'What?'

I keep reading.

'C has struggled at school and has broken down her close relationships with friends and her carers – who have looked after her for eight years.'

Lloyd takes a deep breath. I know what's coming next.

'Do we really want to clean up shit, Louise?'

I smile. 'Come on, Lloyd. You have *never* cleaned up shit. You heaved when you took Dotty and Doug out that one and only time and you needed to use a poo bag! When the boys were babies, I did all the nappy stuff because you always heaved, and the only time you did try to do a nappy on the kitchen table with Jackson, he did a wee in your face.'

I can't help a little laugh escaping as the memory about the Jackson moment resurfaces. It still makes me chuckle, more than a decade and a half later.

'But–'

'So, Lloyd, darling, the reality is that it's not 'we'; it's *Louise* who will be cleaning up any shit.'

Lloyd has little choice but to quietly agree. Especially when I really get into my stride and remind him that it has always been me who has dealt with the vomiting, nursing poorly children, wiping away blood and tending injuries, girls' periods, bed-wetting.

'Enough, already. I get it.'

I've discovered over the years that I should never try to convince Lloyd or the children about accepting a referral. Far from it. In order for it to work, it has to be a family decision, agreed collectively.

That way they can't blame me if things are tricky – which, of course, they can be.

What I have learnt is that the best approach is to run the idea by them and then ask them to 'think about it'. Sometimes we don't have much time to make a decision, but with Camila I suspect we probably do. With a record like hers I can't imagine she has many doors opening for her. A private children's residential home would charge a fortune to take Camila and handle the risks associated with headbanging and society's aversion to 'dirty protest'. The local authority will want to avoid this from a financial perspective, never mind that these places aren't always exactly what they say they are. Some unscrupulous homes will claim they are specialists in anything if it means they can get more money. Sometimes they charge impossible sums: thousands of pounds per week. But the same low-paid staff are looking after the child in the same way they always look after children.

I suspect we can linger on Camila for a few days.

Once I have convinced Lloyd that the list of bodily fluids that I've cleared up over the years in comparison to his doesn't actually mean I want to file for divorce, he recovers enough to tuck into his polystyrene snack.

I leave him to it and walk into the garden carrying a cup of builders' tea. This is my silent protest against the boxes of herbal teas that seem to be jamming up the cupboard. I stick a sugar in it, too. I need a bit of energy. I make my way to the bench where I can look out onto the garden. I'm swiftly joined by Doug and Dotty, who fight over my lap. The cats approach, and arch themselves past my ankles, letting me know that they're there too. I know they love me the most. I am no Dr Doolittle, but I am the one who feeds them.

I find Kendi's number and leave him a message when he doesn't answer.

Hi Kendi, It's Louise Allen. I was just calling to chat about Camila.

I put my phone down and enjoy my pets and the garden. The phone rings again before I'm a third of the way down my mug.

'Hi, Louise, how are you?'

I tell him about Crystal's departure. 'I'd like to put her in a museum as an exhibit of the most perfect young person in the world,' I say.

'Ah, yes. But your children would get jealous,' Kendi says, and I hear the smile in his voice, as I always do.

'They're all going to miss her, too. She was such a good influence, and she was really good mates with Vincent.'

They loved playing badminton together in the garden, though I found it amusing to watch such a tall girl so politely thrash my younger son. To be fair, he took it well.

Kendi asks me what I think of the referral.

'I think I'm reading about a young woman who needs to be heard. Something unresolved is choking her and it's all coming out the wrong way.'

Kendi agrees. 'That's why I think you are the right person.'

Because I know I have the upper hand in this, I say, 'We'll consider this one BUT, given the details in her referral, and I

103

think you know what I'm talking about here, her social workers will have to let me do this my way.'

Kendi chuckles. 'Is there another way, Louise?'

He knows I mean that I don't want the aggro of social workers and their managers offering endless, pointless, exhausting suggestions.

'I think I know what we need to do and, frankly, Kendi, I want to be left alone to do the work.'

'I hear you, Louise. I'll put it to her social worker that you are a highly-skilled foster carer with plenty of therapeutic experience who will devise your own strategy and will only consider taking Camila if your techniques are not over-questioned.'

I laugh. 'Very good. But I don't want my techniques even questioned, let alone over-questioned. And I won't be writing daily logs. I'll write *weekly* logs, but I will keep everyone informed if something noteworthy happens. I'm not buying into their Ofsted-generated paranoia. That's their business, not ours. We want to get on with the work of caring.'

Kendi loves my confident militancy.

'I'll put this to them, Louise.'

I adore Kendi, because what he'll actually do is put forward the most diplomatic version of what I've just said possible, smoothing things over while making it happen. I suspect that the authority will be so desperate that they'll agree to almost anything. If this placement breaks down then the next referral becomes even harder and, with such drastically diminishing numbers of foster carers, beggars can't be choosers.

Getting to see the children, who are all becoming more independent and doing their own thing, is not the easiest mission to accomplish. The best place to get their attention is while they're sitting at the kitchen table, but I'm lucky if I can get all three in at the same time. Lily is always out with her friends, or in with her friends, she is rarely by herself. Vincent seems to have a girlfriend who lives a car-journey away, so there is a great deal of to-ing and fro-ing. They don't seem to talk much and the relationship apparently consists of holding hands around the school field, but what do I know? Jackson is old enough now for independent gym membership and spends most of his time there, although I don't know how much exercise he's actually getting. I've been down to the gym to drop his water bottle off and when I looked through the round glass windows in the double doors, I caught sight of him sitting on some terrifying-looking equipment, but not actually using it. He was scrolling through his phone, which may increase the muscle capacity in his fingers and thumbs, I suppose.

So, I hold the referral, planning to run it by each one of them as soon as I can catch them. The kitchen is the place. They are always hungry and, while they are eating food, they are a captive audience. I nip to the shop to get Lily a tub of low-calorie hot chocolate and Jackson a tub of ice-cream and it comes to over £10. If my eyes could pop out on cartoon stalks, this would be the moment. I present my card to pay and reflect that I genuinely don't know how we all keep going with all the rises in the cost of living.

I'm mindful about what I say about Camila, partly because I don't want her behaviour − or perhaps it would be more accurate to say 'her cries for help' − becoming the subject of gossip. To be fair, the children are generally very good about that. One great thing about being foster siblings is that they have learnt to respect each other's privacy and disapprove of gossip. As do I. On the other hand, I can't not allude to the challenges that her presence might well present. Nobody raises any objections.

Meanwhile, I carry on working on my books and administrating the charity.

Crystal messages me multiple times. She has not yet met her 'Personal Advisor'. As a care-leaver, she's supposed to have one. They're considered a key support figure as a care-leaver transitions into independent living and adulthood, and she's entitled to one up until the age of 25. I send her another contact number I have at the council, but really it's the Leaving Care Team she needs to contact. I hope she's ready to do battle. It isn't always easy out there getting hold of the things that should be part of the package for a care-leaver like Crystal.

It's another two days before I hear from Kendi. I have been patient and not given a firm answer as yet. I'm playing hard-ball with my 'demands' because I know Camila is going to need a lot of support and I don't want to rush into this. It fried my brain having to listen to second-guessed suggestions the last time I was in this position. They always come with that awful language and tone. A tone that makes *me* feel cross, so God knows how the children feel. I'm not a huge fan of the 'there-there-would-another-laptop-make-you-feel-better?' approach.

I prefer the young person to start taking responsibility for themselves and for them to hear, 'Yes, you can!'

'They're thinking about it,' Kendi says.

'I don't know what there is to think about,' I say. It feels kind of insulting. To me, yes, but also to Camila. Her needs should come first, not slopey shoulders and inertia. 'In that case, I think we will pass.'

Kendi knows I mean it. Within an hour I get another call back from him. 'Good news. They've agreed to your terms, Louise. They will not interfere.'

I make a final check with the Allen household before I say yes.

The general consensus is that Camila 'sounds like she could do with some friends'.

I let the authority stew for one more day. I also want to get through some work tasks like getting my book over to my editor. If I can clear my desk, I can also clear my mind.

It's mid-afternoon the next day when I call Kendi. This time he answers the phone straight away.

'Hi Kendi, just ringing to confirm that we'll be happy to welcome Camila.'

II

Lloyd has acquired a dark humour lately. Perhaps it might just be from living with me.

'Do you think we should paint Camila's room with bathroom paint, or easy wipe, or something like that?'

'No! Absolutely not! She's going to be welcomed here as a completely normal young woman. But someone who is travelling through a lot of pent-up emotion. That's all. I am actually more worried about her banging her head against the wall.'

I think he has forgotten that bit. I prepare the room as best I can, attempting to make it look nice and welcoming without attempting to tell her who she is or how she should be.

To that end, less is more.

I leave things missing deliberately so we can go shopping together and I can learn about her tastes, get a sense of who she is. Being 14 years old is difficult for any girl. I think about Millie, my now grown-up, 30-something stepdaughter at that age. I remember how she used to wear her thick, shoulder-length hair like a pair of curtains, with only her nose poking through. I would try to cheer her up by taking her out to a local Italian restaurant for hot chocolate. It was hard work trying to make polite conversation to a pair of hair curtains and a nose. I'd struggle on for a while and then we'd leave. Over the years I learned not to take this personally. I'm just glad I don't have to be a teenager again. It's a weird time.

But I am intrigued by Camila, and this one particular aspect of her behaviour in particular, because I hold a little secret.

Actually, it's no secret at all because I wrote about it openly in my first book, my memoir of my own childhood, *Thrown Away Child*, but not without some trepidation of how it might be received. I still tend not to invite conversation on this particular subject unless I need to, but, when I was a child, I too had a thing about poo, or at least, my own poo.

I have had many (and they are still stacking-up) years to think about it, but when I was younger I kept it secret because I was so ashamed. I would never have told anyone about it. I included it in my first book because I hoped that sharing it could offer some comfort to others who have used their poo to express how they feel. The whole description of what Camila does makes a funny sort of sense to me. This is probably in part why I said yes to her coming here.

Sarah is her social worker and the author of the referral. She is someone who has known Camila for a long time and is clearly troubled by what happens. I can guess, by the wording in the referral, that she is silently thinking 'asylum'.

One of the specific incidents that has been recorded in the referral is when Camila came into an important meeting covered in her own faeces. Everyone was 'shocked' and 'repulsed' (Sarah's words), and so Camila effectively disrupted the whole meeting. If that's not a desperate scream for help, then

I don't know what is. If the meeting about her was disrupted, then I guess that also counts as a successful 'campaign'. By which I mean her 'dirty protest' achieved some kind of result. A challenge to authority.

Using bodily waste as a political weapon has a bit of a history. In 1980, in Northern Ireland, female republican inmates held in Armagh Women's Prison joined their 400 male comrades in Long Kesh men's prison in smearing their walls with their excrement. It was during the Troubles and was part of the protest against British colonialism, escalating when less disruptive kinds of protest had no effect. I very much doubt that a 14-year-old girl has any awareness of that historical moment. Something far more primal will be going on for her, but it is still likely to be a form of protest.

She has also done it on a separate occasion in front of her foster carers. Of course I wasn't there and so I have no way of knowing, but I would guess that, having lived with them for such a long time – eight years according to the referral – it wouldn't have been an action designed to hurt and humiliate them; rather, at least on a subconscious level, it would have been because Camila felt safe to do so.

And, because people are so shocked by human poo, especially its deliberate deployment, the placement ended. I wonder if that was driven by the managers rather than the foster carers themselves. A manager who functions inside an office in an administrative world might have forgotten what it's like to be presented with a real, live situation and might, therefore, be more shocked by it. Yet, for so many foster carers, extreme behaviours are a day-to-day reality. So I wonder if the foster carers could have worked through this, but maybe weren't given the chance. It seems a very great shame for a placement to have come to an end after so many years.

Managers are completely risk averse. They have to be, because it's their job to be. Their job is all about keeping to the rules, sticking within the guidelines, obeying policy to the letter of the law. I know this from personal experience, sometimes to my cost. At the same time, children don't read those memos. And, even if they did, they'd take great pleasure in knowingly breaking the rules. I know I would have as a young person, despite being a quiet child. So I am following my gut on this one. I'm not too worried about shit and blood. They can be cleared up. But I'm curious about why.

Shit smearing felt good, I remember.

Years ago, I attended a training session where the psychologist led a session about traumatised children and poo. What I remember most from this session were the reactions from the other attendees, who were clearly baffled and revolted by the idea of poo being a way for some children to express their emotions. As an 'ex-poo-user' myself I felt ashamed by their reaction. After the coffee break that day I decided to speak up on behalf of all the children everywhere who choose poo, wee and blood as their means of self-expression.

When we all went back to our seats, I raised my hand.

'I used to poo in strange places, and I enjoyed holding my poo in my hand and squeezing it.'

Everyone, including the psychologist who was the 'expert', looked horrified. I resisted the old feeling of shame and instead sat there with an impervious look on my face. I folded my arms in a 'what's your problem?' pose.

Apart from confirming my belief that most people,

including some professionals, cannot see the young person as an adult in the making, (did they really think that Camila and children like me would be poo-users for the rest of our lives?), the experience helped me reflect on why. Because I was terrified of Barbara, my adoptive mother, I would take myself off to the back of the open-air garage at our house. There was a surplus of gravel to the rear. I would make a hole with my foot and do my business, just like a cat.

I also smeared poo under Barbara's bed, hoping she would smell it in the night. Now I know it was a subconscious act of protest. I was too young to know what a protest was then.

It's often said, but it's true: all behaviour is communication. That's why I'm not concerned about the practicalities of the human leaks and liquids. I am going to deal with those in my own, creative way which will not require the over-interference of managers with their zero-risk mindsets. Sometimes risk is the name of the game.

I'm also going to do my best not to pay Camila's chosen media for her self-expression too much attention – for other reasons. She might be trying a bit of shock treatment, but I was an art student in the 80s and saw many live art installations and performances that mimicked this behaviour; the only difference was that the artists used chocolate and ketchup.

Vincent walks into the kitchen in shorts. I'm surprised to notice how hairy his legs have become. My young family are not so young anymore. When did this happen?

I do my, 'Now, are you sure you're happy for Camila to come? There's still time to change your mind' speech.

But Vincent, like the others, is fully prepared, and now curious to meet the young woman with the history of challenging behaviour, who could be confused for an avant-garde artist.

'Last chance. She arrives tomorrow morning.'

I think that Sarah, the social worker, is pleased about the speed with which the placement can begin now that the decision has been made. For some reason, known only to the gods of social work, they thought it would be fine to leave Camila with her birth parents for a week while they waited for me and the Allan team to make our decision.

I suspect that to have been an act of monumental foolishness because, whatever the reason she was expressing herself with shit, blood and headbanging, it will almost certainly have something to do with her parents. Foolishness at best; cruelty at worst.

Thank you, Sarah and team. I can't help thinking that they have already set us all up to fail. But that will not be happening on my watch. They don't know me. They have no idea how their bureaucratic decision will now become the fire in my belly to ensure that this young woman is safe.

Her life will improve.

I explain the 'pettiness' of the interim arrangement for her care to Lloyd. A decade ago, Lloyd would have defended social services. 'I'm sure it's practical rather than petty,' but he no longer does that. He's seen enough to know, as I do, that it doesn't seem to be the interests of the child that are put first. If anything, they seem very low down on the list.

Instead, he sneers and agrees that they are 'arse-wipes'.

It would be easy to become very cynical, but I hang on to thoughts of Kendi and all the great social workers I have worked with over the years. Kendi is, without doubt, my favourite. He is like my great writing friend, Ted, who reins me in when I want to rant and rave, even though she will agree with my sentiment. Kendi is the same, he knows full well how messed-up this system is, but remains dignified and focused on doing right by the children.

I do wonder why our children in the UK, or any number of other developed and industrialised countries around the world, are so fucked up. How we have reached a stage where our parenting skills are so terrible, in spite of the number of books on the shelves written by 'experts'. When I do read those kinds of books, which is rare, they make my blood boil.

I remember when I was pregnant with Jackson, and friends were throwing baby and parenting books at me left, right and centre. I never read one. I remember one of my cool friends, a mum of two who had a huge cannabis leaf tattoo on her arm, gave me a parenting book by Paula Yates called *The Fun Don't Stop*. Things didn't work out too well for its author as I recall. Instead of reading books on parenting, I watched back-to-back episodes of *Midsomer Murders, Inspector Morse* and *Poirot*. I think I learned just as much.

I might be at a different stage of life, but now, as then, I prefer to wait and see, rather than plan an approach. I will ignore the disparaging comments in the referral because I know that shit, blood and headbanging is a very loud request for help. I will wait to see who this young woman is first.

In the evening, I stay up late, fiddling around in the house to make sure everything is ready for Camila and her social worker. It looks as if Sarah has been with Camila for a long time. That is unusual given the turnover of social workers in the profession. I think it will prove to be a good thing. At least, I hope so.

But the morning starts with me completely forgetting that Camila is coming today! Not for long – I rub my eyes, yawn and then it hits me. I throw back the covers to get going. First, though, the morning chaos-chorus.

Now that Jackson is at college and Vincent is in his last year, with Lily following behind soon, I will shortly be in the position of having no children at school. I'm really looking forward to that day. But it isn't here yet.

And, actually, college hasn't quite been the release from parenting demands I imagined it would. I still often end up having to drive Jackson to college. He belongs to that generation of teenagers for whom lockdown had a profound effect that is still unquantifiable. At exactly the time when he should have been out and about, finding his independence and his way in the world, he was stuck inside. He missed out on opportunities for building confidence and social skills. If certain people are on his bus, then I end up having to take him. I hope it won't be too much longer before he is able to get past this. He seems to have lost his nerve in certain situations outside the house but, as he reminds me, living in a foster home makes him more aware of how many people out there suffer with various forms of social distress.

And one of those, right now, is Camila.

Today is one of those days when I find myself driving Jackson to college. That takes an hour. When I get back, I finish off tidying the kitchen, making sure that I have biscuits, soft drinks and coffee cups at the ready, all the little bits that help to say 'welcome'.

I stand at my laptop like a DJ at the decks, sending out emails rapid-fire, not bothering to read them back and knowing that they'll be poorly constructed. Happily, my editor knows my flaws and probably has a chuckle when she reads them. I dart through LinkedIn, though I never quite know what the protocol is there and only tend to post when I have an idea.

Connections with the outside world duly made, I look out of the window and see two people walking by as if they're looking for something. I look at my watch.

'Oh, that will be Camila!'

I run to the front door, but hang back until they actually knock at it.

Lloyd and the children have already been briefed not to talk about the small matter of Camila staying with her parents this last week. We need a fresh start. I suspect, as becomes the case in so many long-term foster placements, that Camila's emotions and attachments will be to her foster carers rather than her birth parents.

The anticipated knock arrives. Dotty is first up, barking and wagging her tail at the same time. I open the door.

I do not see a version of Lady Di from the 1980s. In her place is a pale, blue-eyed, dark-blonde haired girl – with a face like thunder.

Oh, heck. Here we go!

III

'Well, hello, Camila. And hi, Sarah. It's lovely to meet you. Come on in.'

Sarah does not look as if it's lovely to meet *me*. She looks red in the face and stressed.

Camila stands at the end of the hall. Her uncertainty is clear. She doesn't know which direction to move in.

'Through here,' I say, pointing in the direction of the kitchen while trying to manage doors and dogs. Dotty and Doug waggle their tails towards the kitchen. 'Follow the dogs.'

She takes a step inside and looks around. There's no holding back. 'I don't want to be here!'

Sarah looks exhausted. I can see from her red eyes that Camila has been crying and Sarah looks like she might be just about to.

There is a second knock at the door. Lloyd leaps in behind me to open the door to Kendi.

Camila makes it to the kitchen, but then asks, 'Where's my room?'

'I'm glad you asked me that, Camila. Come with me and I'll show you.'

Lloyd scans the room, reads the situation and does what every Brit would do under the circumstances. 'Would anyone like a cup of tea?'

Camila is agitated. Poor little thing. I say 'little' because, in spite of the fact that she is 14, she isn't tall. Perhaps I'm judging her unfairly against our previous house guest, but I'm struck by just how short she is.

She follows me up the stairs, still carrying her rucksack on her back.

I open the door to show her the room. The sun is streaming in, the window is a little open and there is a cat, Mabel, already on the bed offering therapeutic support.

'Shall I take the cat away? That's Mabel.'

'No, don't take her. Can she stay?'

'I think she'd love that,' I say, and smile.

I move towards the door as if to leave her alone. Before I go, I say, 'Are you hungry? Would you like a drink?' I reel off all the available options and then write my mobile number on a bit of paper. 'Text me if you fancy anything. And I wouldn't stay down there if I didn't have to either. I more than understand. Boring adults, eh?'

She doesn't look at me or respond, but I sense a little drop in her shoulders, the tiniest release of tension.

I walk back downstairs to the kitchen to find that Lloyd has supplied everyone with a cup of something and biscuits, plus posh crisps in a bowl. I take a deep breath at the door and prepare myself to start again.

'Hi, Sarah. Has it been a bit of a morning?'

She nods and shares a rueful smile. 'Camila didn't want to come here. And she didn't want to stay at her parents' either.'

'Well, I'm no Sherlock Holmes, but that sounds like she wants to be with her foster carers.'

The rueful smile is replaced by a more tight-lipped one. 'I don't think that will happen. Our policy is not to send children back to a previous placement.'

'Is it?' I ask, politely, while quietly thinking to myself, *we'll see about that.*

Sarah reaches down for her bag and then looks panic-stricken. 'Oh, dear. I think I've left the paperwork in my car. I'll be back in a minute.'

She gets up to leave and Dotty barks at her as if to say, 'What do you think you're doing?' I don't know where Doug's gone. I look at Lloyd and Kendi and tilt my head upwards to indicate Camila.

'She wants to go home to Sian and Gary.'

I read the referral carefully and remember the foster carers names, though I also noticed that their surnames weren't given, nor their address, which does usually appear in referrals. I've often wondered how that sits with GDPR, General Data Protection Regulation that's meant to protect everyone's privacy and control over their personal data but often ends up being misused, or used as an excuse for not providing information that would be beneficial.

Kendi looks a little upset.

'Are you okay, Kendi?' I ask.

'Another broken heart, Louise. It's so sad.'

Sarah comes back in and there's still no sign of Doug. I wonder if he has got out somehow. Maybe when she opened the door to return to her car. I begin to worry.

'Excuse me a moment.'

I stand in the road and call out Doug's name, feeling a little bit sick. My dogs and cats are like children to me. I worry as much about them as I do about the children. Sometimes I think they are just as much work as the children, too. I take a quick look around the house, but know my pooches well enough to know that if they thought there were crisps and biscuits on offer in the kitchen, they'd be sitting under the table, death-staring us into dropping something.

There's only one other place to check. I walk upstairs and gently tap on Camila's bedroom door. Opening it slowly, I'm greeted by the sight of Camila with not one, but two of the household pets in her lap.

My first thought is, *Oh, thank goodness, there he is!* My second is to note how content Camila looks to be cuddled up with them both.

As I turn around to go out, I hear a soft voice, almost a whisper. 'Please can I have something to eat?'

I twirl back around ready to provide waiter-service. 'Of course you can, sweetheart. What do you fancy?'

'A sandwich?'

'Coming right up – text me what kind you want,' I ask. Then, 'Problem averted,' I say when I reach the kitchen once more.

'She wants to stay?' Sarah says, brightening up.

'I just mean I've located Doug,' I explain. 'But she seems fine. She's on her bed with a cat and a dog, so making friends.'

Sarah obviously has another problem on her mind. 'I'm afraid I didn't bring the paperwork. I've checked the car and it's not there. I'm so sorry.'

Kendi smiles his lovely smile. 'It's not a problem, Sarah. I can take care of most of it with the paperwork I have here.' He points to a neat little cardboard folder.

Sarah sighs.

'It's okay, Sarah. Really, do not worry. All will be well. Sometimes these things can be challenging, but let's make the most of what we have here.' There's such kindness in his voice.

I watch the relief flood her face.

'I'm just making Camila a peanut butter sandwich. She'll be fine until she's not, then we will help her be fine again. That's what we do between us. isn't it?'

'Oh, you're all so lovely,' Sarah gushes. 'Can I move in?'

'I'll have to decorate the spare room first,' Lloyd jokes.

She settles back into her chair, and I know that the ice is well and truly broken. I always know when someone feels a bit better because they reach out for a biscuit. It's almost as if the body is saying, 'That fear and worry used up too much energy, I need some sugar!'

I let the three of them around the table crack on with the paperwork. I'm quite relieved to be busying myself with sandwich making. The truth is, I never like this part, and I meant what I said to Camila. I don't blame her one bit for not sitting through this. Lord only knows why the powers that be think a child sitting down to fill in a bunch of forms, in a strange house with a bunch of adults they have never met before, is a good way to begin settling in. I certainly don't. I always try to offer a get-out for children, usually via Dotty and Douglas. 'Do you want to play with the dogs?' usually works. I like to get away from the statutory conversations, too. If anything important is said, I'll find out, no doubt.

I excuse myself with a tray of sandwiches, crisps, Club

biscuit, and a can of Diet Coke, as quickly as I can. I'm never sure if Coke or fizzy drinks are a good idea, but they all ask for them. I've read articles suggesting that diet versions are worse. It seems that, whatever we do, we just can't win. I walk up the stairs, followed by Dotty. She's not actually following me as much as the food. I tap on Camila's bedroom door once again. She is on the bed, now cross-legged, with Doug and Mabel resting in the centre of her lap.

She is also on her phone, scrolling with one hand, and stroking Doug with the other. I don't know whether it's because she's bored, or because the whole situation is just awkward, but I've noticed that kids do that kind of mindless scrolling for both reasons.

Dotty jumps up on the bed and demands that Camila stops scrolling to pay her some attention. There is a slight giggle from Camila – not too much – I suspect she wouldn't want me to think she was actually okay. I shoo the animals off her lap. They line up on the bed seeing which one can make the biggest eyes. I ask her not to feed them, especially upstairs.

'We don't want any more bad habits from them. They are gangsters already.'

Camila tries not to smile but I can see that, like all children, she has a playful streak, however much she might want to suppress it. I leave her to it and walk slowly downstairs, dragging my heels. I'm sure I was like this at primary school after being asked to deliver a message to another classroom. Despite knowing that it was an honour and enjoying the recognition for being seen as responsible, it was also an opportunity to walk as slowly back to my own classroom as possible – knowing that in all likelihood something rather dull was going on in there.

I remember, just in time, that I am, in fact, an adult, and return to the kitchen.

'She's fine,' I report. 'So, where are we up to?' I use the royal 'we', as if I've done something.

'We're just going over medical information,' Kendi says. 'Because Camila was in a long-term foster placement, she is pretty much up to scratch.'

That's a welcome confirmation, and certainly not the case with many children I have fostered. I wait for all the box-ticking on medical to be done, then get up and close the door near the hall so that we can't be easily overheard.

I lean in. 'What happened with her parents?'

Sarah slumps back into the chair. 'Um. It was not a great two weeks.'

I meant originally, but never mind. I'm always happy to glean any detail I can.

'She doesn't have an easy relationship with her mum,' Sarah continues. 'Her dad is much easier to get on with.'

I keep my eyes fixed on Sarah. 'And?' I prompt.

'I don't know exactly what happened over the fortnight she was there, but Camila was definitely not in a good place when I picked her up earlier.'

Sending a child back to the people who are the reason they are in care makes as much sense as a good old chocolate teapot, but saying that won't undo what's just happened. I ask the question so Kendi doesn't have to and can remain looking professional. 'Why was she sent to her parents?'

Sarah looks down to her left which, in interrogation

terms, means she's either lying or saying something she does not believe in, like politicians on TV when they trot out the party line but without conviction.

'There was nowhere else.' Sarah shrugs.

Kendi says gently, 'Really?'

She does the look-down-and-left again.

What birth parents, whose child is in care, would refuse having their child back for a period of time? The local authority will have done this because it's the easy option. But it also sends a very loud message to the parents. If they can be 'trusted' for a week or two then whatever went on before can't have been that bad.

The cynic in me wonders if the parents are being played here for the bigger political agenda. Perhaps this will nudge Camila's parents into thinking they can have her back for good. It's the sort of nudge that could save a local authority a great deal of money in the long run. In this case, I suspect it was probably a blend of 'can't be arsed to look for somewhere' and 'let's stir up some trouble for those pesky foster carers who don't want our long arm of interference'.

I resist saying anything me-ish. After all, I've only just met Sarah and she will be very useful because she knows Camila and will, in time, if we all get on, help us advocate for her. I cast my eyes over the medical paperwork while the grown-ups chat.

'There's nothing in here about excrement, blood or head banging,' I say. 'What happened when she banged her head? How serious was it? Did she go to hospital? Has she suffered from headaches since?'

Sarah smiles, evidently feeling on safer ground. 'After a few head injuries, the foster carers began to deal with it from home.'

'Did they, indeed?' I try to imagine our fostering agency

being happy with that. We would have to report it as an urgent incident and get her to the hospital to be checked out, or be absolutely certain that she was safe, which just goes to show the difference between a local authority and an independent fostering agency – or at least a good independent agency. I'm sure there are some not so good ones.

I need to keep pushing on this. 'So, what incident reporting was there, and can we see?'

Sarah looks a bit sheepish. 'Um, we'd rather keep those confidential.'

Kendi raises an eyebrow. I appear to have found out the sum total of bugger all and that's all I'm getting because Sarah suddenly makes a big show of looking at her watch and noticing the time.

'I'll have to be quick because I've got another household visit, to do an IRO meeting. It's in one hour's time and it's a 40-minute drive from here.'

An IRO is an Independent Reviewing Officer and a meeting with one usually means a review of a child's care plan. We finish off the paperwork as quickly as we can and Kendi says that he'll get copies made and will email them over to Sarah.

That sounds like an hour's work to me – an hour that I know Kendi hasn't got – but he will always go the extra mile to help.

Before we know it, Sarah is standing up and gathering her things.

'Would you like to say goodbye to Camila?' I say, when it's quite obvious that she wasn't planning on it.

'Oh, yes, go on then. I'll quickly poke my head around the door.'

I've been trying to give Sarah the benefit of the doubt.

She's clearly not having the best day, but this reveals a lot to me about her. In my opinion, she should have been up those stairs and looking at Camila and her new room an hour ago. I think we have here a nice, probably overworked, social worker who is letting some balls drop. But I'm still trying not to be too hasty in coming to a judgement. We'll have to see how she pans out. In some ways, her detachment could be a good thing. If we're dealing with shit, blood and head-banging then things may need to become a little unorthodox in the forthcoming days.

I see her out and walk back into the kitchen.

Kendi is clicking his pen, 'Hmm, Louise. I'm not so impressed. She never brought the paperwork. No one forgets to do that.'

I ask if he can request the incident reports for us to have a look at.

'I shall. And if they decline you seeing them, I'll ask to have a look myself.'

I like that about Kendi. He can always find a work-around.

'Can I meet Camila before I go?'

'Oh, yes.' It hadn't occurred to me that, in the chaotic moments of Camila's arrival, they hadn't had a chance to meet. 'One sec.' I text Camila.

Just letting you know we are on our way to see you with our lovely social worker.

Straight away I see the moving dots that tell me she's texting back. *I'm coming down.*

Good. I hoped that would bring her downstairs. She hesitates at the bottom of the stairs, as if she can't remember the way, but Dotty, chief navigator, leads Camila safely back to the kitchen.

'Camila, I am Kendi, Louise and Lloyd's supervising social worker. It is good to meet you. I hope you enjoy your time here at the Allens' house. They are my favourite family.'

He offers her his hand – she is not weirded out by that, and shakes his hand.

'Oh, Kendi says that about all the families. You smoothie, Kendi.'

Kendi chuckles. He picks up his file from the table and puts it in his briefcase.

I love his briefcase, it's so Kendi. He looks like the man from the ministry.

'I will say goodbye and wish you all a good evening. Send my regards to Jackson, Lily and Vincent.'

Lloyd walks him to the door, leaving me alone with Camila. I turn around to look at her.

'My word, Camila, you have gorgeous, striking eyes. You really do.'

She lowers her head, shyly, but I can see a bit of a smile threatening once more.

'Now, sweetheart, shall we take the dogs out and I'll show you where we live?'

'I'll get my shoes,' Camila says, very quietly.

There is a knock at the door. It's Sarah.

'I'm so sorry. I was rushing and I forgot to give you Camila's stuff.'

Lloyd comes outside with Camila and me to pull out old suitcases and laundry bags full of clothes and things. There is quite a lot of stuff. This is why I never fill a room up before the child arrives. We leave everything in the hall and call the dogs.

'We can sort it out later. Let's walk.'

IV

For the first few days, Camila is quiet. But she does manage to come down from her room a fair bit, and is building up her presence in the household.

She is confident enough, for example, to ask for a snack. I point out this display of good manners to Jackson and Lily, who are very much of the help-myself-whenever-I-feel-like-it persuasion. Vincent is much better at asking, though he usually does so while actually eating the snack. She is a funny character. She manages to slot straight into the family while still remaining distant from everyone.

Camila's room, after a few days, is exactly what I would expect from a teenager: she is confused by the furniture arrangements, mistaking the obvious wardrobe for the floor as a home for her clothes. But Lily has been here far longer and does the same, so there's nothing in Camila's behaviour to worry me overmuch. Yet.

On balance, I'd say she is settling in okay. Or at least, as okay as a child who is trapped in trauma can be. She has lost the people she loves and has been plunged into a new life that she didn't ask for. It's weird that a child can live with foster carers longer than their birth family, but removal from them isn't recognised, enough, as loss. Camila will be experiencing a form of grief for that loss, there's no doubt. And so will her former foster carers. I don't think I know of any foster carers who have had this loss acknowledged. We aren't given a thought. There isn't any support. I know it's sort of what we sign up for, but it's hard.

Harder still for a child.

I have such a strong feeling that Camila must be missing her foster family. It seems so arbitrary, such a weird rule or policy that foster children aren't allowed to go back to a placement and the preferred approach is for them to 'keep moving forward'. Camila was removed from her birth family for a reason (and I will find out, I'm sure). But whatever the reason, however much abuse and neglect a child has suffered, it's never an easy thing to go through. Then she is, at speed, removed from the family who have cared for and loved her for over eight years and put back with her birth family. Are these bloody managers deliberately trying to destroy a child's mental health?

But there is a level of resilience in Camila; she is evidently a tough cookie. She is also happy to keep accompanying me on dog walks, which is good for getting her out of the house and making sure she has some fresh air. It's also a good opportunity to tackle the subject of school. Not too much, initially. For the first couple of days, I just float it as an idea.

I remember myself hating it when adults wanted to talk about school, because it was never really 'talk' in the real sense of the word. It was only ever an attempt to get me to go back, stay out of trouble and do some work. Sometimes the value of that makes no sense to a child who is only hearing white noise and can't think like that.

But after a week of settling in with us at home, I'm well aware that I do need to get Camila back to her old school as soon as I can. As ever, it's not local to us, so transport will be an issue. More importantly, I'll also need to find a way to make her *stay* at school. In preparation, I speak to the pastoral team at the school about setting up a phased return. The reality is that there's no way we can expect all this change and turbulence in Camila's life to be conducive to a straightforward return.

Mrs Green, the pastoral lead, is supportive and gives me a decent amount of her time, for which I'm grateful. Experience has taught me that teachers are just as busy, if not busier, than social workers. That kills the opportunity for really building a relationship through the small things, the little nuances that there used to be time for. There is no space for social niceties. There's no, 'Hello, how are you? Lovely to see you,' anymore. I think schools have become places of unacceptably high stress-levels, with staff who quickly become institutionalised.

This blinds them to the necessity for that kind of empty talk that is so important to oil the wheels of communication. They don't see what they have become to a child. They want to do the right thing, but in being so fixed on that, they forget some of the basics. I don't think it's their fault. When more and more children seem to be collapsing emotionally, they are torn between different demands on them. There aren't enough hours in the day to devote to that growing level of need.

'So, we're only talking about a few hours a week, initially. That's all,' I say to Camila on one of our daily walks.

Camila doesn't say anything, but shoots me a look that suggests the second word she's thinking is 'off'.

I think of the tools in my armoury and settle for good old-fashioned bribery. I've already learnt that she likes the all-you-can-eat buffet at a local Chinese restaurant.

Monday is the start of the week, of course, but it's also the night that the buffet is half-price. If she manages to go in, I'll take everyone out to celebrate her successful start. At 50% of the cost, it isn't bad value, especially when the men in the house have hollow legs.

We obviously can't do this *too* often because of the waistline and bank balance, but I could *just* take Camila and leave the others at home. Only two all-you-can-eat is better than six all-you-can-eat places, I tell myself. It's a hardship I'm willing to undertake... And it will be worth it if it does have the desired effect of encouraging her back.

On Saturday morning, before she is due to begin the phased return, we have a breakthrough. Camila raises the subject of school herself. I let her talk, layering my response with 'hmms' and 'yeses' and 'I sees' as she tries to explain how she feels when she's at school. She doesn't like certain subjects, and many teachers come under fire.

'Sometimes I hate them!' She spits out the words with venom. 'They're still going on about that bloody video.'

A rude AI film about one of the teachers was, apparently, being pinged around the school some weeks ago, before she came to us, and Camila got caught sharing it and was accused of involvement. Apparently, she didn't make the film, or so she says. I don't know whether to believe her or not. I just know that the young people I meet grew up with tech in a way that

I didn't and are capable of stuff most of my generation thinks only NASA could do. So I suspect she may have had a hand in it somewhere along the line. I have no idea what the film actually contained, or who the teacher was. She won't be drawn on that.

But it's a reason why, in my opinion, they shouldn't allow smartphones into school. We wouldn't open up the school gates and invite an endless number of paedophiles, con artists, murderers, charlatans, perverts, terrorists and lunatics to just come right on in. And yet, that's exactly what we do when we place a mobile phone into the hands of a young person. There remains, currently, a collective global sense of denial about the true impact of smartphones.

If I had my way, every school would be a mobile-free zone. And teenagers wouldn't have them at home, either.

My birth children were not allowed phones until they went to secondary school, and when they did get them, they weren't state-of-the-art, they were our old ones. We regularly did random checks to see what they were looking at and who was on their contact list. Both boys now laugh and say how easy it was to hide porn from us, but they also both say they wish they hadn't seen what they saw. Lily's mum bought her phone which gives me zero rights. The social workers might advise me just to take her phone off her and put sanctions in place, but there speak individuals who have never tried to do it themselves and are clearly clueless. Camila came with a phone. I have no idea what's on it or who she is talking to. We let these people, one after the other, not just in through the front door, but up the stairs and into the children's bedrooms.

I control these thoughts, a well-worn theme in my brain, while trying to listen intently as Camila talks about some of the other things that have happened at school and the way she is spoken to. 'Sit still, pass a pencil, walk quietly.'

I realise that she is actually describing demands that are being made on her.

We've looped back around the woods once and normally this would start us on the homeward stretch, but I veer right to take us on a different circuit, into a field, and hope I can keep her talking. The dogs will either hate me or love me for it, I'm not sure. First, I thank her for telling me. Then I try a question.

'Is it that you don't like being told what to do, then? Would you feel better if you were *asked*?'

It seems to hit the nail on the head.

'Yes! Exactly!'

It isn't the actions themselves, it's because they come as demands.

What seems to happen with so many adults working with children – teachers, social workers, police, you name them – is that they label children in care or children who are experiencing a difficult home life as 'non-compliant'. A sense that this is just who they are, part of their personality. They must have been born like it. It begins a downward spiral of consequences that inevitably leads to them being called 'troubled' or 'challenging' or 'defiant'.

But they're not. It's a phenomenon known as Pathological Demand Avoidance. They aren't born with it. How could they be?

I'd put money on this being my own state of mind when life in my home was difficult, which in my case was most of my childhood. I certainly wasn't defiant; I was *too* compliant. That was part of how and why I was abused. But I did repeatedly find myself in situations where I must have seemed oppositional.

The source of the feelings that Camila describes as we walk (again) around the field lies deep within her subconscious. They arise from the need to have some control over her life when so much of it is changing and is out of her control.

Losing autonomy feels horrendous. It's instinctive to fight to keep something: a little island that she can still stand on, recognise and call her own.

We possess – and, once again I deliberately include myself here; my own experience and hindsight, having had many years to reflect – a desperate need to express, in whatever way we can, some sense of balance. The oppositional appearance comes from an attempt at equalising.

If Camila feels that she has been abused, ignored or devalued as a result of not being included in decisions about her life, she will, I believe, do this naturally and intuitively. Her behaviours are a way of trying to create balance, albeit a misguided one. A version of tit-for-tat.

I'm sure that, in my very young mind, pooing in the garage was the same. I was not aware of consciously making that decision; it was much more automatic than that. A need. Camila's previous foster carers may not have understood this entirely. It sounds like the school certainly don't. I'm not too sure Sarah and her managers do either. If only more people were prepared to understand this for children in care, to run their hands back along the metachronal rope, as it were, they might find what it's tethered to, or caught and stuck on.

I'm very grateful to Camila for sharing her accounts with me so frankly, and I tell her so again. She looks a bit surprised when I thank her.

But I've travelled similar roads before and I've been doing

this long enough to know that, because Camila has shared this and I have acknowledged it, there will be some sort of backlash. Of course there will.

This is what is sometimes difficult for people who don't do this kind of work to understand: *everything* is about balance. Camila has leaked out some big stuff today and that isn't always as simple as the old maxim about a problem shared would have us believe. Actually, the sensation can be very uncomfortable, and I suspect she'll cope with that sensation by trying to replace it with what feels familiar. For our new young family member, that is probably going to be something destructive.

When we get in, I let her disappear into her world up in her room, just as if a breeze has carried her. I put the kettle on and stare out of the kitchen window for a few minutes, contemplating the impossibility of her situation. The cycle of a young person being misunderstood. Of her foster carers not being supported in the most helpful ways and perhaps being underestimated. The interference of a risk-averse manager (which, ironically, tends to create more 'risk' in the end). All these factors have exacerbated Camila's woes way beyond the obvious trauma that must have gone on in her home to warrant her, and her younger brother, going into care.

Sometimes fostering is like a jigsaw puzzle that has been dropped on the floor. There are bits missing and the cover image on the box has rips and tears and coffee stain rings on it. I can't quite see the whole picture, but I will when I find a few more pieces.

Meanwhile, I brace myself for whatever is coming.

V

Monday comes around soon enough. I make light of Camila's return to school. Those educationists know not what they ask of some children. Not all children were meant for the system they have designed. When Jackson started school, I cried my eyes out, because I knew he was such a gentle soul that he would be picked on and struggle. Being kind these days is often seen as a weakness and, sure enough, all the way through secondary school he was bullied.

It still hurts. Sometimes I would lie awake wondering what to do for him. He told me that he was fed-up with being picked on for his size. He was taller than most at the time and stocky, so he stood out physically from his peers. I would watch him leave the house each morning and walk along the road with his head down. Heartbreaking for a mother. I cried most days.

I phoned his tutor to explain that I thought that Jackson was being bullied. So, the bugalugs walked up to Jackson, while he was standing alone (as he always was) and said loudly, 'Your mum phoned and said you were being bullied. Are you being bullied?' It won't take many gos to guess who overheard that entire stupid conversation. Yes, the very bullies who made

Jackson's life hell. Of course, Jackson never told me anything else after that. Why would he? I'd only made things worse. He was miserable and I was awash with guilt. I felt that I must be somehow to blame, perhaps because I was giving too much attention to the foster children in our house and not enough to my own son. Since he left school we have talked openly about his experience, which is why I never entirely believe the adults' view of things.

Camila has been very eloquent about why she doesn't want to go to school. In my assessment, it's a classic case of being let down by a system that is broken and wasn't fit for purpose anyway. I would love to meet Sian and Gary and be able to unpick exactly what has gone on, but I have no doubt that Sarah will make sure that doesn't happen. She's been told not to let it happen and she'll follow her orders.

But, they always underestimate foster carers like me, so we'll see. I've had plenty of inexplicable experiences with social workers who take their directives from managers twice-removed from the situation they are managing. I've earnt my stripes.

'Fingers crossed, Camila, my dinner depends on you,' Lloyd says, with a wink. Everyone is happy to 'take one for the team' and go out to eat this evening.

Camila smiles. She has a nice smile and wonderful eyes. Those dazzling blue eyes have sunshine in them and her smile, too. She has a very 'sincere' face. I suspect Camila is the sort of child who wears her heart on her sleeve – once she knows you. Though she is still playing her cards close to her chest for now. Life is tough if you are open and honest. I'll need to show her, as I did with Jackson, that being kind should never be mistaken for being weak.

She makes a big show of saying goodbye to all the animals before she leaves. The animals love her. She's definitely made a bond with them. Sometimes I walk into the sitting room to see her reclining in the armchair, not watching TV, but staring out of the window with both dogs and one cat on her lap and the other two cats near, one on the back of the chair lying down with an arm reaching out on her head and the other cat lying across the arm of the chair but also touching her. I don't often see all the animals at once, like this. They usually have some pet politics and pecking orders going on. I think this is recognition that Camila is kind and calm. They trust her and seem to be drawn to her. When she stands up they drop off her like leaves and follow behind her.

'Did you have animals when you were at Sian and Gary's house?' I ask.

'We had two dogs and five cats. Two were mousers. There were also chickens and a Shire horse called Monty, and he shared his field with Andrew, the sheep. They're best friends and when it rains, Andrew stands underneath Monty for shelter. Sometimes a crow would sit on Monty while Andrew stood under him.'

That's quite the image, for someone who's heading out to school. She's obviously holding on to happy thoughts. It sounds idyllic, beautiful.

Not like school.

The women on the front desk are less than warm when we arrive. I know they are gatekeepers, but they could still do their work with a welcoming smile. I'm only there for a couple of minutes, but even in that short space of time I hear too much shouty-voice from nearby teachers. At one point, as what looks like a panic-stricken Year 7 boy is stopped as he hurries through reception, I feel like saying, 'Oh fuck off, his shoelace is undone. Point it out, don't shout at him.'

I'm gone for over an hour as I drive Camila to school. Inevitably, her school is a significant drive away. On my return, Cinnamon is on her hands and knees retrieving something from behind the washing machine. She is a brilliant cleaner who knows all the tricks of the trade. Our taps are always gleaming and the shower grout is no longer black, but has returned to something closer to its original buff colour. It's fair to say that having Cinnamon in my life has transformed it. We live in a large, too large, house that we got at a good price years ago because it needed so much work doing to it. We thought we had a steal. Oh, how we misjudged the amount of work, not to mention the cost of it all. Lloyd and I have quietly agreed that, when all the children leave home and we retire, we are going to live in a young house, not something that appears in photographs in the local museum.

It's only a short time before I'm back on the road to collect Camila after morning one of her phased return. I park the car outside and walk up to reception, where I can see through the glass-front that she is seated on a chair covered in red fabric.

I smile and wave through the glass and she looks horrified. That's good; she is a by-the-book teenager in that regard. She signs out and off we go to the car.

'Fancy a Starbucks?' I ask as we drive through town and approach a large roundabout that splits off into the shopping zone and contains all the usual eateries and shops.

'Sit in or drive by?'

She looks at me.

I laugh at my own stupidity. 'Not drive *by*, obviously. I mean drive *through*!'

We get to the speaker and I ask what she wants.

'Java Chip Frappuccino.'

I have to say it out loud three times to get it right which also makes her laugh.

A female voice asks me what we want.

I give it my rehearsed, 'Java Chip Frappuccino, please' with full concentration.

She asks if we want anything else. The list on the plastic board in front of me is bewildering, so I say, 'No, thank you.'

The female voice asks, 'Any allergies?'

I find myself saying, 'No, thank you,' again.

It's automatic politeness; I don't actually think she is offering me allergies, but Camila thinks this is hilarious. 'You're so old, Louise.'

I laugh, because she's right. When I was Camila's age there were two kinds of coffee: freeze dried or Camp coffee. The latter was made from chicory and wasn't even coffee. And don't get me started on the price these days. I try not to visibly flinch as I pay.

I leave Camila to enjoy her energy boost from the jabbafabbacino or whatever it was, while I navigate the next few roundabouts, waiting as long as I can before asking her how today went.

'Alright.'

I interpret that as fairly upbeat for a teenager who apparently hates school.

'Lloyd will be pleased. He's been fantasising about sweet and sour pork and duck pancakes.'

When I eat at the 'eat-all-you-can-you-greedy-woman-buffet', I abandon all health foods and pile my plate with brown and beige food covered in satay and curry sauce. I add prawn crackers for a bit of colour difference. I'm also salivating at the thought of tonight's feast.

For lunch, I make Camila a peanut butter sandwich, this time with honey at her request. She asks if she can take the plate upstairs.

'Yes, but please bring it back down.'

She won't. They never do. I have to go hunting for plates, bowls and cutlery. I emptied out the composter in the garden a few weeks ago and found eight teaspoons. Your guess is as good as mine.

We all have a lovely evening at the buffet and Camila is praised, because even though she's not paying it's kind of her treat.

'And there's more of this if you can keep up the good start at school,' I wink.

We have to go in two cars as we don't all fit in one with two foster children.

Back at home, Lloyd and I sit on the sofa nursing our food-babies. I'm quick to put my elastic-waisted pyjamas on and stare at a Scandi murder. They do it so nicely. Their murderers are more complicated and macabre than ours. They're planners. And the police in Scandi programmes look like university lecturers. It's all very satisfying. I must have dozed off because I suddenly wake myself up, snoring. I look across at Lloyd who's fast asleep. I wake him gently and point him in the direction of the stairs.

I let the dogs out. Dotty runs around the garden barking at

everything. Doug takes himself to bed. I look up and can see Camila's light on. Once the dogs are in bed I walk around with Mabel doing my 'perimeter checks' for the night. Mabel likes to check on everyone too. I lock up and head upstairs myself, tapping lightly on Camila's door. 'Are you okay, sweetie?'

She nods.

'Well done for being so good today. Can I have your phone please, poppet?'

She hands it over and turns over to face the wall.

I ask her if she wants the side light on or off.

'On.'

I can see that Camila is trying really hard to 'be good'. I can also see that she is wearing a mask. She is polite and compliant. Too compliant. And I understand it. I can relate to Camila, perhaps more than any child we have looked after. I feel a connection. Not in terms of attachment besties, but because in her I recognise so much of my younger self. I know that there is trauma beneath the surface and, for some reason, Sarah isn't forthcoming with the information on that. There's no point in wasting time second-guessing why we're not allowed to know, I don't want to sacrifice my energy to conspiracy theories. She might simply be too busy, stressed out or incompetent, and might not think Camila's past is important while she's focusing on the future.

I think it's essential.

But we'll get to that a bit later. Right now, we need to help Camila to keep going to school, no matter how much she dislikes it or how hard she finds it. Part of me understands entirely why she doesn't like school. When I was young I was told I had a problem with authority. I really didn't and I still don't. What

I have, and always did have, is a problem with the abuse of authority, like the incident with the shoelace in reception this morning. That abuse of authority manifests as intimidation, coercion, or manipulation to exploit those with less power. It's unfair. Most of the children who end up in care have already suffered abuse by someone, perhaps physical, emotional or neglect.

There are some great teachers out there, but schools as institutions can treat children like shit. Not all teachers are good people and so, to mitigate, we create more rules and tougher sanctions. When a child is shouted at, the whole class hears it – and feels it. There is a move towards toughening up our children while they are at school. The word 'resilience', if applied wrongly, can be dangerous.

Perhaps even worse, some schools are 'silent' schools which means that the children are not allowed to speak in corridors between lessons. What sort of Victorian horror is that? I say just ban phones, then let them be kids!

I pull the door to behind me as I leave, shaking my head to myself.

VI

The rest of the first week back at school is largely uneventful for Camila. She seems to be okay at attending for mornings only. That she only has to get through a half day seems more manageable. On Friday, I do as I promised and take her out for another buffet for completing the week. This time I don't include the entire family, thereby saving a small fortune.

Camila gives us full permission to shorten her name to Cam or Cammy. She much prefers it, and so do I. It's more affectionate and less stuffy. I look up the name 'Camila' and discover it means 'religious attendant' or 'helper to the priest'. I sometimes think we become our names. I have definitely become 'Louise' according to Lily and my sons: *renowned warrior, destined to stand her ground with courage.* I think that's probably pretty accurate. But helper to a priest? Not sure about that one.

She's settling in, for sure, but I catch her sometimes, when the mask slips. She keeps smiling but it's a tired air steward's smile. Not insincere, just not very real. It keeps me wondering just what's brewing under that mask.

A second week goes by and school days are back to normal,

which means that Cam can be on the bus for school, along with a load of other young people. I begin to see some changes.

She starts to spend increasing amounts of time on her phone, far more than I like to see. I know that my threshold for screen-time is less than that of most parents, but even taking that into account, there's a shift. It isn't just the attachment to her phone, though. She has become secretive about it, swiping away whatever she is looking at whenever I come near. It's annoying, but very teenage. Perhaps not enough to be concerned about. But more worrying is the way that her mood has dropped. She has less 'zip'. But she remains outwardly polite, so again there's little to put my finger on directly. It's a feeling as much as anything.

There is much I don't know about Camila because she is so guarded. She's not unusual in that; she reminds me of plenty of other children when they first arrived, but I see so much of my old behaviour in her that it's disarming. I haven't run my ideas by Kendi yet, mainly because I need to be sure and check my assumptions. But I'm fairly sure that Cam is seeking equity, and I use that term very deliberately – to mean fairness and justice with an understanding that we don't all start from the same place – and distinct from 'equality'. The trouble is, achieving equity requires acknowledgement from those in control of her environment, and for them to make adjustments to account for the imbalance. I simply don't think that the leadership team at her school believes in offering equity and justice for young people. I don't like her school. I didn't like it the first day I went in. I regularly chat to her tutor who, it's fair to say, doesn't come across as the most nurturing of people. He's a bit older, and I get the sense that teaching is a second or third career and he regrets the switch. He seems to think that Camila is fine because she isn't getting into trouble. She has only a handful of behaviour marks. But I think children like Cam will be looking for opportunities to disappear. Her way of getting through school is very quietly, a school ghost. This is where it can become dangerous because the quiet ones tend to be overlooked.

'She's not engaging with anything,' I say to her tutor. 'She needs as much help as the loud children. She's slipping through the cracks.'

But Mr Sands isn't much help, and there's little I can do without his support. I'm up against the weight of a whole institution.

Instead, I keep nagging poor Kendi to get hold of Camila's case notes, or at the very least, fulfil his promise to demand sight of them so he can feed back to us. How are we meant to do our very best for the child when we don't know her issues, the nature of her abuse? It's actually crazy when I think about it.

In the meantime, I keep watch, observing carefully and looking for clues, on the alert for the appearance of any red flags.

Camila observes conversations at the table, though so far contributes little. We've always been a chatty household and discuss just about anything, though Lloyd refuses to talk about anything vulgar at the table. We have, on occasion, had conversations that mention body bits – which is too much for him. He gets it from his mum, who is very old-school and prefers not to discuss politics, religion or money. Personally, I love discussing these subjects. They are, it seems to me, the foundation of our existence. Camila is interested in the world, certainly. There's plenty going on beneath the surface. She's busy forming her world view. She is, for example, the only child in the house who fully understands recycling – despite me trying to educate the rest of them for years.

Vincent brings up AI images.

'It's so obvious when something's AI. They're banal and ugly.'

I wonder where he's got the word 'banal' from, while Jackson totally agrees with him.

'But AI is the thing that will kill our planet,' Cam says quietly.

I surreptitiously shush Vincent, who is looking incredulous, with my hand, in order to let Camila speak.

'The mining and production of the metals used in AI hardware causes soil erosion and pollution. Too many electronics aren't properly recycled. Electronic waste just causes further pollution. The material used inside these devices contaminates soil and water because they aren't being disposed of correctly.'

She goes on to say that AI will remove the wrong kinds of employment from our existing workforce.

Lloyd looks up with an appreciative nod.

I smile. 'Cammy, that's such an informed and intelligent point of view.'

She puts her head back down to look at her food, but I can see that she is smiling. I can tell that the others are impressed, too. Have we got a little Greta Thunberg in our midst?

So Camila is quiet, yes, but there is a lot going on in her head. She is a thinker, but still very young. Unless she has a sounding board to develop her views, these little seeds of discovery will harden, wilt and die. I think she is super bright and just needs to do her life her own way. Something else I see strongly in

Cam is a desire for justice, but in a kind of brutal, eye for an eye way. Less good, perhaps. Punishment equal and similar to the offense committed. Fine in biblical times, perhaps, but not these days. The trouble is, it's a method of justice that can just perpetuate cycles of behaviour. A kind of a trap that actually never changes anything at all, only hardens bad feelings. Also, and I don't want to speak too soon, so far there's been no sign of any poo, or any headbanging.

Jackson and Vincent seem to like her because she's a bit different. Lily is doing her best to include Camila in things, but she can only do so much. They seem to have an indifferent relationship, despite being close in age. Lily has tried to encourage Camila in various activities from hanging out, going to the shops, or watching a film with her, but Cam is resistant most of the time. She does enjoy a bit of baking; the girls make some very expensive chocolate Bueno cake together using a recipe they got off TikTok. It ends up costing me £15 to cover the cost of the ingredients and we aren't invited to taste a thing, but they have a good time doing it, so I refrain from commenting on the mess they make of the kitchen and quietly clear it up.

Soon, her first month with us is up.

Sarah wants to come and see Cam. I thought that, with a new placement, social workers should come within the first two weeks, but not any more, it seems. Everything has changed. When a local authority is broke, inevitably it does things differently. Scarcely. The delivery of services has diminished to dystopic levels, though no one will acknowledge this publicly.

'You'd better eat first, Cam,' I joke, 'the days of sandwiches and cake on these visits are long gone. You're lucky to get a drink.'

Camila chuckles. She has a deep voice, but it's soft at the same time, and when she chuckles it sounds like the deep purr of a tiger.

'When I lived with Sian and Gary—'

My ears prick up at this. It's the first time she has mentioned the names of her former foster carers unprompted. This is great, I think.

'—Sarah used to take me out for lunch. We went to a National Trust place a few times. I liked it there. It had a lovely restaurant.'

She was sad when that stopped. It's a shame that the local authorities no longer see the value in 'little' things like lunch in a nice restaurant. It's so good for them in all sorts of ways. Far more use than some of the hare-brained schemes they seem to spend money on, as far as I'm concerned. But I'm beginning to get a picture that life with Sian and Gary was good. She has some happy memories. She smiles when she talks about them. I'd go as far as to say that she clearly felt safe and loved. I need to find out more.

Sarah duly arrives and wants to take Camila out for a coffee. Cam and I share a smile. They're gone for an hour or so, and then, when they return, Sarah comes out with a classic social-worker announcement that reinforces the notion that foster carers must operate like robots.

'I've given consent for Camila's parents to contact her when they want on her mobile. It's unrestricted.'

No matter how often I hear this shit, it still amazes me.

'Why didn't you tell us you were planning to do that? Or consult with us? Sarah, you know that it becomes very hard to foster and look after a child when their parent is sending constant earworms to undermine the placement.' Yep, this is all part of the we-don't-give-a-hoot-about-you, just do what you're told approach to foster care, and it drives me mad. 'Surely there are considerations to be made here about Camila's security and safety?'

This new dynamic effectively makes us like a long-term car park. Somewhere to leave the child for a few weeks before a return to the birth parents is made. And we've been here before, several times, with different children.

The pattern so far has been: a phone is given without discussion, social worker gives consent to parent(s) to access child(ren) 24/7. Then the parent coerces (read 'grooms') the child into wanting to come back home. Despite the child going into care, the parents' lives haven't moved on. Not much work has gone into working with the families. Usually, the parents have become proficient in the art of 'social' dodging, which means saying what they know the authority wants to hear. The 'social' are happy to have another child off their books and not have to fund any longer.

Once this formula is in progress and the child says they want to go home, the social workers say, 'There's little we can do; they are voting with their feet.'

How handy for them.

But the reality is that, most of the time, the children are caught between misplaced loyalty, bribes, coercion and grooming.

Now I know this, I feel like the wind has gone from my sails. I was so intent on helping Camila to find a proper way forward. Do I put in as much effort as I was, knowing the inevitable outcome?

I have tried to give Sarah the benefit of the doubt, but she's gone even further down in my estimation by playing this card.

'Why is Camila in care?' I ask, quite openly.

She looks awkward. Good. Let her.

'Er, neglect. Her parents were busy with their work. They had a number of businesses they were running.'

She bolts for the door as fast as she can, before I can press her any further.

Neglect, my arse!

I don't know why Sarah is being quite so cagey. It could be any number of reasons. But, in my experience, some social workers have struggled with child sexual abuse. It's weird, considering they signed up to protect children. But I've seen plenty of social workers, and teachers and other professionals (though not usually the police) actually squirm when it comes to child sexual abuse.

But it's the first thought many of us have when we think of children in care, especially girls. Being 'busy running businesses' is not a good reason to put children in care, or at least I hope not. That's a lot of families at risk of losing their children. There's definitely more to this. I have to be careful not to project my own experiences onto Camila, but sexual abuse would explain some of the similarity I sense between her behaviour and my own at a similar age.

I get straight on the phone to Kendi who, it transpires, also wasn't consulted about the unlimited phone contact. Nor can he shed any more light on why she arrived in the care system in the first place. He agrees with me that Sarah's explanation sounds flimsy at best.

I wonder if Sarah has her own children. If she does, would

she allow them to have unlimited contact with people who the courts felt were so unsafe that their children needed to go into care?

I very much doubt it.

VII

The protectiveness about her phone increases. My concern now is about the contact Cam may be having with her birth family.

In the past, I've mistaken the behaviour of children around phones for the involvement of County Lines, when in fact it was the mother of the child or older sister whose interaction with the child looked remarkably like grooming. Which just goes to show how easy grooming is.

I get a call from her tutor at school.

'I just wondered if you knew if Camila was seeing an older boy?'

This is news to me.

'Well, we think she's seeing him. He waits for her outside school and talks to her before she gets the bus. Not every day, but quite a few days a week. He's not a student at the school and he looks older. We wondered if you knew who he was?'

'No, I don't know anything about a young man. How old?'

'Hard to say, but beyond school-leaving age.'

'Are you concerned?' As usual, my thoughts dart to County Lines. Is he a road man trying to recruit her into County Lines? Given my past experiences with other foster children, my mind can't help but travel there first before coming back to other possibilities – like maybe she does actually have an older boyfriend.

Mr Sands doesn't say that they are concerned exactly, just that it has 'been noted'.

I thank him for letting me know and think about what to do next.

I wait until Cam gets home, when I rustle up a peanut butter sandwich with honey. I know she loves them. I offer her a coconut water, as they are all the rage now, thanks to TikTok – who have no idea how much this fad adds to our weekly shopping bill.

Cam puts her rucksack on the table and, as usual, stares at her phone, scrolling, scrolling scrolling.

'How was school today?'

I almost wince as I hear the words come out of my mouth. I know it's up there as one of the very worst possible questions I ask young people. I usually get a shoulder shrug, or 'I don't know', maybe an 'alright' at best. Sometimes they launch into how unreasonable a particular teacher was today. I know that when they say 'they're picking on me' and I say 'what did you do?' there's usually just cause: they have been caught in the act, and it's themselves they're cross with, really.

I get the bland response that questions deserves, and Cam is pretty nonchalant.

That is, until I say, 'Cam, who's the young fella waiting for you after school?'

Her cheeks colour straight away, then, as any good teenager will do, she looks around and away, as if trying to find someone else to blame or to make it my problem and my fault.

I fix eye contact and let her know that my stare says, 'Well, I'm waiting?'

'Uh, he's a friend,' she manages to squeeze out.

'How lovely it is that she has friends,' I say, as though talking to an imaginary audience. 'And not all of them are from school.'

She performs the classic eye-roll. 'He's just a mate. Anyway, how do you know about him?'

It's a good question, to be fair. Do I reveal my sources? I decide that I'm going to have to or she will end up never trusting me.

And this *is* a matter of concern. Why is a young girl of 14 meeting up with an older boy?

If he's 'just a mate', then why the blush? I always lose my initial confidence with children when they lie. They are so good at it and make me feel like a silly old fart.

But my reply that the school has got in touch only leads to another withering eye-roll. She slides her bag from the kitchen table and takes the plate. 'I'll eat this upstairs. And, before you say it, yes, Louise, I will bring the plate back down.'

Great. Not exactly a masterclass in interacting with a teenager.

I know I have to write all this in the logs, so I do it straight away, as bullet points, to keep things factual and clear. It's not always easy reporting on children at this level. It can feel like interference. I feel like I'm ratting on her, but I know all and sundry would come down on me if I didn't report everything that was considered a concern.

Then, just as I'm trying to work out what to do next to handle this situation carefully, I see a text from Sarah.

Hi Louise, we've arranged for Camila to see her family this weekend.

155

Oh, marvellous. Just what we both need!

This adds evidence to my working theory that either social workers don't listen or they don't care. I have, on several occasions, put the case forward that Camila would not benefit from more contact with her parents. Yet now, Sarah is telling me that she has arranged for Camila to stay with her family this weekend. A second text follows.

And for once a month from now on.

I head upstairs, blowing out my cheeks as I go.

I tap on Cam's door, and decide not to soft-soap it. 'Are you okay with going to your parents for the weekend?'

She shrugs her shoulders. 'They didn't ask me. Sarah told me in a text I read on the bus.'

Camila's weekend contact, arranged by Sarah, also includes a contact worker to collect Camila and drop her back. I'm not sure why that's needed. Lloyd and I are happy to drop her off and collect her. In fact, I'd much prefer it; that will give her time to see how she feels and give us time to help her in and out of the contact. We know that, aside from the fortnight before she came to us, she hadn't lived with her parents for over eight years. I imagine that returning for a whole weekend will be unsettling all over again.

Apparently, they are trying this on another weekend for Josh, her brother, too. That definitely sounds to me like a plan to get both children back to their parents. Cynically, I'm seeing this as a cost-saving exercise, but eight years is a long time and perhaps things have changed. Whatever circumstances led to both children being removed into care might now be totally different.

Might.

We wait around in the morning for the contact worker to arrive. They don't turn up at the allotted time, which means that Cam is pacing up and down, apprehension increasing with every step. This is not how it should be. A smooth passage is what's needed. Instead, Camila is waiting to sit in a car with someone she doesn't know to visit people who are parents only on paper. The anxiety levels are mounting.

I feel for her, I really do.

Nearly an hour later, we receive a curt text.

Jane has cancelled. Here is the postcode. Can you ensure that Camila gets to her parents house by 12.

No question mark at the end, because it isn't a question.

Bloody cheek! is my first reaction.

Messing Cam around, messing us around, assuming we can drop everything at a moment's notice, and then giving us orders to suit the people who have abused the child.

I remember a fellow foster carer's advice to me years ago. 'Don't let ignorance and incompetence come between you and doing what's best for the child.'

So, I do some first rate swearing and angry muttering in the garden while I hang out the washing. I will not drop everything. I will go when I am ready. When I walk back into the kitchen, I give Camila a hug. That came out of nowhere. I just felt like giving the poor girl a hug and didn't hold back. It's a shitty situation.

'Change of plan, I'm taking you, sweetheart. The contact worker has cancelled.'

'Why have they cancelled?' Her voice is small.

'I have absolutely no idea but, actually, I'm glad. I couldn't understand why you were going with "Jane" anyway.'

Camila smiles at that and brightens. 'Me neither.'

When we're in the car she plugs in her music and we listen all the way, only stopping off to get overpriced lattes en route: £5 for a plastic cup. Mine is cold with lavender-flavoured ice at the bottom. Who'd have thought? To my surprise, it's rather nice.

We drive towards what looks to be a very nice area.

'Is this where you grew up?' I ask.

Without hesitation she says, 'I grew-up at Sian and Gary's. I hadn't been here for years, until just before I came to you.'

This is madness, I think to myself, that I still know so little and Sarah isn't helping me grow the teeny bit of knowledge I have.

Why do they insist on keeping us in the dark?

I pull up outside a large, cream-coloured house. It's a nice house, well-kept. Everything looks clean and tidy. I get out of the car and wait for Camila to come around the car. She has her rucksack slung over one shoulder. We crunch over the gravel and I notice a new white BMW and a black sporty Audi as we head up to the wide, wooden front door. They obviously have a penny or two.

Rob and Gabriella come to the door together. They make a very attractive couple, both dressed casually, but expensively. I immediately see the resemblance, though it's much stronger in Rob than Gabriella.

'Hi, Louise. Thank you for bringing Camila over. Come on in.' Gabriella's tone is super-friendly, even though we've never met before.

There is no reaction from Cam other than a timid smile.

I resist the opportunity to be nosey (though, as a writer,

that's hard), but this is about Camila. Until Camila says, 'Louise, please come and have a coffee?'

The little uplift at the end of her sentence sounds like she is really saying 'help'.

We walk through the hall. It's wide, light and bright, and spotlessly clean. This is a seriously sizeable property. The floors are immaculately varnished blonde wood, the walls are white and the ceilings are loaded with spotlights. We are escorted through to a large, open-plan kitchen where the blonde wood has given way to pale grey floor tiles and the sun pours through the bi-fold doors onto a well-manicured (but easy-to-keep given that much of it is artificial!) garden.

I sound critical, I know, but I have noticed that people who love gardens and plants are nurturers and tend to have a nurturing approach towards looking after children, too. Is the opposite true of people who don't like tending a garden. It's too much of a sweeping generalisation, but if you are a gardener, you know that plants only thrive when they are planted in the right place and given space to grow, not surrounded by horrible weeds and brambles that are a threat to survival. I feel like human beings are no different. We should water and tend the flowers. If we don't allow the weeds to have nourishment and oxygen then flowers take over just by growing well, blocking out the weeds that eventually disappear – until next season when we do it all over again. But this is a garden with a lot of landscaping and white gravel (how does it stay so white?) and not much in the way of flowers. Lots of invitation for weeds to grow. The house is terrifyingly clean and ordered, and that hasn't been done for my benefit because Jane, the contact worker, was due to drop Camila off, probably at the door.

We engage in polite conversation. They are a little bit patronising. I think they assume that, presumably because I'm a foster carer, I'm a bit dim and old-fashioned. I try to be as warm as I can, but the reality is that I can't wait to leave. Their house echoes. It's filled with hard materials and not many soft furnishings. Practical and stylish rather than homely. I notice, on one wall in the kitchen, a large board of neatly-arranged photographs of Robbie and Gabby on holiday. On boats, jet-skiing, canoeing, with wild animals in Africa, they look like they have been to all the countries in the world – which explains the unhomeliness of their home; they are away a lot. I scan the room for pictures of Camila and Josh. There are three pictures in silver frames on the shelf. One is when Camila and Josh were quite young and the others are school photos that have been sent to them by the children's carers.

I take it all in. On a trip to the loo I check out their wall of CDs. I'm always fascinated by other people's musical tastes. I'm surprised to see Outkast. I remember that song, 'Hey Ya!' I was dancing to that before Jackson was born. It was sometime in the early 2000s. Are they even old enough to know it? Just about, probably. The Killers and Adele. I'm guessing Gabby likes Adele and Robbie likes The Killers, but who knows? There's also lots of Nirvana and some lesser-known artists, but not so much recent stuff. I guess people don't buy CDs anymore in an age of digital downloads.

It doesn't tell me much, but I'm all eyes and ears as Camila's safety touchstone. So, I see a house and lives that could offer everything to children, but there is something wrong. Something is definitely missing from this presentation of success. And Camila definitely looks uncomfortable.

Rob seems more pleased to see Camila than Gabby does. There is love in his eyes when he looks at his daughter. But there is also sadness, I think.

As soon as I can, without being rude, I say, 'Right, I must get going and beat the busy Saturday traffic.'

I pick up my bag and head towards the door. To my surprise, Cam hugs me to say goodbye. She does this in front of her parents and it all feels a bit awkward. I don't ever feel like Camila is manipulating, or putting on a show. She's a kind soul who cares a great deal about people and has a keen eye for what's going on in the world. I think she doesn't want to be left here, but there's not much I can do about it.

VIII

I made a mental note about a nice bakery and vintage shop that we passed on the way to Rob and Gabby's house and stop to take a look on the way home. I have a jolly old time, especially in the artisan bakery, where everything looks delicious. I buy soda bread, a whole Victoria sponge, some Florentines, donuts and croissants for breakfast. It doesn't disappoint. Until it comes to paying.

'That will be £31.50,' the young girl behind the counter says.

I feel as if I'm stuck somewhere in the mid 2000s at a moment like this. I'm shocked every time I go to the shops. When Jackson was born, a tin of Heinz soup was about 60p. I remember because I loved it and it was an easy lunch while I was at home on maternity leave. Now it's about £1.70. The state pension, which I'm inching towards, is £170 per week. If that's all you have to live on, a can of soup will have to be a home brand. I genuinely don't understand how most people live. I can tell that, at Rob and Gabby's house, they are very much into healthy eating. I spotted two bullet juicers on the counter and three different sizes of air fryer. We have an air fryer; Jackson went through a stage of using it but has now gone back to the hob and oven so it's become one of those almost redundant kitchen gadgets.

I return to the car and my journey is filled with thoughts of what I've just seen. Rob and Gabby seem perfectly nice, but I'm sure the Wests seemed nice when they put on a polite show for the outside world. That soulless house bothered me, but if you are wealthy, with no kids to pay for, and probably no mortgage, what do you do? They clearly travel a great deal, and they're still young enough to follow what's happening in music and fashion. All lives move on. People grow up, or they're meant to, and have their own children. Sometimes it goes wrong. I wonder what happened with Camila's cool parents. I think about their music collection. I equate times and attitudes to music. Love songs from the last century were about being in love, feeling happy. Now love songs seem to explore the darker sides of human nature, or the saddest. Many are about misery and some aren't about love, but hate. At least that's my assessment, given what I hear when I'm in the car with the children and they play their music.

I realise that I'm home and the way back has been a blur. I don't remember driving. I must have turned on my automatic pilot, certainly once I was back on the roads I know, lost in thought about what's happening with Camila in that house.

I display the spoils from the bakery, which starts me off thinking about the cost of living all over again. My phone pings. I see that it's from Camila, so I open the message straight away.

Are you all okay?

Now, that's not the right question for her to be asking here, that's for sure. She knows we are more than likely to be okay. This is trying to find a reason to make contact. This is an insecure girl wanting support. I look up at the kitchen clock: it's only been two hours since I saw her.

Hi Cam, how are you getting on? I text back.

K. She replies.

Because, evidently 'okay' is far too many letters to type. Or perhaps not. Maybe she's signalling more than that. My children tell me that actually, a single 'k' is low-key. A lack of strong emotion in a text message, or perhaps a kind of dismissive, disinterested response. An extra letter to make it 'kk' softens the tone. So 'k' on its own is probably less than okay. Or, I could be reading too much into it.

I ask her what she's doing.

I'm at Nando's with them and it's awkward.

Then you probably shouldn't have your phone out at the table messaging me, I think. But I message back: *Oh nice, what have you ordered?*

I hate it here, fast food is bad for the environment.

Ah, I see. I think that maybe her parents might not be up to speed with green issues, judging by the gigantic carbon footprint they must clock-up with all that travelling. I suspect Cammy is thinking the same. Or perhaps she's struggling to talk to them because she just doesn't actually know them very well, nor they her. The best place to have taken Cam would have been to an independent street-food or vegan and vegetarian restaurant. They probably think that all teenagers like going to Nando's. But they don't know Cam's preferences yet, and how could they? Cam has been in care more of her life than she had lived with her parents. This weekend *is* all about them getting to know each other. And, if this weekend is all about the local authority manoeuvring Cammy into a position where she'll want to go home and live with her parents, I suspect that this particular money-saving initiative might be doomed to failure. It's so hard. I wonder if she has many memories of living with Robbie and Gabby. I'll find a way to ask her when she returns. Gently and carefully. 'Cam, do you have any childhood memories from living with your birth family?' probably isn't going to get me very far.

The people I'm really interested in are Sian and Gary. I'd love to be able to have a good conversation with them, but without a surname, I can't get anywhere.

And then it hits me. Good God, sometimes I can be so stupid! I could just *ask* Camila what their surname is.

I'm so stuck in the systems-thinking of GDPR and paperwork and all the rest of it. Sometimes it's hard to work out who is being protected here, the local authority or the child.

I wish Cam a good meal and then send some food emojis, hoping none of them is rude, then call Lloyd to join me for first dibs at the bakery treat.

He takes one look and shakes his head. 'No, thank you.' He pats his tummy. 'I need to look after myself.'

I can almost see the halo around his smug head, but he's right, and now I don't want a pastry either. Never mind the fact that I've spent over £30. Still, at least I know someone who will. I call the children down. I still think of them all as 'the children' even though they are all in their teens.

Vincent is first down. He pulls a plate from the rack and puts one of everything on it. He saws away at the soda bread and makes a mouthwatering sandwich with ham, cream cheese and sundried tomatoes. I definitely have foodies in the house these days. I'd like to think I've raised them that way, but it's really TikTok who've done it. All great, I think, in spite of costing me a fortune.

I check my phone again. Nothing else from Camila. No news is good news, I hope. But with my phone in my hand I reflect for a moment on the way that we just got on with things before the advent of the mobile phone. This level of texting and WhatsApping is so excessive: family groups, friends' groups, foster carers' groups, and plenty of groups I have no idea why I am in. Each new group or 'chat' fries my brain. It's not 'chat' if I'm doing it with my fingers.

I sit outside on the garden bench with my two chums, Dotty and Douglas. Their company is always easy, not least because I don't get texts from them. Mind you, if Dotty was a human I have no doubt that she'd be swiping and texting all the time, or at least until she decided to gnaw on her phone and kill it.

Next I take the pooches out for a walk. I breathe in the fresh air and enjoy the birds singing.

It's my birthday soon and Lloyd asked what I wanted. I couldn't think of one material thing. These days I appreciate, more and more, the simple pleasures of life: a good night's sleep, a cold glass of water, five minutes in the garden with the dogs. Birthdays mean less, but I did ask for a little dinner party for a few friends to help me celebrate. Maybe with a few cocktails. Now, that is my idea of a good evening, one which involves a cocktail or two.

I once made the mistake of sharing with a supervising social worker the fact that I love cocktails. That must have gone down in the records somewhere, because shortly afterwards we were in trouble. It was a Saturday and we'd been working hard in the garden. We were looking after a teenager, Adam, who'd gone out for the day with friends and was meant to be home by 7pm. When he didn't appear, I had to contact the out-of-hours team. It transpired that he'd got stuck somewhere with no money.

'No, I can't pick him up,' I explained to the team. 'I've had a cocktail.'

Next thing I knew I was being investigated for alcoholism and put on a training course. Now we are supposed to keep any alcohol in the house locked up. And they wonder why they can't keep and recruit foster carers.

I grew up in a house that hated drink. Both my adoptive parents had fathers who were obnoxious drinkers, so we grew up in a temperate household, hearing nothing but vitriol towards booze and those who drank it. Therefore, as soon as I could, I was knocking back the booze without a clue what I was doing. Civilised, sensible drinking of alcohol can be good, and often it teaches children how to be safe with booze.

I was furious about what happened with Adam, but as foster carers we soon learn that sometimes it's better to just nod and smile, make the social workers feel clever and important and get back to looking after the children. Sometimes I wonder if we are allowed to have a life at all.

We try.

We have a nice, quiet weekend. Lloyd and I watch a film in the evening and the teenagers mostly eat. They seem to be hungry all the time. It's a cliché, but it really does feel as if they might eat us out of house and home. I go for low-cost collateral damage as far as possible, buying crumpets, muffins, bagels and nice bread for them to make sandwiches and snacks in between meals.

I don't want to overdo it, but I do check in with Cam on Saturday evening to see if she is okay.

She texts back immediately. *I'm fine, bored!*

I ask her what she is doing.

I've had a Facetime with my grandparents from Spain. They wouldn't shut up.

If she hasn't spoken to them in a long time then I imagine this must have been awkward. To her, all these people feel like strangers. It must be tough. I suspect they all want to pretend that nothing has happened, and that her return home means that they have magically clicked back into being a family.

Experience (and common sense) tells me that it really isn't that simple.

IX

On Sunday Cam texts to ask if I can come and get her in the morning. I wasn't supposed to be collecting her until 7pm and the request kind of messes with the day I'd planned. Still, it was only domestic bits and pieces, so it'll just be that some of the chores don't get done.

I haven't got her parents' contact details, other than the address I dropped her at. Sarah gave me nothing more than a postcode; Cam had to point out the house. They never used to be this precious. I think it's down to a shortage of staff. Presumably that's why 'Jane' didn't arrive yesterday morning to take her.

A fellow dog-walker I know told me that she used to be a support worker, but she left because she was getting so much aggro from the parents and the social workers when things hadn't been arranged properly. She concluded, and I don't blame her, that a little job in the supermarket and walking her dog was better paid and easier work.

I realise that not being given Gabriella's or Rob's number isn't an insurmountable problem, though. I use my brain, unlike when I was trying to figure out how I could find out

Sian and Gary's surname. I simply ask Cam for her parents' mobile number.

But there's no reply.

So I simply sigh and say that I'll collect Cam at 9am as she asks.

When I get there to pick her up, she's already standing outside the front door with her bag. No sign of her mum or dad, and I still don't have their number.

She gets in the car.

'Morning!' I say with a bright smile. 'How are you?'

She reaches in her bag for her headphones and puts them on. That is as much of a reply as it appears I'm going to get.

I smile again, to let her know that's fine, and start the engine.

Just before we move off, I glance up at the front bedroom window, assuming that the main bedroom is at the front of the house. I see that the curtains are drawn. I look back at Camila and gently tap her on the arm. She looks at me and pulls off her headphones with a raised eyebrow.

'Do your parents definitely know that you're leaving now?'

She shrugs and pulls her headphones back on.

I wonder what to do. I can see how this *could* look and how it could blow out of proportion if I don't do the right thing now. But I'm not entirely sure what the right thing is. I don't want to wake her folks up. I root about in my bag and pull out my notebook. I find a pen in the coin tray by the gearstick and pen a little letter.

Cam isn't looking, she is busy scrolling through her phone. I write:

Hi, Gabby & Rob,

Camila asked me to collect her this morning. I didn't have your number, but here is mine. She asked last night. I assumed you knew she was leaving early but I'm just making sure she told you.

Best, Louise

I get out of the car and walk to the front door to post it through the letterbox. It's that Sunday morning sort of quiet, where the sound of gravel underfoot mixes with birdsong. Suburbia has its appeal.

As we near the retail park, I ask Cam if she would like a drink, maybe some breakfast.

She lifts up her right side of headphone. 'Yeah, please.'

'Sit in or drive through?'

'Drive through, please.'

And that's the extent of our conversation. She does not speak and I don't try to engage, knowing full well that sometimes young people – and indeed all of us – simply want to be quiet. I respect that entirely.

But when we are safely settled back at home, I feel I can ask, 'How did it go?'

'I was bored. There's not a lot to do.'

That doesn't give much away, but Cam clearly doesn't feel like talking and I suspect I'm being fobbed off with the easiest blanket statement a 14-year-old can muster on a Sunday morning. I will get my metaphorical tweezers out later to unpick this event, but for now I do nothing.

Sunday soon becomes Monday, bringing with it school – and resistance. Cam hates going to school so much. It's clear how much she drags her heels about going. She is scowling and petulant as we get ready to leave but, good for her, she's still doing it.

And I'm still in the dark about quite what's going on for her, a position I hate being in. As far as I can see, the relationship with her parents is on a hiding to nothing. Her parents haven't texted back to acknowledge my note, or communicated with me in any way. I'm slightly miffed. As far as I'm concerned, it's just bad manners. Bad manners are because of ignorance or arrogance. Given everything I've seen of Rob and Gabriella, I'm leaning towards the latter in their case.

We drop into town after school. I have a few things that I need to pick up. At the end of the shopping precinct a woman is wearing one of the red jackets of the Big Issue sellers. Cam reaches into her bag for some money to buy one. Again, I'm struck by her maturity and the choices she makes. It's not something that every 14-year-old would spend their money on, but Camila feels social injustice in her core.

On the way home, we talk a little bit about the problem of homelessness.

'It will never be solved until the government sorts out enough affordable housing and provides better welfare support,' she tells me.

As ever, I'm struck by the way she has thought about these things. Parroting things she's heard elsewhere, perhaps, but she's engaging with ideas that some kids her age just wouldn't stop and think about. She cares deeply about the world and is more thoughtful about how she wants to live in it than most of her peers would be. It strikes me that she is interested in philosophy.

I suggest it as a possibility for the future. She's smart enough to study at university.

'Nah, I'm not going to university,' she says. 'It's a rip off.'

I feel it's rather a shame that she has that view. I know that some universities are better than others and I think she'd be great at engaging with the principles of philosophy. To me she seems like a highly-intelligent young woman who is struggling to find a place within any of the systems she is currently forced to inhabit.

Again, I think about how to channel this kind of thought and energy. It's great that she has ideas and wants to engage with things, but she needs an outlet. She needs to be able to escape the online echo chambers, the bubbles of people saying the same thing. She needs her thoughts and ideas to be challenged in order that she can develop them.

At home, I think Vincent and Jackson might even feel a little intimidated by Camila. They seem to sort of dance around her, not quite avoiding her, but certainly not engaging with her in the way that they have done with other foster siblings before. They like her, and they are all polite to each other. They send funny things on the family WhatsApp group, which some of our ex-foster children are on, too. But it's all at a distance. They never really post anything concerning themselves, or share more than they have to. Perhaps they leave that for their other platforms.

On the other hand, perhaps it's also to do with their relative ages as much as anything. I think I can see changes in how the boys are with foster children because they are now on the verge of becoming young men. They spend more time in their bedrooms, as does Lily. That doesn't hurt, because so does Cam. She spends some time with Lily but the reality is that Lily has her own group of friends and at her age, being told to take someone else with you can be rather irksome, to say the least. Awkward for Cam, too.

So I do my best to try to tempt each of the teenagers out of their isolation with nice food. It doesn't work often, because they are all on different meal schedules and eating plans, so there is less togetherness at the table – apart from Vincent, who will reliably eat all day long and still come down for dinner.

Cam has actually taken to making her own food. I think this is the first act of independence. She belongs to the generation who spent crucial social development time in lockdown. Cooking and eating independently isn't a big problem, as long as that feeling of independence doesn't go too far too quickly.

But overall, I think that Lloyd and I find Cam easy to live with. Other than the problems at school, she is no bother at all.

The first few days of the week tick along, but on Wednesday afternoon I get another call from school. This time I am asked to collect her because she has received a suspension for two days for 'defiance'.

'I'll be there in 45 minutes,' I sigh, knowing that first I have to write up the report, as I always do whenever there is a significant incident like this. In doing so, I notice that my last one, about the last time school contacted me when the young lad was waiting for her outside school, has received no action whatsoever. It makes it feel like a back-covering exercise, rather than a real attempt to support Cam. I make sure I reference the fact that there has been no development there in today's log, partly to ensure that it's clear it's not me who has failed to communicate.

In a belt-and-braces approach, I send texts to Kendi and Sarah updating them about the suspension and saying that I have *Re-added concern re: the young man meeting Camila.* It also means

I now have this on my phone as well as via the social services system. I have become a meticulous record-keeper.

Camila is quiet in the car. I avoid being 'cross' or judgemental about whatever has happened to result in the suspension. I start chatting about the dogs.

'I've still got some work to do this afternoon, would you mind taking them out for me?' I ask.

I actually love taking the pooches out to enjoy the fresh air and birdsong, but I feel like Cam could do with some of that to herself today. She smiles and nods.

I wait a few more minutes before asking a different question. 'Have you heard from your parents?'

She sends a quick, quizzical look in my direction, then says, 'Yeah, but they don't have anything to say.'

'Well, it must be hard for them,' I say, 'I guess they don't really know you, not at this stage of your life.'

This time she keeps her eyes fixed ahead. 'Exactly. So why the fuck am I staying with them?'

I feel very much the same way. But I have to be careful here.

'Have you told Sarah how you feel?'

'Yeah, but she doesn't care. She just says I need to give it time.'

This seems to confirm to me that the Allen family are nothing more than the parking bay while the authorities try to get Cam back to her family. And it doesn't feel right at all. Sian and Gary flash to my mind and I ask the question I meant to ask before. 'What's the surname of your old foster carers?'

She turns sharply to look at me. I try to keep my expression impervious, features carved into grey rock. I have a terrible poker face.

'Ellens.'

I clock that name and say no more.

But Cam is intuitive. That's partly why she suffers as she does. I suspect she knows I'm going to find them.

But we say nothing.

Over her two suspension days I put my work to one side and spend a lot of time with Cam. We take the dogs on a long walk to a nature reserve. She is so knowledgeable about the names of trees and birds and how the natural world works. Much more than me. I make a joke about her being like David Attenborough.

She smiles, sadly. 'Sian will cry her heart out when he dies.'

That little statement tells me so much. Cam misses her parents. Not her birth parents, whom she knows so little about and has so little in common with, despite looking like her dad. No, she misses her foster parents.

We talk some more. I do my best to gently tease out more information. Each time I do, it points to the same thing: she loves Sian and Gary. She is ill at ease with Gabriella and Rob.

'How often do you hear from your mum and dad,' I ask.

'Not much. They occasionally drop a text saying hello, but not much else.'

'And Sian and Gary?'

'Nothing. Sarah told them that they shouldn't contact me, so that I could have time to settle.'

'How do you know?'

She tells me that she always sat on the stairs and listened to social workers when there were meetings, that's how she knows what's going on.

'I didn't like how the social workers treated Sian and Gary.

It wasn't fair.'

Interesting. She doesn't like the way that Sarah treats her as if she's a child, either.

Given what's she's already said, I feel confident enough to ask her about the breakdown of the placement.

'I'd had enough of all the talk about seeing my parents more. It made me feel unwell.'

'Unwell how?'

She tells me that she can't really explain it. 'Just as if my head was going to blow off. Like all the feelings were too much. I had to do something.' She looks up at me. 'I tried cutting.'

I'm not shocked. 'Did it help?'

'No. To be honest, it just didn't work for me.'

But, she does start talking about poo. Ever since she was a little girl she had caught her poo in her hand as it dropped.

I was more than fascinated by this.

'I did that too, when I was very young,' I share.

I wonder if it's more common than we think. I wonder if perhaps, when we are in an environment that smells different to us, or that the people who are caring for us change, or some other trigger, that our primitive, primal feelings and intuitions rise to the surface.

Is it, perhaps, totally natural to sniff your own poo? Animals do it. They sniff their own poop, and that of other animals. I see the dogs do it all the time. Are they checking that they are okay? Maybe this is more okay and less shameful than we are led to believe.

Listening to Cam tell me this gives me a whole new level of understanding and awareness.

We grab a coffee in the cafe, and while she's in the loos, I do a bit more internet research, discovering that it isn't, in fact, unknown for teenagers to engage in 'fecal smearing'. It can be a way of expressing emotions, seeking attention, or *a reaction to underlying psychological issues like anxiety, depression, or trauma*. It doesn't surprise me in the slightest.

When she returns, I broach the subject of the AI created little film at school that seems to have got a lot of young people into a lot of trouble.

She looks at me with a smile. 'It wasn't that bad. They completely over-reacted. They let things slip all the time at school, the wrong things. But the petty shit? They love that, really go to town on it. They've got their priorities all wrong.'

I can't help but think she has a point. She's really quite perceptive.

'What they should be worried about is bullying, but they haven't a clue. It's out of control and that's why I hate that school.'

I let that statement settle, then ask her if she is being bullied.

The shrug again. 'Yeah, most of us are. The bullies bully each other and people like me because I don't bully and I think they are all twats.'

Now we are getting to it, I think.

'There's loads of bad shit at school. Boys sexually abusing girls, putting their hands up their skirts, touching girls. Most of the boys do it, because the ones that don't, and are actually okay, get bullied too. And they worry about a fucking AI video.'

I nod agreement.

'The teachers don't do anything about it,' she says.

Since today is a day for being open and sharing, I broach the subject of the young man who waits for her outside school.

I'm no longer worried that he has anything to do with County Lines. That is not Camila's tribe, not even slightly. I *am* worried that something untoward is going on. Is this man a paedophile? I hope that I'm barking up the wrong tree there, but what's the nature of his relationship with Cam? I don't understand his presence.

'Who's the boy who waits outside for you?'

She pauses. 'It's just Fred. My protector.'

It strikes me that 'protector' is a strange word to use. I press a bit harder. 'Who is Fred, though? How do you know him?'

'He's been my friend since middle school. He was my old neighbour when I lived with Sian and Gary. The school gets all worked up because he's a few years older than me. When I was younger no one said anything. Not Sarah, or anyone else. No one minded that we played together. There were a load of kids in the area, we all used to play around each other's houses. It was normal. But not now we're older, it's now a threat to humanity if kids not chronologically the same age talk to each other or like each other. The world is fucking mad!'

I have noticed that the children are sort of brainwashed into thinking that having a relationship with anyone outside their year group is somehow dodgy. If a boy is seeing a girl in the year below, he is automatically a 'pedo'.

Lloyd is four years older than me. I've been out with men in the past who were older than me by a few years or more. Only once I went out with someone who was younger than me. It didn't last long because it was like having a little brother in tow.

It's well-known that girls seem to mature faster than boys. Is it surprising that a teenage girl wants to hang about with someone older? She's so mature, in so many ways. I'm torn between my instinct to protect her and giving her the benefit of the doubt.

I think I can give her that; can I do the same for Fred, though?

X

The two suspension days are up. Cam goes back to school. Reluctantly.

But a few days later, she's suspended once again for her 'difficult behaviour'. Details aren't really forthcoming, but that word 'defiance' is used again.

Because Camila has missed some school and had so much upheaval – leaving her home and family, which is what Sian and Gary represent – she needs to be cut some slack. If she'd just been removed from her birth family, especially if she had been happy in that domestic environment, I have no doubt that the school would be thinking very differently. It's just another example of how foster children's attachments aren't taken seriously, and these emotions are not properly recognised. This is, almost certainly, a kind of grief that she's suffering.

Instead of being supported, she's being punished.

When she gets home, she goes straight upstairs to her room. I tap gently a little while later and see that she's fallen asleep. I leave her to snooze.

The stricter disciplinarians out there might think this is rewarding bad behaviour. I disagree. When children, young people and adults struggle to regulate, it's usually not as simple as 'they're bad' or 'misbehaving'. It can mean that they're struggling to cope more broadly. They don't have a hold over their emotions and are overpowered by them.

It's another sign to me that this is grief.

To say 'pull yourself together' doesn't always work, tempting though it is. It's tempting because when those around us are unregulated, our lives become much harder to navigate and we end up having to work harder ourselves.

I think this is what happens in classrooms, when teachers have 30 or more young people to deal with, some of them are going to be like the can of Coke that's been shaken, ready to fizz up and explode when someone tries to open it.

My gut feeling is that as well as all the complicated feelings she has about her former foster carers and her birth parents, Camila experiences this world as someone who cares more deeply about things than some. I watch her take information in. She is always questioning and has a natural sense of justice. All to the good. But being like this, for some reason, seems to cause discomfort in others. Especially those who are, perhaps, in denial about something, or have limitations in their world view, a very 'local' view of the world. I think Camila is one of life's disrupters. Just her very presence seems to agitate some people.

Personally, I love this. I admire independent thinking. But school isn't always a place for independent thinking, even though it should be. I just don't think some teachers *get* children like Camila, and, instead of treating them as the intelligent and sensitive beings they are, they are punished.

I think it's perverse that Camila was taken away from the

people she loved. For, to all intents and purposes, smearing her own poo on herself. A dramatic act, perhaps, but a protest. Not the best, but probably all she could manage to do at the time.

Sarah gets in touch to say that she's coming round to take Cam out. This could go either way. I sense that Cam is probably a lot sharper than Sarah. Cam has also expressed her displeasure at being patronised by her social worker. But Sarah is a grown-up, and a professional, and they've known each other a long time. Originally I thought this was a good, and relatively rare, thing – to have had that level of consistency over years. Now I'm starting to wonder whether it's a case of familiarity breeding contempt.

The idea that Cam is in care because she has busy parents really doesn't cut it for me. If that were the reason, then half the bloody world's children would be in care. I'm certain that Camila is hiding some sort of trauma experiences, whatever they may be.

For once, Kendi is letting me down on this. He hasn't managed to pull out anything further. That's really not like him at all. He must be very busy, or there is something that we aren't allowed to know about.

I am guessing – and it is only a guess – that if we knew what it was, we could argue for Camila *not* to be returned to her parents, a course of action which I am increasingly convinced is the master plan here.

Too many children, who seem settled with their foster carers are somehow making their way back to their parents. The 'voting-with-their-feet' argument is a load of tosh. We're talking about vulnerable young people with mixed up attachments and immature prefrontal cortices in their teenage brains. The latter being the bit of the brain responsible for, amongst other things, decision-making, and an area still undergoing significant development while they are adolescents.

On one level, Camila scares me. Her need for justice is so strong. I have been like this myself. Being in care certainly sharpens your sense of social justice. Combine that with having a kindness of soul – not the kindness that is easily exploitable – but one which is empathetic and determined, and underpinned with knowing what is right. That's a formidable thing to face. Which is why it doesn't always go down well with authority, especially the kind which exists in schools. But again, I wonder if it all comes from a place of trauma.

Sarah messages me to let me know that Camila is going to stay with her parents again this weekend.

Did you read my report from last time? I ask.

Her response is non-committal. *Early days. It must be hard for all of them.*

Oh, she has this off to a fine art, as they all do. If the foster carer protests just a little too much, they send back a platitude. I hate the platitudes. They must have a special social workers' thesaurus for platitudes, plus an instruction manual on how to break down placements and throw allegations at foster carers if they become difficult.

Moreover, there's no question of a lift over there from the support worker; the assumption is that I'll simply drive over once again on Saturday morning and pick her up on Sunday night. I don't mind doing it, of course I don't. It's the lack of consultation that I mind. No checking in to see if that might fit with any plans that the Allen family might have for the weekend. What if I had been busy, or we were going away? They never think of that.

And in the midst of all of this, is a child who is being pulled in too many different directions.

I feel a kind of kinship with Camila, that I don't often feel with the children we take in. I think it's because I can see that we're similar – or at least she's similar to the way I was when I was younger. And that's why I can see that, if she is not heard and seen with support and love and understanding, she'll do something more serious. She's already had two back-to-back suspensions from school.

The content of the email about her that I received from school was worded in such a bland, non-personal way that it has wound me up. No wonder Camila gets incensed. Again, there's little detail but it doesn't sound as if her 'crime' was all that bad. The word she used the other day to describe the way teachers pounce on her behaviour was 'petty' and I think that's pretty accurate. They aren't tuned into her needs at all, and they are also keeping us at arm's length. We aren't being treated with the same courtesies as 'parents' would. They're excluding us from meetings and correspondence, as though we somehow don't count because we're 'only' the foster carers. It's annoying at best, and I'm actually finding it quite depressing.

So, Camila is off school for 'defiance' and Sarah thinks that sending her to her parents, where she clearly is not comfortable, is a great way to settle her. Terrific.

Camila is upset about the world anyway, why create even more problems for her? She's still a child who hugs a teddy at night. How can she deal with all the emotions that the adult world is throwing at her? The pressure to be with her parents and the business at school is too much.

Almost as if to add insult to injury, Gabby texts to see if I can drop Camila off on Friday afternoon, instead of Saturday morning. So *now* she chooses to use my number, at long last, because she wants something. I get the impression that she's quite a pushy woman. It's already Thursday. This was not the arrangement and just another example of how everyone seems to be taking the mickey. On the upside, I at least now have her number.

I walk upstairs and ask Cam if she wants to go tomorrow night. She looks at me as if I've asked her if she wants to poke her own eyeballs out.

'No.'

That's good enough for me. I text back: *We will see you on Saturday morning at the arranged time, depending on traffic.*

I feel agitated. I feel powerless. I feel complicit in something that I know is the wrong choice.

And I feel like this is all going to go horribly wrong.

Poor Cam. I go back upstairs and sit down on her bed while she fiddles about on her phone by the window.

'Cam, sweetheart, I am so, so sorry about all this crap.'

She looks up from her phone, surprised I think.

I carry on. 'I don't know how you feel about seeing your parents, you don't say. But I can imagine it's pretty tough because you don't know them like you used to.'

She looks out of the window and her expression is sad.

I go on. 'Sarah seems keen for you to spend time with your parents. Has she been encouraging it before?'

'Yes, even more since I left Sian's.'

I do some maths in my head. She's been with us for around two months, and she had two weeks with Gabby and Rob while her placement with us was sorted out.

186

In for a penny. 'Did you want to leave Sian and Gary's?'

'No! That was never meant to happen!'

Ah. Here it comes.

'I feel like it was all my fault. I love them, they are my parents, really. I wish I could just go back and rewind time and make it all not happen.'

The vehemence with which she speaks makes me realise that it isn't just a kind of grief she's feeling, it's also guilt about what happened and her part in it.

She didn't want to leave. This was an overreaction from the social workers. Placement breakdown my arse. I knew it. This is exactly what Lloyd and I had thought was the case.

I desperately want to talk to Sian and Gary to find a way to put things right. I know it would be frowned on. From a social services perspective it's unacceptable. And I'm worried that Kendi would disapprove.

But what else can I do? This whole situation isn't sitting well with me. None of it feels right.

'I know that feeling,' I say, because I do. 'It's tricky.'

She nods sadly, and looks away again.

'Do you want to go to your parents this weekend?'

'Honestly? No, not really.' She pauses. 'I'm not sure I like my parents very much. I have nothing in common with them.' Another pause. 'They live a pretentious, shallow life.'

Well, that is quite an opinion, especially coming from a 14 year old, but it's her opinion and, knowing Cam as I have come to in this short time, her opinion matters. It's her own intuition, and it's from the heart.

XI

I wait until much later, when Lloyd and I are sitting on the sofa after the day's work is done and the teenagers are all in their dens, before telling Lloyd about the conversation I had with Camila.

He thinks very highly of Cam. He refers to her regularly as a 'lovely young woman', and she is. It's not an empty phrase. He doesn't always say that about the teenage girls we have fostered, and his description acknowledges her maturity as well as her good-nature. We don't see any of the 'defiance' that the school evidently does.

We agree to let this weekend happen, not because we want to, but because we don't have any power to change it. But, if she is unhappy, we'll write up a report and make it really clear. I already know that we'll get accused of writing in the wrong tone. It will be too personal, or not personal enough, or some other crap. Honestly, we're always damned if we do and damned if we don't in this game. I also resolve to text Kendi first thing in the morning to let him know our concerns and share Cam's thoughts.

On Saturday morning I feel Cam change. She becomes

quieter and quieter, the closer we get to her parents' house. This is so hard for her. As each day passes and we become even more fond of Cam, it gets harder to know that she is being put through this emotional discomfort again and again without doing anything about it.

Having gauged Cam's feelings now, I will start to put some feelers out to see if anyone knows the Ellens. It's high time I found Sian and Gary. They live in the next region so fall under a different local authority, or agency. I don't know and I don't want to ask Cam too many questions because I don't want to make her complicit in any way. Lloyd is the only one who knows.

Years ago, I wouldn't have told Lloyd what I was doing. In the early days he was very much 'by the book' in every aspect of our fostering lives. Then he began to realise that that book didn't exist, that the goalposts change all the time. National 'minimum standards' in care are a nice idea, but Ofsted and the Department for Education have no way of knowing, let alone ensuring, that those lovely standards are being upheld. When things go wrong, there are internal investigations. That just sounds like marking your own homework to me. And who doesn't give themselves the benefit of the doubt when they're doing that?

We arrive at Gabby and Rob's house. They aren't waiting at the door this time, so I walk with Camila across the gravel drive up to the front door. Crunch, crunch, crunch. The sound beneath our feet takes on an ominous timbre because I know that we are marching towards somewhere that Cam doesn't want to be.

We stand at the door. I ring the bell which has a camera attached to it. I resist the temptation to stick my tongue out.

Rob opens the door. 'Hi Cammie, hi Louise. Gabby won't be long. She's just coming back from town, she's had her nails done.'

Two things flash through my brain. One, why didn't she do this at some other point, when Cam wasn't coming? The second is, why didn't she arrange for Cam to have hers done too? That could have been a nice mother and daughter bonding thing to do.

Something inside me says, 'Don't leave Cam alone.' I can see she's uncomfortable, but it's hard for her to hide. She just stands behind me awkwardly. I continue to stand in the doorway smiling, but without saying anything, until he gets the message and invites us in.

'Have a seat,' he gestures to the stools up at the island in the kitchen.

I watch Cam slide her rucksack onto the floor by her feet. I put my handbag down on the floor too.

There's another uncomfortable pause before Rob smiles and asks if we would like a drink. 'Coffee, tea, juice?'

'Water, please,' Cam says.

Rob dashes over to the big fridge and fills a glass half full with ice, then pushes on the water handle. He puts it down in front of Cam. They have the same make of coffee machine as us, but theirs is the big flash one with all the bells and whistles. We only ever have black coffee at home because neither of us have bothered to learn what to do with the little pipes and taps that froth things.

I ask for a cappuccino.

It's not to be difficult, rather to give him something to do and help slow down the awkwardness. I'm also keen to see what those pipe things actually do. While he has his back to us, busy making a fussy, frothy coffee which evidently generates a good deal of noise, I take the opportunity to have a good scan of their home.

It feels like a workplace, I decide, with some home comforts. There are desks and computers everywhere.

'What is it you do, Rob?' I ask.

In a few moments I am presented with a very nice cappuccino. He puts the coffee in a coffee shop style white cup and saucer.

'I run a building company.'

'Oh, that's lovely,' I say, realising that I now sound like an interested auntie. 'And how long have you been doing that?'

He seems quite pleased to be asked. 'Oh, about 15 years, I suppose.'

'How lovely!' I say, wishing I could find another adjective, but words seem to be failing me this morning. 'And do you enjoy it?'

He flaps his arms around vaguely. 'Oh, you know.' He looks like an awkward teenage boy, I think, not quite looking me in the face.

I'll take that as a no then.

He scratches his neck and puts his hands in his pockets. He doesn't look like someone who is happy in his own skin.

I make my coffee last as long as I possibly can, but time goes on and there's no sign of Gabby. Now it really does get awkward.

'I'm not sure where she's got to.'

Gabriella is over an hour late to see her daughter and I want to get on with the day, but I can tell that Camila is feeling desperately uncomfortable. I look across at her and see that her whole face seems to say, 'Can we go now please?'

But we hang on, making small talk. I manage to get a tour of the very low-maintenance garden while looking at all the houses out the back. Some have put on huge extensions. It's bifold central around here. The gardens are quite long and wide and they can all afford good, strong, tall fencing with trellis, which all the neighbours have taken advantage of and grown clematis and honeysuckles on. I would, too.

It's nearly two hours later when Gabriella finally comes in carrying several shopping bags from different clothes shops: All Saints, Asics, Castore, Crew Clothing. I hope she's got something for Cam in all that.

No apology, or acknowledgement, beyond a, 'Oh, you didn't have to wait for me.'

I bid my farewells and put my second coffee down. Cam looks utterly fed-up. I give her a little squidge of a hug, which is meant to be reassuring but will, no doubt, come back to bite me in some report somewhere, but there's no way I can leave that child here without her knowing I'm on her team.

I let out a big sigh when I get back in the car and reach for my water bottle, glugging down a good half of it. If I'm honest, I'm a bit caffeined-up and can feel a headache coming on.

Back at home I check my phone several times. No messages from Camila, so I can only assume that she must be alright.

I hope you're having a nice time, I text.

It's not until much later in the evening that I get a *yeah* back. Nothing more.

That's not good. I wonder what they are all doing?

When I collect Camila the following evening at the

appointed time, she is waiting on the doorstep. The headphones are on and she walks straight to the car and gets in without a word.

Gabriella says, 'Teenagers, eh?' with a little conspiratorial smile.

I don't return it. She doesn't have any right to say that because she hasn't looked after her children to understand how, for them, their teenage years will roll out. Every child is different.

'Did you have a nice time?' I ask.

Rob smiles. 'We went bowling, then got a burger.' His eyes dart from side to side a bit nervously. 'A bean burger.'

We drive home with Cam looking out of the window, away from me, headphones on. A bundle of body language that shouts: DO NOT ENGAGE. I don't push her. I notice that her hands move from clasped tight to almost wringing. I sense that the person beside me is all coiled up, ready to explode.

As we walk towards our front door, I ask Cam if she wants any dinner.

She shakes her head and heads straight upstairs to her room, not quite slamming the door behind her, but closing it in a firm, do-not-follow way.

We carry on with our evening, but after about an hour I pop upstairs to check on her. I knock lightly on her door.

There's no response. I wait for a moment, then knock again, slightly more firmly. I turn the handle. And walk into a horrific sight.

XII

Cam is sitting on the floor with shit all over her hands.

On the wall she has written in big letters I'M NOT WORTH SHIT and I HATE YOU and FUCK.

I look her in the eye and say, very calmly, 'Go and have a shower. Bring out your towel and clothes for me to wash.'

She pulls her knees into her chest and sinks her head down onto them. 'Sorry.'

She looks so broken and distressed. Everything in my bones says 'be kind.'

I say nothing.

Whilst she is in the shower, I take pictures of the walls. Then I grab the bathroom cleaner, kitchen cleaner and bleach, old cloths, marigolds, kitchen roll and the outside bucket that we use for washing the cars.

Lloyd looks at me with a questioning eyebrow.

'You don't want to know.'

And I mean it. I'm saying it with love because Lloyd will only start retching if he tries to help, and I have no desire to add vomit to this delightful scene.

I fly back upstairs to make sure no one is anywhere near

her room. I hear a cacophony of music from the different bedrooms: a sound clash between Lana Del Ray, The Killers, and Taylor Swift. I also hear the shower going, which I take as a good sign.

Flinging open Camila's windows lets the fresh air in and the foul smell out. I put on the marigolds and work quickly. The shit is still soft and easy to wash off. Good. But it means I soon need to change the water. I run to the other bathroom, tip the bucket down the loo and flush it away. I repeat this action four times, as quickly and efficiently as I can.

Lloyd is standing on the stairs. 'Is it what I think it is?'

I nod and say nothing. I can still hear the shower going. Hopefully the hot water is helping her feel better, so she can begin to regulate herself and feel calmer.

With the cloth held out in my hand I pour on some bleach and wipe over the skirting boards that were dribbled onto. I dash back to change the water once more and start on the wooden floorboards. The room smells of cleaning products, but it's better than what it did smell like. I push the window open even more.

I grab the bucket and all the paraphernalia and run downstairs, shoving it in the conservatory. Another dash back up the stairs and a sniff of the air. No shit here!

I tidy up a bit in her room and make the bed, which is mercifully unscathed. It all looks fine. You'd never know. I lower the window. The windy bluster outside has helped circulate the fresh air. I turn the big light off, leaving the side light on. It's just a softer atmosphere. Just like magic, Dotty and Doug enter the room and jump on Camila's bed. It feels like creating a stage set. I leave with the door slightly open.

I tap on the bathroom door. 'Cammy, are you okay, sweetheart?'

A very quiet 'yeah' in response.

'Would you like a cup of tea or hot chocolate?'

'Hot chocolate, please.'

I begin to head off down the corridor but stop a few steps down on the stairs. I hear her come out of the bathroom. She has rolled up all her clothes and put them by her door. I hear a sweet voice, 'Hello Dotty, hello Doug.' I continue to walk down the stairs, past Mabel on her way up. She must be on her way to see Camila, she always knows when she is required. I leave Cam to her furry support workers and go into the kitchen, where Lloyd is sitting at the table with a glass of wine next to his laptop.

'Shall I pour you one?'

'Yes, please.'

I smile and breathe out. 'All is well.'

I wait until the next morning to send the photos with a report. I hate doing this. I feel that I am complicit in taking Cam's dignity away. But I must. And, if I don't, they will haul me over the coals. I word it carefully, in a way that strongly suggests that this is a reaction to her stress, a form of self-expression. I feel quite pleased with myself when I add a sentence at the bottom that reads: *nothing says I feel like shit more than shit.*

Well, the shit storm has happened – and in more ways than one. Smeared poo grabs the attention of Sarah within seconds. My word, nothing seems to move a social worker quicker than poo.

I've organised an urgent TEAMS meeting. Do you want to end the placement? is Sarah's first response.

Wow. Let's not think about how Cam is feeling. Let's worry about cost. They are terrified that we'll pull the placement and they'll have to pay a vast amount of money to put her in some high security therapeutic whatever. That is a situation they do not want.

Kendi is kind as always and springs into action. He tells the team, not asks, that they fund a therapist.

I laugh, as I know that with current CAMHS (Child and Adolescent Mental Health Services) waiting lists we could be looking at months, or years, to see someone.

We foster carers, with our gallows humour, used to jokingly say (not to the children but amongst ourselves) 'They have to have killed themselves to get an appointment.'

Now that almost seems to have become the sad truth.

The urgent Teams meeting is rather annoying as I had other online Zooms planned. I sigh and cancel them.

Within an hour, Lloyd and I are sitting in front of the computer in his office looking at a wall of faces we have never seen before, plus Sarah and Kendi.

In the maelstrom of clearing up and writing reports, I haven't actually shown Lloyd the pictures I took, so when they all start talking about the 'seriousness of the incident', I show him the images on my phone. He looks horrified.

I also show him the 'after' pictures and he looks relieved.

I'm finding this meeting rather interesting, if I'm honest, from the point of view of what seems to me to be an overdramatic response. I'm not sure if it's because I come from an art background or because I was expecting it, but I'm not repulsed by Camila's chosen self-expression in the medium of excrement. I was the one who cleaned it up and I'm fine about it. I've cleaned up human shit many times before. I've dealt with adults, children, dogs and cats who were unwell. This was relatively healthy shit, so to speak. And her poo-graffiti was a creative act, of sorts.

Piero Manzoni was a conceptual artist from Italy who became known for his provocative pieces that asked questions about art itself. In what most people consider to be his most shocking work, *merda d'artista* or 'Artist's shit', a work of the early 1960s, he filled and sealed 90 tin cans with his own faeces. And, in 2015, tin 54 was sold at Christie's for £182,500. So, there is money in shit. Quite literally.

The words 'smeared' and 'smearing' are, in my view, being overused in this meeting. All these professionals, and I use the term fairly loosely, are giving their tinpot hypotheses and many are doing so with wrinkled noses, as if they can smell the faeces in the air. So I wonder how much of their theorising arises from their personal revulsion.

I think about a friend of mine who used to run an Airbnb. She let it out to a young couple. I say 'young', although for both of us, our definition of that term has shifted over time. It now covers most people I encounter, it seems, as I've aged. Everyone else seems young. But my poor friend found her beautiful, boutique-style cottage covered in shit. Human shit. They had, it seems, had some kind of kinky sex session. She was furious, but powerless. They had her over a barrel because, if she said anything, they would write a negative review. She had to throw all the bedding and even the mattress away, along with the towels and a rug. She had to redecorate the whole cottage. So, in the context of her experience, wiping up a bit of poo used as graffiti doesn't seem so bad.

I can see that Lloyd is becoming agitated by their assumptions about how traumatic it all must have been for us. And it's annoying me, too.

But at least they all agree that Cam needs support. CAMHS is mentioned again. I don't hold my breath, and not just because of the waiting lists. For so many children whom we've fought for in order to access CAMHS and other services, the outcome has been disappointing to say the least. But they all know that, with this little 'occupation' of Camila's, they will struggle to get her in anywhere else cheaply.

It's interesting to hear them talk, and it reminds me of when I taught at the university and there was a student of mine who wanted her own room in halls, so she said on the application form that she was a bedwetter. That got her her own apartment.

But if she is able to access a form of therapy, then maybe it will help her with the original abuse which, despite Sarah's dismissive nonchalance, I think is very real. Something happened to Cam in the past, and whatever it was, it was something significant.

'So, ultimately,' one of the faces on the screen says, 'I say we let Camila choose. Art therapy, equine therapy or guinea pig therapy.'

It turns out that guinea pig therapy is an actual thing.

I can just imagine her face when we ask her to pick.

I think my preferred version of therapy in my own world is watching the washing machine go around. I always feel better after. I don't have to talk to anyone and I'm convinced the eye-movement of following the drum around must have a scientific benefit.

But there'd be no money-making opportunity from that and it seems as if, unless you can monetise something it's worthless.

Someone else leads a conversation about employing more therapeutic parenting. Lloyd and I have done a few therapeutic parenting courses. Mainly because when we changed to a new fostering agency, they had a preferred provider and insisted that we undertake another set of courses. They were dismissive of the ones we'd already attended.

So now, we've done PACE, which stands for Playfulness, Acceptance, Curiosity and Empathy. It's all about how adults interact with children to help them feel safe and build secure attachments, especially those who may have experienced trauma.

And we've done 'Conscious Parenting' which is all about self-awareness and emotional intelligence in parents. The focus is on getting parents to think about and understand their own triggers, biases and patterns, which in turn helps them to respond to their children with greater compassion and understanding, rather than reactivity.

We've also done 'Proactive Parenting', which is kind of a different version of the same thing: anticipating potential problems and situations and trying to address them before they escalate, rather than reacting to them after they occur.

It's all very similar, just newer academics who cook up a catchy name for their new, signature technique, even though they're all saying roughly the same thing.

I have to be honest, at times it can feel a bit like joining a cult.

What I do is take bits that I think are useful and blend them into the Louise Version of therapeutic care, the one where the foster carers, said parents, are allowed to think and feel and are *not* turned into robots. Sometimes I raise my voice and swear – because I'm human.

Kendi already thinks we're good therapeutic foster carers, though, honestly, the bar is low. They perceive making cupcakes together as therapeutic which, of course, it can be but that's what I mean. It's a lot of big words for simple things. I often think this chitter-chatter is a distraction from the bigger issues that are going on for children, and a way to try to compensate for the lack of expertise and resources available.

Later, after we've all eaten and the others have disappeared into their rooms, I ask Camila which therapy she would prefer. Initially she says 'art', then changes her mind.

'I mean, I can do that here whenever I like, with you.'

Which is true. My art studio is open any time she wants it.

She can't make her mind up between horse or guinea pig.

'Well, no need to make a decision tonight. Give yourself a chance to think about it before you choose.'

I think it's going to take more than a horse or a guinea pig to help Cam, whatever the experts say.

XIII

With all the stuff that has been going on with Cam, I've taken my eye off the ball with Lily. She is starting to behave in ways that say, 'I want your attention.'

'Is that girl staying much longer?' she asks me.

I wonder quite when Cam became 'that girl'. The honest truth is that I can't say that the two of them have been besties. As a fostered child herself, Lily is usually brilliant at welcoming the newbies, but they've never quite hit it off. They are both at an age, I suppose, where they want their own worlds as far as friendships are concerned. Lily has taken to going out a lot with her mates.

They are an okay crew on the whole: a wash-up of friends she has had for a few years and a few new ones. There is a leader of her little gang and it isn't Lily, although I would say she is next in command. Funny how these friendships pan out. I have noticed with Lily's lot that when there are just three of them they become quite bitchy to one. Two gang up together. I see this play out a lot.

I don't know exactly why Lily is feeling so bruised. I always try to include all the children in as much as I can, or at least offer the same to all of them. I think that's the trick: to ask if they want to join in, then they can say 'no' rather than accuse me of favouritism. This was a complaint when they were young. They've all accused me of treating Vincent as the favourite in the past. I had to explain that it only seems that way because Vincent causes the least trouble. The suggestion that they can't have it both ways, that they might be responsible for the way they are treated at home, was something of a revelation.

But it's true that Cam is the priority right now.

'Do you want to invite Fred to come over?' I ask.

The face she pulls is almost funny, but leaves me feeling concerned. Is she hiding something? Or does she just consider us to be too much of an embarrassment to introduce someone she knows well to us?

I tell myself it's the latter. Any time I've said to any of the children including the older ones, now with their own children, 'Why not invite your friend over?' they have resisted. When they reach a certain age it seems they'd rather sit in a bus shelter all evening than have their friendly Louise offer nibbles and drinks, non-alcoholic, of course. It's kind of funny because Barbara, my adoptive mother, was hideous to my friends. She could be rude and menacing and generally deeply embarrassing. Consequently, I would arrange to meet my friends anywhere but home. That's why I try to be as relaxed as possible about friends and as welcoming as I can. I would far rather they were here, where I can keep an eye on them, than perhaps getting up to the stuff I got up to.

Sarah has arranged to visit Cam again. She has a specific agenda this time. She wants to talk about the poo situation – good luck with that; and the Fred situation – again, good luck with that too. I'd like Sarah to talk to Camila about how often she wants to see her parents and what the shape of those visits needs to look like for Camila. I can see a distinct link between parents and poo.

When I see Sarah at the door, I say hello and all that stuff, but then get straight to it. 'Can you ascertain what Camila *actually wants* to do about seeing her parents?'

'Yeah, no problem. I'm planning to cover a number of subjects with her today.'

I ask where they are going.

'We'll go for a drive,' Sarah says.

I ask if they will stop off for a coffee somewhere. Starbucks or Costa. 'Cam likes those.' Those kinds of places are perfect for public sector workers and care kids.

'Probably not,' she says, with a little shake of the head.

I suspect I know what's happening here. She can claim for her petrol, but not coffees. For goodness sake! I go to my bag and pull out my purse. Luckily there is a fiver in there. I know that Starbucks is Cam's favourite and whatever she orders will be about £5. I'm not paying for Sarah, she can sort herself out. Sip on her water bottle, perhaps.

The care system is truly broken. It was only last year we were told that they could no longer buy cake with the coffee for children when they do their sessions with social workers. Now it seems they have cut out the coffee. Should this system even be looking after children if they can't even afford a damn coffee? I say 'coffee' but what Cam and Lily drink is more like a pudding in a cup. The boys don't do these sorts of drinks. They would rather have fruit juice or an energy drink. *Prime*, when that was a thing, a few years ago. But I don't suppose the energy drinks are any better; probably worse. I read a newspaper article where a teenage boy was critically ill after drinking 13 of a certain brand of energy drink. It's a ridiculous number. I'm not surprised it made him ill, but that's the thing about children and teenagers: the bit of the brain that controls moderation isn't fully switched on.

I wave off a grumpy Camila as the pair walk off towards Sarah's car.

I notice that Sarah's car looks worn out. I decide that she must have her own children, I can tell by the items visible on the parcel shelf. I always wonder if social workers can shut off from being a parent while working with children in care. I know I wouldn't be able to. I would want for them the same as I want for my own children. But it also feels to me as if Sarah is under the cosh. She looks haggard and increasingly defeated. She is like so much of the social care workforce: an army of predominantly women who work hard under difficult conditions and juggle their own family's needs, just like nurses, teachers and foster carers. It seems to me that more and more of them are going part time, especially the supervising social workers. I understand why, but it can result in frustrations when they only work certain days and nobody is covering in between. Young people like Camila need consistency. I remind myself that, unusually, Cam has that; she's had Sarah in her life for years now.

While they are out, I catch up with my emails. I don't get very far because after an hour they are back. I see Sarah's car pull up again outside. It seems such a small amount of time, but the reality is that an hour a month is all they get. In that time social workers have to get to know the children in their caseload

205

and make massive decisions about their lives. An hour isn't long enough. How long does it take to break the ice anew each time? How can they make the right decisions based on the evidence from an awkward hour where the children can say, or not say, just about anything.

The door goes, and in walks a rather solemn-looking Cam followed by Sarah. Cam disappears straight upstairs.

'How did you get on?' I ask, anxious to know about what I perceive to be a vital conversation about Camila and her feelings about spending time with her parents. 'Did you talk about her contact visits?'

'Erm, sort of. Camila is going again this weekend. I must get going, bye,' she turns and is gone almost before I have any kind of chance to respond. I say some terrible things under my breath.

I walk upstairs to see Cam. She is sitting on her bed with her phone, texting rapidly with both thumbs.

'Are you okay, sweetheart?'

She doesn't look up.

I feel sidelined from whatever is going on. I ask again, 'Cam, are you okay?'

When she has stopped texting she looks up.

'No, not really. I don't want to go to my parents this weekend.'

'Did you talk about this with Sarah?'

She shakes her head.

'Look, you don't have to, darling, if you don't want to. I'll send everyone an email. I'll say you're busy or tired or how about you just don't feel like seeing your parents this weekend. How about the truth?'

Cam looks down at her phone as a message pings in.

'Sarah isn't interested in what I think. She never has been. They just want me to live with my parents again, but I don't want to. I don't like them.'

This last statement hangs in the room like a herd of hippos.

'It's not easy, is it?' I say. 'It's okay not to want to see your parents.' Dare I push further and try to get closer to the real reason she doesn't want to be there? I don't want to ask leading questions.

I'm just trying to formulate the next sentence to broach the subject of why when she blurts out, 'They're sexual deviants.'

Okay, well, there we are. It's nothing if not direct.

'What makes you say that?' I ask.

She looks up. 'Because I remember seeing dad's arse fucking some woman and my mum licking her tits. Will that do?'

I am momentarily wrong-footed. This is not quite the direction I was expecting the conversation to go in. But I can't do anything but go with it.

'Blimey, Cam. Were your parents into sex parties?'

'Yes, they were at it all the bloody time. Men and women fucking all over the place and that room!'

'Room?'

'Yeah, I remember it in grandad's garage. My mum must have read *Fifty Shades of Grey* and turned sex fantasies into one of her many shit businesses.'

I lean against the wall by the window. I remember girls from school who had cool, lefty hippy parents who used to have swaps. I knew because I stayed with one of them. Her parents were at it above us in the attic room and we could hear all the moans and groans. I never fancied it myself.

If ever I wanted a cup of tea it's now. Why on earth do I want a cup of tea when I'm hearing about sex and perversion?

'I'm so sorry, Cammy. That's hard to live with. And you were so young.'

I do some rough calculations. She must have been around five years old when she was removed into care. She obviously saw a lot. My mind boggles.

'Does Sarah know this?'

'I've tried talking to her about it, but she changes the subject.'

I am genuinely baffled, because most social workers I know would be all over a disclosure like this. Even if Cam wasn't involved, just being exposed to these things, seeing them, is abuse in its own right. It could be causing all sorts of confusion and conflicted feelings, especially given how young she was.

'It's certainly no problem to cancel the weekend visit,' I say. Perhaps we could go and do something?'

'If you cancel then Sarah will be wanting to know why, and I can't talk to her. She's too stupid.'

That is a bit harsh, but I am curious as to why Sarah doesn't seem to have acted on these things. Not least because perhaps what Cam saw as a child is what is impacting on her need to shit and smear and all that headbanging stuff from before. It's not bloody rocket science. I think we may have found the root of Cam's issues.

XIV

As always, I feel disloyal to the child when I write up Cam's log at the end of the week.

The process confirms to me that logs are as much about protecting us as they are about the child. I note the details of Cam's disclosure, keeping everything as factual and pragmatic as I can. That is, until I find myself writing:

I wonder if this is the root problem for Cam. If it is, then specialised therapy would be needed.

I'm not sure if sitting stroking a guinea pig quite cuts it for some of these kids, no matter how sweet an activity that is. Cam is quite keen to bin her equine therapy. I had assumed she would learn about caring for a horse, creating a good relationship with a horse and learning to ride, but no. She is with some much younger children and has mostly been standing around keeping the younger kids away from the back end of the horse while they dip their hands in paint then make handprints on the horse. They take photos then hose the paint off. That's the best bit, apparently, because Camila shoots the other kids with water and chases them until they're told off.

Camila has attended two equine therapy sessions and has decided not to attend anymore. She feels that her session, which she shares with three younger children, isn't giving her what she needs.

I've seen the costings for the equine therapy sessions – £500 a time – and now think I might buy a horse and stick it in my back garden. A great earner for people with stables.

If they are doing this in groups of four at a time and they are all paying 500 quid, that's an obscene amount of money. And what are they getting, exactly? Once again, my mind boggles. I wonder how many kids they have in the stable a day? I'm definitely in the wrong business.

The going rate for a decent therapist seems to be about £70 per hour, so I don't understand why it's so hard to get funding for a therapist. Who knows what goes on in the offices at local authorities?

I also have to report on the change in Cam's demeanour over the last few days. It feels to me as if she is brewing up to something again. She is quieter than usual, and angry. I check her room regularly because she has taken to putting poo smears and smudges on the lower part of the wall by the top end of her bed. Whenever I see it, I dash in with bleach and bathroom cleaner to spray and wipe. She knows I am doing this, though we never mention it openly. It has become a kind of unspoken arrangement that I will clean up after her.

And, to be honest, I don't mind. It's probably a more dignified way of going about things, and more useful than patting coloured handprints on to a horse's bum. I am working intuitively with Cam, probably more than I have done with any other child. After her disclosure I am beginning to understand more about how she feels and why this particular self-expression feels necessary to her. I leave her to it. Giving her space seems to be working for us. I have no idea if this constitutes therapeutic parenting.

I'm doing what seems to feel right.

I'm mostly ignoring all the suggestions from the social workers, even kind Kendi. At times, the number of suggestions coming at you from different directions can feel overwhelming. And it almost always means more work.

Sometimes it seems better to do nothing, or very little, until the next idea reveals itself. Maybe it's not therapeutic parenting, it's 'laid back parenting', which, as we're older now, we tend to do far more of. When you've been doing this a long time, like us, you pick your battles and know that most times, things will turn out fine. A good night's sleep is worth more than gold.

On Friday morning, the phone goes. It's the landline which means it's most likely to be a social worker, the NHS, or one of the schools. That's if it's not some dude trying to sell us loft insulation. I recently found myself chatting to an automated call. It was that clever. I did feel like a twit, so now I slam down the phone if I am not sure within a second that it's genuine.

This time it is. It's Camila's school.

She has been caught sending another explicit AI-generated image around school again.

'We think she was involved in the creation as well as the distribution. Therefore, we'd like to request that you pick her up immediately.'

Great. Just what we all need.

'We also need to inform you that this time, given the sexual nature of the image, we will be reporting it to the police.'

Uh oh, this sounds more serious than before.

In spite of Cam's dismissive attitude, I knew that somehow

we weren't done with this AI business. AI-generated images have developed to astounding levels of accuracy. What is she doing generating sexual imagery? If indeed she is responsible. In my heart I think she probably is. And if she's distributed it amongst her peers, then that counts as child sex abuse too. She might not know that and may have inadvertently committed a criminal offence.

There are different types of image editing software, I have learned. 'Inpainting' allows users to change elements of an image – add bits in or take things out. Kind of what I used to think of as airbrushing. 'Roop' enables users to swap the faces of individuals. This is the technique that's used to create most of the deepfakes that circulate, adding the faces of celebrities into existing scenes. But 'open pose' AI is the one most likely to be used in the creation of AI-generated child sexual abuse images and in pornography. It refers to a computer vision library that tracks key points on a person's body, such as joints and body parts, within an image or video. All words and phrases that I wasn't familiar with until very recently.

I let Lloyd know that I have to get Camila, then apologise to the dogs and promise them that I will walk them later. Dotty does one of her famous 'sneeze' communications to let me know she isn't happy.

The receptionist in the school's front office looks like she's sucked a lemon, but I realise this isn't personal. She always looks like that. I am asked to wait while the headteacher comes.

There's no sign of Cam.

I sit down and feel like *I'm* the one in trouble. I notice a few kids walking out of the school gates with adults wearing lanyards. Are most children needing 1:1 these days?

It's not the head who arrives, but one of the deputies, who introduces himself as Mr Forester. He looks a bit flushed.

'Mrs Allen, thank you for coming, but Camila has gone.' He chooses his words carefully, and I can't help but feel like they're insurance talk for, 'We seem to have lost Camila'.

I am quite annoyed because this will now all come to me. The police, the reports, the hours on the phone in follow-up conversations. Given that it's Friday, Mr Forester and his team will simply go home for the weekend.

I sigh and step into Detective Chief Constable mode, one of my many 'hats' I can wear as a foster carer. This is the best when I need to establish a few facts.

'When did you last have eyes on her?'

Ms Snotty-Pants Lemon-Sucker in reception lowers her head.

Yes, I thought so. She must have been the one who watched her walk out of school. I thought they had to be buzzed out.

'Why was she allowed out of school without me? Particularly given that you asked me to collect her?'

Oh, the blushing reaches almost cherubic levels.

'Er, we're not entirely sure.'

'What time did you notice her leave?'

Mr Forester says, 'It was around 10.45am.'

I look at the clock on the wall. It's now a quarter to 12, so she's been gone for an hour. I rub my chin like *Columbo* and inhale then tut. 'Has anyone been out to look for her?'

Mr Forester shakes his head.

'Well, that's slack isn't it?' I didn't intend to be so blunt, but the words popped out before my brain had a chance to stop them.

I reach for my phone to text Cam and ask her where she is. *Are you okay and shall I come and get you?*

'While I'm waiting for her to answer, might I ask what the image was that has caused all this drama?'

I am invited into his office where I'm shown a print out of what looks like the headteacher having anal sex with Sarah, the social worker.

Oh my, if ever there was a cry for help, this is it.

I sigh and instead of showing disgust, which is probably what he's expecting, I say, 'It's about time her social worker started to pay attention and listen to her.'

Before I leave, I check my phone. Nothing from Cam.

In the car, I call Lloyd and relay the morning's findings. It occurs to me that the school has not yet called the police. Interesting.

I wonder how Sarah is going to take the news about an image of her and the headteacher having anal sex. I mentally write my report as I drive. I'm going to explicitly link all of this to the recent disclosure about her parents' sex orgies. The inappropriateness of her experience requires expert intervention. I also resolve that, no matter what, there is no way Camila is going to her parents tomorrow.

As well as sending emails I also text the local authority to tell them what has happened, making it clear that this is about explicit AI generated sexual images of her social worker and headteacher.

I get a curt, *Thank you for letting us know* in response. Hmm!

When there is no word from Cam by 2pm, we decide that we should now report her as a missing person.

XV

I'm worried, of course, but I'm pretty sure that she will be with Fred. I think about what I would have done in her situation. I'd have fled somewhere I thought I'd be safe and cared about and understood. And for me, at the same age, that would have been into the arms of my ideologically-similar boyfriend, who 'got' me. Even though she has denied a romantic liaison with the mysterious Fred, her blushes have told a different story.

Meanwhile, all the social services offices are closed. The responder on the out-of-hours team asks me to let them know if anything develops, and to inform them if Cam comes home. She's not daft; she knows that doing anything like this on a Friday afternoon is very different from, say, a Wednesday afternoon. I'm the one who will be doing all the liaison work.

I call Kendi who, like me, knows that *she knows* about the Friday thing. It's so frustrating. He says that he will leave his phone on, but also call the out-of-hours team.

I need to get hold of Sian and Gary.

And, so far, no one has had any luck. Or at least, I should say, Sarah hasn't delivered on that one, even though I know Kendi has pushed her on it. I set Sherlock Allen to work, scouring Facebook. I know I will probably get my wrists slapped for it but, frankly, I don't care. I need to find out more about Fred so that we can bring Cam home. It doesn't take long to locate them online, and I'm annoyed with myself for abiding by the ambiguous rules for as long as I have done. GDPR can be misused in more than one way. I find Sian first, then see a picture of her and Gary together. Now, I'm well aware that what you see online only tells one side of a story and people are going to present their best side, but they do look like nice people. They are both teachers and, judging from the kind of posts and memes that they share, they look the sort to genuinely care about children.

I message her.

While I wait for that to do its thing, I go up to Cam's room to see what's what. Dotty follows me up the stairs, no doubt to lick something revolting. I open Cam's door and can see what look like fresh dents in the wall. Uh oh. This must be her head banging. What a shame. I thought we'd been spared that. I'd hoped she might have felt that she didn't need to.

But I get it. Everything is so hard for her. And the more I think about it, the more I think I really do get it. I also see more smearing on the wall. I wonder if Fred knows about this. I doubt it very much. She will want to keep this side of things to herself, I'm sure. I clear up the smears and tell Dotty off for being a poop-opportunist, making sure she gets nothing.

There's nothing else to give any clue about where she might have gone.

I head back downstairs to check my emails and my Facebook.

The miracle of social media: Sian has replied. And, sensibly, she's given me her number. I get my phone from the kitchen and sit down at my desk. That posture and location makes me feel more serious and formal than sitting in the kitchen or on the sofa would.

'Hello?' her voice is tentative.

'Hi, it's Louise Allen here.'

'Hi Louise, it's good to meet you, or at least meet you over the phone. We've been so worried about Cam. We'd love to have seen her for a visit at least, but Sarah advised against it, so that it didn't mess up her new placement as she settled in — which makes sense, of course.'

I tell her that the police are looking for Cam, but she already knows.

'Don't worry, she's safe.'

I was right about Fred. Camila is with him at his family's house, not far from where Sian and Gary live. 'But we haven't seen Cam ourselves or got involved today, because we knew it would come back on us, so Fred's parents have kept us in the loop.'

It's a relief to know, but I realise that I was calm. I knew, somehow, that she would be fine.

Sian is friendly and ready to talk more. I ask her to tell me more about Fred.

'Nice lad. She's known him for years. He's one of a group of childhood friends that she's hung on to. She's been close to Fred since they were young. He cares for her, even though he's a couple of years older. He always has done. They were always doing things together, just hanging out. We knew she'd miss him being around the corner.'

Sian was very sad that the placement ended. 'Cam is a good

girl. A kind girl. We miss her. You've probably seen already how caring she is. How switched on she is about social issues.'

I share some of the things she's talked about at the dinner table, and Sian laughs.

'Yep, that's Cam!'

'We felt taking Camila away from all that she knew was wrong, but the decision was taken out of our hands. Sarah assured us that Camila was okay; we've been in contact with her a few times to make sure that she was settling in with her new carers, but she didn't give us any detail about where she'd gone.'

I talk about the smearing and headbanging. 'I'm not worried about the poo, so much. I just keep clearing that up,' I explain. 'And I think it's reducing. But the head banging is new.'

Sian talks about how they tried to get support and help at various points, but none of it was actually very helpful.

I joke about the cost of the horse therapy and guinea pig therapy.

'I know. It makes you think we're in the wrong job,' Sian says.

My thoughts exactly.

We talk a little about Cam's birth parents.

Sian is quite scathing. 'I suspect that it's her mum who is the root of Cam's problems.' She explains how they tried to develop a good relationship with Camila's brother, but plenty of obstacles had been put in the way. 'So far, that's been difficult,' she admits.

We sit for an hour or more discussing all the different aspects of Cam's situation. Sian suggests that I wait for a message from Camila. 'Check your phone in around an hour.'

I decide that I like Sian, very much. She seems like a smart woman, very warm, and someone who clearly cares about Camila. I've never felt that Cam was staying long term with us. She is definitely a child that is passing through. And I'm convinced she needs to be back with Sian and Gary, whatever the local authority's policy is.

And Sian's right on the money. In an hour or so I receive a text from Cam to say that she'll be home in the morning.

I call the police to tell them that she is safe and with a friend. Then I call the out-of-hours number to update them, too.

Her room is tidy and poo free. I play the poo part down in the logs I write. I don't want this passing need, what I'm sure is very temporary behaviour, to become what she is defined by and known for.

I fall asleep, dreaming of scenarios where I can get Cam back to Sian and Gary.

In the morning, Lily starts the day by stomping round the place, slamming doors and muttering loudly. I know her well enough to know that she is clearly advertising the fact that she is not in a good mood.

'Are you due your period?' I make the mistake of asking, because she can be grumpy around that time of the month. I don't know if girls' periods are worse these days, but there seems to be a lot of drama around period time. Hot water bottles, chocolate, days in bed. I wonder what would happen if all women took to our beds when bleeding; the world would end, I think. I'm definitely from a generation of women who refused to allow our periods to stop us from doing anything. Lily, on the other hand, seems content to roll over and eat chocolate.

But no, she claims it's not her period. 'It's Camila. You're only interested in her. She's your favourite.'

It's shifted from the perception that Vincent is the favourite child, at least. But, to be honest, I *have* paid Camila a lot more attention lately. I'd never share with the children precisely why, though. It's none of their business and I would hate for a bitchy slip of the tongue, and for the news to travel. Camila is entitled to privacy.

I realise that I'm going to have to handle this carefully. Lily is clearly becoming a bit jealous, which I understand. And, unlike Camila, who seems to need a different level of interaction, Lily still needs a mummy figure, and that figure is me. Despite all her bravado, Lily has been with us a long time and these days I can read her like a book. Once Cam is back home and settled I will take Lily for a drive out on her own. She can sit next to me and blast her music. She may even talk, who knows? But she definitely needs my attention and fostering is often all about balance.

I check on the boys, too, in case they are also feeling put out by the fact that lots of my energy has been directed at Cam. Weirdly, they seem incredibly self-contained right now. Dare I even say happy? Jackson has been positively cheerful around the house. They are both a bit more secretive than they once were. Vincent especially so.

I think on this for a while. As a foster carer, I tend to go for the worst-case scenario and work my way back, hopefully to something less dramatic. Then the penny drops: extra time in the bathroom, the appearance of new face washes, skin and hair products. Not to mention fragrances. They are pursuing girls!

Lloyd is busy working on the big arched window in the stairwell. It's huge and, for a while, we had a big piece of plastic flapping in the wind as part of it was being replaced. Some things can't be rushed, especially when we're doing these huge tasks ourselves. It's always a learning experience and a slow process, but way cheaper than paying a carpenter to make the repairs. That would have cost thousands of pounds.

I run the idea that the boys might both have girlfriends and he laughs.

'Where have you been? How has it taken you this long to notice?'

I've definitely taken my eye off the ball a little on the home front, I think. I change the subject.

'Cam should be back soon. Her text said 11am.'

She walks through the door just after 11am, claiming that she got the bus. She didn't because there isn't one that comes in at this time. Fred must have dropped her back, or his mum did, but we go along with her version. We need to keep her calm and I have not yet met a teenager who tells the absolute truth all of the time, so why would Camila be any different? The other thing I tell myself not to do is launch into a 'safe sex' or 'you're underage' conversation. I think if I did, she might feel like turning around and heading right back out of that door.

Lily is hovering about, being nosy I suspect.

Cam looks up from the stool in the kitchen where she is scrolling on her phone, but connected to the plug socket as she's recharging it at the same time.

'How's your head?' Lily says.

'Fuck off.'

Ah, teenage girls fighting for dominance. Delightful.

Lily walks out of the kitchen and, still in Cam's ear shot, asks me loudly, 'When is she going?'

I knew the two of them weren't bosom buddies, but I wasn't aware that they had reached the point of stand-off, or bitch off.

'Excuse me, young lady, you're so shady,' I intervene.

She sneers at me. 'What? She's a loon. She bangs her head against the wall. Can't you hear her?'

'Lily, Cam struggles sometimes. Please leave her alone. She's not hurting you.'

But this isn't enough for Lily. 'She comes here, takes over, gets all the attention and never speaks. She ignores me and, when she does speak, she's a tard.'

'Lily, that will do,' I say as firmly as I can, assuming that will be the end of it.

But Cam suddenly comes through the kitchen door and shouts, 'You fucking bitch!'

A five-minute slagging match ensues. Lloyd comes in from the garden side of the window to see what's going on, as does Dotty, who starts barking at both of them as if to say, 'Chill your beans girls!'

Eventually they each storm off in opposite directions. Lily goes up the small side stairs to her room and slams her door very loudly. Camila marches out through the middle door into the hall and stomps up the stairs.

'Be careful!' Lloyd calls out. 'I'm—'

Bang, crash.

Too late.

We rush after Cam to find her entangled in Lloyd's big metal stepladder that had been leaning up against the wall.

I'm not entirely sure whether she pushed it or, perhaps more likely, crashed into it, but either way she's scuffed the new paint.

Lloyd's face is silently crying out, 'You stupid girls'.

We peel her off the metal ladder and notice blood coming from her forehead, the spot where I think she has been banging her head against the wall. I gently lead her to the kitchen and hear Lily's bedroom door close on the way. She has evidently been listening. I clear the blood off Cam's forehead and look to see the damage.

'Hold this against your head,' I say, handing her a piece of kitchen roll. 'Do you want a couple of paracetamol?'

I imagine this will ache soon.

She says no, initially, but concedes after half an hour. It's a deep cut and the bruising is coming up already. I decide to take her to the Cottage Hospital, where they put five strips across her cut.

'I think she'll live,' I text Lloyd while she's being fixed up.

Then I message Lily to see if she is any calmer. I tell her that Camila bumped her head and needed a few stitches. She sends back a laughing emoji.

This is bad.

What's happened to my sweet little girl?

XVI

The girls actively avoid each other over the next few days. I berate myself about the fact that I hadn't seen this coming. I know that I must not be seen to give one any more attention than the other, and deep down I know that Lily is right on one level: she hasn't had her usual quota of attention because I have been focusing on Cam. Lily has no idea about the poo, but I can't keep the head banging a secret because the house shakes when she does it.

The doctor at the cottage hospital explains that she has mild concussion. 'Watch her,' he warns, in his Hispanic accent.

'I will,' I promise. I will watch her like a hawk. And somehow I will find time to spend time with Lily. The latter isn't as straightforward as I'd hoped. Lily is a typical teenager and has far better things to do than spend time with me.

The rest of the weekend passes uneventfully enough. I write up the logs and email them over to Lloyd, who is much more patient and much better at uploading them than me. I get tired of all the different systems and processes in tech that mess with my brain.

The girls continue to avoid each other and, when I talk to them individually, they bitch about each other.

They have each created a list of things they dislike about the other. I dare to say that this might be 'transferred fears and anger' and my helpful attempt at analysis goes down like a shit sandwich.

They only seem to like therapeutic language when it suits their story.

On Monday, I leave early to catch a train to London to meet my friends, James and Daniele. James is an art critic and Daniele is one of the world's leading aromatherapists. They have invited me to work on a project with them, creating some illustrations for marketing a new business. I'm excited because I am desperate to make art once more. I do more admin around fostering than is sensible and, if we foster carers are not careful, we can easily lose sight of doing what makes us happy. When that happens, we're not always the best people to be looking after these children. Once again, it comes down to a matter of finding balance.

But I'm in a buoyant mood as my brain fizzes with ideas for the project on the way home. We pull into a busy station and Lloyd calls. The connection is bad and I can't hear him properly. It sounds as if he's telling me that someone has died.

My mind rushes through a list of people I know are ill, or at risk. Then I assume he might be telling me about a famous person. But why would Lloyd be phoning me about someone I've never met, I wonder, as I ask 'who?', loudly, several times.

Then I hear the name 'Dotty'.

'No!'

I can't quite register what Lloyd has just said to me.

Not Dotty. Not my little dog. Not one of my best friends ever. She can't have just died. How? When I said goodbye to them all this morning she seemed fine. I put on my sunglasses and look out of the window but my eyes sting with the blend of salty tears, moisturiser and mascara.

I sniff and wipe my face with the back of my hand. I wish Lloyd hadn't told me till I was home. This is hideous. I can't do anything from here. I can't even talk to them, the signal on the train is rubbish. By the time I get to my station I have a thumping headache and a rash across my forehead.

I sit in the car for a minute and drink some water. I feel like my whole world has shifted and isn't turning properly on its axis. I cry all the way home while I'm driving. I cry for Dotty, for myself and for Douglas. Those two little pooches have been 'married' for 13 yrs. A lifetime. They went everywhere together and have been inseparable.

I console myself as much as I can with the thought that Dotty lived a full and lovely life. I need to pull myself together because there are other things going on at home. I'm a little worried about what is happening between Lily and Camila. And now that I say their names inside my head they suddenly sound like two debutantes from a Jane Austin novel.

The wind has been well and truly removed from my sails and I don't have the energy for one of their arguments. Not this evening. I park the car. Normally Dotty would be barking because she could recognise my car from the other end of the road. But there is no sound. Nothing. No friendly 'hello, Louise' woofs from my little four-legged girl.

My eyes start burning all over again and my head is killing me.

I open the shed door and see Jackson sitting on the garden bench holding one of the many children's patchwork memory quilts that a group of lovely ladies make for, on the whole, totally ungrateful children who don't get the concept of a memory quilt, which is why we have acquired quite a number of them. Jackson has carefully wrapped the little quilt around Dotty and placed her in one of our old IKEA baskets. He has picked some flowers and put them down by the side of the basket.

I sit next to him and stroke her face, her dead little face. She looks like she was smiling.

'Her soul has left her eyes,' Jackson says.

He has always been the softest of all the children. He slips away when Lloyd comes out with a glass of wine for me.

'Oh, that's kind, but I would much rather have a couple of paracetamol and a glass of water, please.'

He returns a minute later with the substitution.

'Where are the girls?' I ask.

'They're working on a poem and a painting for you.'

'Together?'

He smiles and nods. 'We all know how much Dotty meant. To you, especially.'

I smile too, sadly.

Lloyd goes on to explain what happened. 'Lily took both dogs out for a walk and they had their snacks as usual. Then Dotty went for a lie-down in her favourite sunbathing spot and dozed off as she always does, with the sun warming her fur. We walked past her, quietly, so as not to disturb her. Everything seemed normal. Except that she seemed to sleep for hours.'

It sounds like a very peaceful end. 'What made you realise?'

'Well, someone knocked at the door with a parcel and I thought it was unusual that Dotty didn't bark. It was then that I realised she'd gone,' he adds gently.

227

I go to check on all the children. Jackson is still red-eyed and sad. Vincent is gaming, but he stops as soon as I come in to ask me if I'm alright. He seems okay. Lily has done a lovely portrait of Dotty from one of the many photos on her phone. Camila has written a beautiful poem and is genuinely upset. When I tap on her door and go into her room she stands up and gives me a hug. I check the wound on her forehead and ask her how she is.

'I'm good. Really. How are you, Louise?'

I make a joke about the reports I have to write up. 'I wonder what they'll think when I write "Camila ran into a ladder" on the page?' We both smile and she seems calm. I take a surreptitious glance over at the poo wall and see nothing there. Maybe the bang on the head was what was needed. I have also given her the role of poo picker-upper in the garden, on Cinnamon's suggestion. This is really helping, I think. I have no idea how or why, but handling others' poo seems to have stopped her need to use her own – at least for the time being. Cinnamon also says she should clear up her own shit. I'm not so sure about that.

I have a quick look at my inbox. There have been a few emails from Sarah about Camila visiting her parents again. Not dealing with that tonight. I'll pick that one up tomorrow. Right now I need to go to bed.

I lie in bed, shedding more tears and missing my little friend, Dotty.

XVII

When I wake up, I don't feel the pizazz of a new day. I feel tired.

Dotty has been 'laid to rest' in the conservatory. Jackson didn't want to leave her out in the shed overnight. I stroke her little face each time I walk by. There were no illnesses, no trips to the vets, it was just her time. When we got the dogs, the boys were young. We have watched them all grow up together. I've seen other children and their dogs do the same when I'm in the park. I notice the cycle. Eventually the parents walk alone, the child becomes a teenager and the dogs die. Even though I've seen it happen any number of times, somehow I never thought this time would come to us.

In the afternoon, I have the long drive to horse therapy for Cam. She has two more sessions booked, in spite of her waning enthusiasm. The therapy isn't going too well and it takes out a significant chunk of my day. There is no signal, I can't work in the car, so they really do feel like wasted hours. I sometimes try to read a book but always fall asleep. Day or night, my brain is programmed to snooze if I read.

I'm not sure what we should expect from the horse patting

and painting and I know that those with horses will say that it's all about establishing trust with the horse, but I'm not sure if I'm seeing much change for her. It really does all feel a bit pointless.

On the way back, I ask her if it's any closer to helping her. By way of answer, she just laughs.

'Tell me more about it?' I say.

'There's this cat who comes into the yard and sits on my lap. I spend most of the time playing with the cat rather than the horse.'

Her words give me an idea. One which will save the NHS, or children's social care, whoever is paying, £500 per week and it will only cost me something in the region of £200, I reckon. It would be nice if they helped us with that, but I already know they won't. (And that, in a nutshell, probably reveals quite a lot about the craziness of spending patterns and priorities in children's social care.) I don't say anything to Cam, but make a mental note to begin looking online for kittens when we get home. I'll try the rescue places first: the local well-established ones that I know of.

In the immediate aftermath of Dotty's passing, both the girls seem to have put their knives down and are behaving more amicably towards one another. I have always known that Camila was 'just passing through' and will not be with us for a great length of time. Or at least I have always had that feeling. You learn to tell. But I'm now starting to get the same feeling about Lily. Something has changed with her, something more than just 'growing up'. We've been through such a lot over the years, but I am sensing a kind of withdrawal from us. She has become more secretive, which I know is normal at this age (unless you're Jackson, who tells us everything and must have been born with a truth switch).

I fear that we haven't fully recovered from the time, not so long ago, when her birth mum became over-involved. Lily still talks to her without supervision. There's nothing I can do to stop her. I might be misreading it, who knows?

But maybe my experience with Lily is also influencing the way I feel about Cam and her birth parents. Again, who knows?

I'm probably not thinking straight. I'm still grieving for Dotty. It's just been such a shock. I never expected her to die. I thought Doug would go first. I don't know why. But Dotty's death has broken my heart. It's funny how we can become so attached to animals. I guess that's the idea with Camila and the horses, that she will make some kind of a connection, that she would be 'cured'. And even though I was sceptical from the start, and I'm long enough in the tooth to know better, I can't help still wanting to believe that every CAMHS councillor, GP, paediatrician, every individual and every group of professionals I meet, truly will have an answer and a fix. Ever the optimist! I have to be, or I couldn't do this job.

The reality is that's rarely the case.

Healing takes time and there aren't usually any shortcuts, however difficult that is to hear.

I'm not convinced that patting a horse, or holding a guinea pig, is much help, but a kitten in the home… that might be. I know she loves animals and I know that the nurture that children give animals is the nurture they need. And, it's a lot cheaper and easier than trotting all that way to stroke a horse.

I tell Kendi and Sarah in an email that I'm going to get a kitten for Camila.

Kendi is enthusiastic when he texts back. *Wow, that's a great thing Louise. I'm sure Camila will love that.*

The local RSPCA branch has a litter of kittens that are just about to go on their website. I ask about colours. There are two white and grey kittens among six kittens of all colours and patterns.

'I think the mother was a bit of a gal with the alley cat toms,' I joke with the volunteer on the phone.

I try to bring kittens and cats into the conversation at dinner time, without explicitly stating why, just to gauge reactions. Lily is pretty grumpy.

'Yeah, whatever. Can I talk to you about money?'

She wants some more, of course. I do wonder where all her money goes. She has a Saturday job in one of the local cafes to supplement the pocket money we give her. She complains that it's hot in the kitchen, but she is only in and out of there, spending more of her time out front serving customers. She is a bit precious about it and seems to genuinely wonder why it should be necessary to work at all.

Both Jackson and Vincent have also found themselves Saturday jobs. I say 'found themselves', but it's fair to say that they had a bit of help from mum. I promised that we wouldn't take their pocket money (currently £15 per week) away, but we did expect them to start working in order to supplement it. They all need to understand how money works, and that it doesn't just appear out of thin air: you do have to work for it.

In a world of media influencers I think there's a danger that money seems easy to come by. Only one in a million will make it, I try to make them see. The rest are surplus to requirements.

I'm determined that these teenagers understand the value of work and money, so I refuse Lily's request on this occasion.

Cam is happy because her scheduled contact for this weekend has fallen through; Gabby has cancelled because of a work commitment.

It's a few days before Sarah gets back to me. She apologies for her 'tardy' reply. Then writes in her text:

I'm not sure if getting a kitten is a good idea, what if Camila goes back home?

Ah. And there we have it! A tacit admission of the plan all along.

It makes me wonder again if there was any kind of build-up to 'Poogate', the final straw that jettisoned her from her foster family.

I don't care what Sarah says, I decide, we're going to get a kitten and that's that! She can take the kitten with her if she needs to. Or it can stay with us after she's gone.

I think that being subtle about a kitten is the wrong approach. Lily has Mabel, whom she got as a kitten. Mabel really helped Lily at the time, but Lily did get bored with her as they got older – which is fine and perhaps only to be expected. I have a house full of animals. One more won't hurt. I'm also thinking about Cinnamon's suggestion that I get Camila to pick up the poo. It might be genius after all: looking after a kitten, cleaning out its tray and having to deal with the poo might make for a lightbulb moment.

Before I say anything to Camila, I go and find Lily. She is quick to put the phone down and look innocent. It's either something bad that I haven't got the brain power to think about right now, or her mum, up to something, wanting something.

'How are you?' I ask.

She shrugs and makes a face that either says yay or nay, I'm not sure.

I come straight out with it. 'I'm thinking of getting a kitten for Camila, to help her—'

I don't have time to finish before she has jumped up, 'Yes, love that!'

I'm pleased. I wasn't entirely sure that would be her response, so that's great. But, before I have even had time to leave the room she has sent a message to the group chat: *Cam, you're getting a kitten!*

Camila comes running to find me with a huge smile on her face.

'Is it true?'

I smile back. 'Yes, Cam, it's all true.'

I tell her about the litter of six at the RSPCA. She's straight on her phone looking it up. They have put the kittens up on their website. She immediately falls for one of the ones I guessed she would, whose fur is mostly white with a little grey.

Right, let's go get it!

XVIII

I anticipated just taking Camila to the RSPCA to collect the kitten.

No such luck. Jackson and Lily are ready and waiting by the door. Vincent is gaming and has planned to meet his new girlfriend in town for coffee later on. Not sure if that's a metaphor or not.

So four of us get into the car. I begin to punch in the postcode of the RSPCA to the sat nav. I have scribbled it down on a Post-it note. Suddenly, three phones are thrust into my face, displaying the route.

'Thank you, my darlings, but I need the sat nav in front of me so that I can see what's coming up. By the time any of you tell me to turn left or right, we're usually driving past the turning. You'll understand when you're all drivers.'

There are huffs and puffs of frustration at my slowness, but I know it's all excitement to meet the kitten, and the atmosphere is good humoured. They're tripping over themselves to be kind and helpful. I knew they knew they had it in them…

Even with the aid of the sat nav, I still drive past the turning I need and have to look out for a place to turn around, much to the amusement of the non-drivers. We eventually find the location, tucked away down a little lane. Out we all get and all I can think is 'poor little kittens', having to look at four humans who will be staring at them and poking and prodding and ooing and aahing.

We walk through a corridor of cages, each seems to have its own private garden to the rear. It's a lovely set-up. We go past several grumpy-looking cats which makes me wonder if this is like fostering: everyone wants the little, angelic, fluffy ones, but in reality, 50% of children in care are teenagers and not always angelic.

I walk by the older cats, feeling like I need to take them all home. Then I imagine the chaos and change my mind.

Jackson is asked if he would kindly mind not taking photos of a huge ginger tom who looks like Garfield. He apologises and puts his camera away.

'Why?' I ask, a little confused.

The RSPCA lady explains, 'Ah, well this particular cat is protected by GDPR, due to being involved in a crime scene.'

I don't know quite where to put myself. I want to laugh and make jokes about cat burglars, but the lady looks very stern, so I look to the children to discourage them from making similar witticisms.

We carry on walking in the direction she points us to, eventually reaching a large, empty cage. We look beyond, to the en-suite garden, to see six kittens. Two are tumbling around together, two look like they are beating each other up, and the last two are sleeping. It feels uncannily like a scene from my home.

We are allowed through the door into the garden, one at

a time. Camila goes first, using the hand gel pump before she enters, as directed by the lady with no humour.

She beams as she reaches down to say hello to the mostly-white cat. That's her baby.

'I think that's the one she has her heart set on. Is that kitten still available?'

She is, although I can't help feeling that old grumpy-drawers would like to stop us from taking her if she could.

Camila is beside herself when I give her the nod to say yes.

Jackson and Lily take it in turns to visit the kittens next. Cam can't stop smiling and, my word, what a beautiful sight this is to see. She can look a bit solemn at times, as can most young people, I've noticed. But when she does smile, her smile reaches properly to her eyes and, to me, that has always been a good indicator that the owner of the smile is a good person, a sincere person. Jackson and Lily do their best to convince me to let them have a kitten *each* too. I remind them of the disclaimer I made at the beginning of this outing.

'Multiple kittens is not an option.'

But they try harder and are very persuasive.

The lady with no humour saves me. 'We only allow one animal per household.'

Phew. They mutter away about 'injustice' to potential cat owners while I ask what's next.

We have to fill out the online form, which slightly annoys me given that we are here, right now, in real life and not online, but Camila has already done it.

Amazing! We come back next week with £90 and a cat basket.

Annoyingly, I remember that we threw the wicker ones

out a while back. I think for a minute about what we can use, then, as we walk up to the exit, we walk through the shop and I find myself letting Camila choose the colour of a new one. She picks burgundy and cream, very grown-up. Then we buy kitten toys, treats and very expensive food. Off we head back home, via Starbucks, which costs me another £19. It would have been more but I forgo a hot drink and sip my water. I'm not going out with this lot again, I decide. One at a time is much cheaper.

Camila doesn't make it into school at all this week.

'There's no point. I'll only get into trouble for absolutely nothing.'

The 'defiance' and rude, attention-seeking behaviour have escalated even further lately, or at least according to her tutor, who tells me in an email that *Camila struggles with the word 'no'*. Well, hold the front page. Me too!

I feel more and more on Camila's side in terms of the school's attitude. Our mix 'n' match therapeutic parenting style seems to work at home, but school finds it impossible to 'manage' her. Basically, I don't give her a hard time or annoy her. But I can see how teachers could poke this little bear and see some sharp pointy teeth. I think the correct therapeutic term is 'co-regulation', the process where a child and a teacher interact to help each other manage emotions and behaviours. It involves a responsive and supportive relationship, which Cam doesn't have either with her tutor or with the school leaders. Co-regulation is a kind of dance between two people's nervous systems, where one person's regulation can influence the other. We've reached a kind of impasse at school. There just doesn't seem to be any give on their part.

To me co-regulation can only work when the adult is emotionally mature and, in real terms, mostly quite chilled.

I am much better at it than Lloyd, despite him being known as the more laid back one of us. I have worked hard on myself for years and I think have successfully squeezed out of my nervous system any traces of my adoptive family's behaviours, plus what I have seen and heard of my birth family. I have, if you like, 'modelled' my behaviours around children on people I know, love and trust. People like Sue and George. Both are retired teachers and long-time family friends. Sue was a wonderful headteacher whom I learnt so much from while I was chair of governors at one of her schools back in the 90s. I loved the way she was, both of them were, with children and young people. Both are of the firm belief that conflict achieves absolutely nothing.

I know it. I've watched good people become reduced to big screaming babies while caught in an argument with a child. That's about being out of control. When the adult is out of control the child can feel terrified, or forced into fight-or-flight mode.

So being home is fine by me.

Camila is very happy to just relax and, sometimes, that's all children need to do. They are on screens at home and at school all day. Their eyes and brains must become exhausted. I don't know why school isn't a safe place away from most of the technology for them, but schools are desperate for funding – or ignoring the research – so let tech companies in, some of whom provide their kit for free. It isn't free, though. They are stealing our children's brains. I am, finally, seeing a bit of resistance and some backlash though. The boys and to some degree,

Lily, are not spending as much time on their phones or tech as they once did. Vincent does still love gaming, but he monitors himself. I wonder if they see tech a bit like food. They spend a few years wanting junk food: pizzas, Mackies and KFC. Then they become more self aware at the point at which they become sexually hormonal and start taking more of an interest in their appearance.

The boys are definitely more body conscious these days. I have noticed a lot more fruit going from the bowls, not to mention face packs. They steal the latter from my drawer in the bathroom. They seem to be starting to treat tech the same way, seeing it more like junk food, and other activities, like their increasing hobbies, are the equivalent of fruit and veg. Jackson has taken up the keyboard and discovered a band called Sleep Token who he plays on repeat. Vincent has been using one of Lloyd's old Pentax cameras to take pictures. He loves going out with the huge film camera around his neck.

I suspect Camila is also excited about her kitten, whose name is still being decided. I think we've moved on from all pet names being based on *Harry Potter* characters, which is definitely where we were for a good while. It's strange to think that one day children won't know who or what *Harry Potter* is, or perhaps the wizard will be as enduring as some of the other children's classics over the years. Who knows?

The first part of the week goes quite nicely. Cam is no trouble and I'm able to get plenty of work done, even though she's at home.

I call the RSPCA and ask if we can come and collect the kitten in the week, rather than waiting for the weekend. They agree. I don't tell the others, because I need them to go to school and college without fuss, but on Thursday morning I wait till they've disappeared, then say to Camila, 'Are you busy today?'

She laughs.

'Because if you have some time, it turns out that we can go and collect the kitten today.'

She gives a little squeal of delight and is fed, showered and ready within half an hour. Actually, that's not so surprising. Camila has a good, natural look, clean and fresh. She doesn't do a lot of make-up and always seems to wear denim and white. Her hair is shiny and thick. Today she looks like the epitome of good health.

I pop my head around Lloyd's office door, where I discover him on a call to his Swiss clients. I wave at the screen as I have also known them for years.

'We're off to get a kitten,' I reveal.

The Swiss clients all aww and coo. I like to do my bit for international relations.

The cat box is already in the car. Cam has folded up an old towel from the bottom of the airing cupboard. She also has a packet of treats and a few toys at the ready. I know the kitten will not be interested – only in her neck and hair, much as Cam might like this.

En route, I ask her how she is.

'Fine. Can't wait to see my kitten.'

'Have you decided what you're going to call it?'

'It's not it, it's a him.'

That tells me. 'Sorry. What are you going to call *him*?'

'Mikey.'

'Nice,' I say.

I turn the conversation towards more difficult areas and ask her how she feels about visiting her parents. She is not quick to answer. Her head goes down and she says nothing. I push it.

'Are you comfortable there, Camila?'

She looks at me. 'Yes, it's very comfortable.'

I laugh and say, 'No, sweetheart, are you emotionally comfortable?'

'No, I'm not. I don't like being near mum, she's–' she breaks off.

'She's?' I repeat, and it goes quiet, that question mark hanging in the air.

'It doesn't matter,' she says after a while.

Well, it clearly does matter. When people say something and then withdraw it, I know I have to respect that – but it's bloody infuriating.

'How do you get on with your dad?'

She thinks for another minute and then says, 'He's alright, I guess. Emotionally unavailable, controlled by my mum.'

Interesting, and quite a mature way of putting it. I wonder if she's heard those words, or thought them herself.

'What about your brother?' I ask.

'Josh is alright, I think. I dunno, really. He hardly speaks to me. He's in a new residential home. A nice one.'

'What defines "nice" then?' I ask.

'I dunno. The people are nice, the food?' She pauses. 'He's thinking about joining the army.'

I smile. He's what, 12? 'It's early days,' I say. 'He might change his mind a few times yet.'

I can't tell you how many young boys in care say that they are going to join the army. Always the army. Not the navy or air force, but the army. Maybe they feel as though the army might be their next family. I wonder if it's what residential or foster carers want for them. We have a problem with recruitment to the army, and an attitude prevalent amongst young people that the military is an outdated institution with a culture that clashes with modern values. Not so for kids in care, I don't really know why.

I ask her if she wants to see Josh. 'Maybe we could ask Sarah if Josh can come over, or we could meet him out or go to the residential home?'

'Yeah, that would be good,' she concedes.

'When was the last time you saw him?'

She thinks it was a few weeks before she left Sian and Gary's.

'That's quite some time,' I say.

She pipes up, 'I message him a lot.'

We are soon at the RSPCA and we walk to the reception to be greeted by a rather tubby, curly spaniel. We say an enthusiastic hello. His co-worker soon appears with an inquisitive face.

'Hi, we're here to collect one of your kittens?' I explain.

She is much younger than the grumpy woman last time. She smiles and clocks Cam's very excited face, 'Your kitten?'

Cam nods.

We follow her through the sheds and grass areas to the dormitory zone where we were last week. Cam looks at me, her face turns into one belonging to an excitable child. It's a lovely face to see.

'Now, which one is it that you're after?'

Cam points. 'The mostly-white one please.'

The lady reaches into the ensuite garden and lifts up the kitten. 'This one?'

'Yes, please.'

I watch the next bit with much interest. The kitten is presented to Cam, who is beaming from ear to ear. She takes the kitten and holds him. The kitten scrambles up to her chin and buries itself into her hair. Cam is in love and can't stop smiling.

This has got to be much better than patting a horse's backside. I'm sure of it.

XIX

Once we're home I put the litter tray and all the accessories and poo bags in Cam's room. I smile when I come back down into the kitchen to see Cam stroking little Mikey on her lap.

'So, the way this is going to work is that for now he needs to stay in your room and you must clean up his poo immediately. To start with, after the journey and stress of being in a new home, he may be a bit loose, but it's really important that you keep the litter tray clean and fresh.'

She looks at me, smiles and nods. 'Don't worry. I've got this.'

And she has. The next week runs in miraculous fashion. Cam keeps little Mikey's litter tray in perfect order. She scoops out the poop and wipes the tray, puts the kitchen roll in the poop bag and brings it all down. Lloyd has put a little hook and eye at the top of the outside of Cam's bedroom door, so she can make sure Mikey stays in the bedroom; the draft from the window can blow the door open but Mr Mikey is safe and content in her room. He is up the curtains like a shot. It's so close to summer holidays that I'm indulging Cam's negativity about school. There's little learning happening in the middle of sports' days and summer concerts and swimming galas and all the rest of it. I'm not going to invite confrontation by forcing the issue. She'll have the summer to recover before she does it again for another year, then she can leave.

All is well until Sarah sends a text asking me to take Camila to her parents at the weekend. I'm well aware that this will go down like a poo sandwich with Cam, but I'm just the messenger.

(Though we all know that messengers do, in fact, get shot from time to time.)

Camila is cross, as I knew she would be.

More than cross. She is in a heightened emotional state. It makes her very quiet, certainly not keen to talk. She stays in her room with Mikey who, thank God, is there to keep her therapeutically entertained. It's absolutely clear that Camila loves to love! Children having their own animals is sometimes a good way for them to learn to nurture, to pour out that natural need to care.

But, it gets worse.

Sarah sends a message to say that Camila's parents are coming to pick her up. I have no choice but to agree. It's done without wriggle room and, once again, it's left to me to tell Camila.

When I deliver the news, she seems unsurprised.

'Did you know already?' I ask.

'No, but I guessed. They did this with Josh last week. He was annoyed too.'

'Why is it annoying?'

'It just is. I don't want them near my home. They never went to Sian's.' She pauses. 'She wouldn't let them.'

I can't help but feel that I am now the villain in this. It

makes me feel bad. I've let her down. I should have fought for her, not rolled over and let this happen. I am pathetic!

Despite having her beautiful little kitten that she holds like a porcelain ornament, I can see her mood deteriorating. The reality is, I don't want her parents here either. This is her safe space, our safe space. I've never known it to work out well when the mums and dads start coming to our home. We foster the children; we don't sign up to deal with the birth families, though I see this work creeping into the lives of foster carers more and more. I remember when we started, we were told, 'You concentrate on the children, we deal with the families and parents.' But that was a long time ago, before the local authorities started going bankrupt, and when there were more – and more experienced – social workers available. We seem to be soaking up more of the social workers jobs, as are teachers and the police, though the police have taken a much tougher line. Still, when we see the police face to face, they are usually very kind and supportive. We are all working much harder and less smart, it seems.

When Friday night arrives, I try to gauge how Cam is feeling. She's not hungry and just wants to be alone, or alone with Mikey. I knock on her door and try to talk about what my babysitting duties will entail while she's away. She shrugs her shoulders to everything, is non-committal and disengaged. I can't get anything out of her. I feel frustrated because she was doing so well. Dare I say that she was beginning to shine?

'Look, it's not too late,' I say, rather desperately. 'I can cancel your parents.'

'No,' she says. 'There's no point. Sarah will only move it to next week, the fucking twat!'

Oh, I hear you, my sweetheart, I think, but I offer a non-committal 'hmm'. I am long enough in the tooth to know that things a foster carer says that they feel and think can sometimes be thrown back at us. Before I go to bed I check in on her again. She and Mikey are curled up asleep together. The weather is hot, close and a bit suffocating. I wonder how long Mikey will last before he's stretched out on something cooler to touch than Camila.

In the morning I wake way before I need to. My internal foster carer's alarm clock is in panic mode. I head to the coffee with purpose. No one is going to stop me.

'Shit!' I yell, as I tread in something wet and lumpy, waking everyone up. I have, it transpires, stood on a pile of cat sick. Great! My favourite way to start the day. I hop to the sink via the kitchen roll and clean up my foot. I turn around to switch on the coffee machine and knock over a wine glass that's upside down on the drainer. It goes all over the floor and I'm barefoot. I tiptoe gingerly towards the door of the conservatory to find the long-handled brush and pan.

I tiptoe back in once more, muttering expletives and unintelligible sounds under my breath, like Muttley the cartoon dog from D*astardly and Muttley in Their Flying Machines*. What a way to start the bloody day. I tip the pan into the bin, then worry about all the animals who might tear into the bin bag. Probably none, I tell myself, but then I worry about the bin men. I remind myself that they wear huge safety gloves and are grown-ups. I get Henry, the downstairs vaccum cleaner out and suck up the remaining glass. Somehow it's got as far as the fridge on the other side of the kitchen. It shattered a big distance. I am still not used to Dotty not being here. She is buried under the apple tree and I have taken to going out and saying a little hello to her when I make my coffee. It's just so quiet without her. But I appear to be making a great deal of noise myself this morning.

There is an enormous pile of washing on the floor that wasn't there last night. Jackson must have brought it down after I went to bed. He must be having a friend over, because he is hoovering his room. And that friend must be female, I deduce, because he wouldn't go to these lengths for one of his male friends. I load up the washing and lean down towards the washing cupboard, but there is no washing powder. Where the hell did that go? I have a slight Basil Fawlty moment where I want to shake my fist at the sky and have a punch up with our creator, but I breathe deeply, make my coffee and head over to say hello to Dotty. I miss her most in the mornings. She was my best friend. At this time of day she would be following me around chatting and waggling her tail. She was always on the go. I think she must have had a canine form of ADHD.

I check the clock and jump into the shower, getting rid of the last bits of cat vomit from between my toes. When I'm out and dressed I knock on Cam's door. I go to open it, but it won't open. The hook and eye is across at the top. That's strange. I unlock it, open the door and go in. I see a very sleepy kitten look up at me and yawn. I also see a load of shit on the wall and no Camila. I quickly shut the door and put the hook back in the eye and head back downstairs. Maybe she's in the kitchen.

Nothing. She is nowhere. I go to the front door and it's unlocked.

She's gone.

XX

I go into a state of panic instantly, then decide that it's no good just panicking on my own. I need someone to panic with. I dash in to tell Lloyd, waking him up.

'Cam has gone.'

His response is, 'For fuck's sake.'

I won't be writing that in the logs.

Then he adds, 'Is the coffee on?'

I nod, but wonder where his sense of urgency is. He comes downstairs and stands by the coffee machine, looking out of the window.

'I'll text her,' I say.

Hi Cam, are you okay?

Okay, it's not going to win the Pulitzer Prize, but I suspect that will only be the first of many texts. I should have known by the way it began that today is going to be a long haul of a day. It's only 7am on Saturday morning. There are hours and hours left, and who knows what's going to happen with the rest of it.

Cam replies. *Yeah.*

Well, at least it's a good indicator that she is alive. Often, children are not that far away when they bolt. I walk to the car area and the sheds. She's not there. I decide that I must call out of hours, and then the police. This takes a while and I'm still barefoot. I can't find my slippers. I get through to the police and our out-of-hours line and then Cam's local authority, who just have an answer machine. I look for my trainers and decide that, while there isn't much happening I will take Doug for a walk. Someone from our out-of-hours team calls back and says that I need to phone Cam's parents to let them know.

Like a squeaky child I say, 'Can you do that?'

The answer is no.

I decide that I'll tackle that bit while on the Douggie walk. I call Camila's mother and get her answer machine. 'Hi, Gabriella, it's Louise. I'm sorry, but we will have to cancel today. Camila left the house very early this morning. We think it's because she didn't want to see you this weekend because of her new kitten. We are guessing this is why she's gone.'

I get my excuse in because I know that at some point they will probably try to blame us. We well know how the allegation process, or should I say 'Kangaroo Court' process goes. I also send a text message to her saying roughly the same thing. I take a long time on the walk. I need to clear my head.

When I get home I report to Lloyd that I have contacted her parents.

'Well, they're outside in the car,' Lloyd tells me.

'Oh, bugger, really?'

I don't want to invite them in because that would be too weird. Also, on a Saturday morning without warning the others tend to waft about in just T-shirts and boxers, or shorts in Lily's case. That's my excuse and I'm sticking to it. The reality is that I will probably not see my little darlings till gone 11am, given the teenage capacity to sleep in at the weekend, but they don't have to know that.

'Did you speak to them? Did they see my message?'

Lloyd explains that he spoke to them at the door and asked them if they had seen my message, which arrived while they were talking to him. They probably saw me come in with Doug so will want to talk to me, no doubt. I sigh, give Doug a gravy biscuit, hang his lead up, then walk to the front door. They are in a white BMW. It's a new car, quite shiny and ostentatious. I think about my little yellow Citroen Cactus which I think I must have had for over 10 years. If I have my way, it will last me another 10. I honestly don't think I could cope with learning all the tech in a new car. I imagine myself in a Tesla and know that I would have a meltdown.

I walk over to their car, trying not to listen to the failure voice in my head that is helpfully chattering away. 'Go on, explain to this girl's parents that you have lost her. She's gone and you didn't notice!'

I try to put myself in their shoes. What would I be doing if my child had gone off while in the care of someone else that I hadn't chosen to look after them? I would be losing it by now. Gabrielle's window goes down slowly, like we're in a gangster film.

'Hi,' I say, well aware that I'm not winning any awards for eloquence today.

'Any news?' she says.

'No, not yet. Although she has been in touch via text message.' I am just about to launch into a retelling of the whole scenario, and probably tie myself up in knots while doing so, when she says, 'Will you let us know if you hear anything?'

The window goes back up and off they go.

I go back indoors to the kids, who all want to know what's going on. I tell the story to Lily and the boys. Before I know it, Lily is up the stairs to check on Mikey. Seconds later she is back down holding the kitten with a face that says WTF?

'Why is there shit on the wall?' she shouts.

'Oh, is there?' I say. 'Perhaps Mikey had an accident.'

'Right. And when did Mikey learn to spell *Cunts?*'

Aah.

XXI

I contact Sian and Gary once more to see if they know anything. After all, Sian knew exactly where she was the last time Cam went AWOL.

Sian is quick to reply.

No, sorry, but we will put some feelers out.

I feel the same sort of shame as I did earlier with Camila's parents. I feel like a failure. I feel guilt-ridden that I seem to have lost Camila; none of *them* did. This feeling sits in my stomach and it makes me feel sick. I hate feeling like this.

I check on the other children, the ones I haven't managed to lose, to see how they are. They are fine, as always, enjoying the drama, but in a measured way. Mostly wanting to help out and be supportive, but I know they are being nosey too.

'So, was the poo on the wall Camila's poo?' Lily asks.

I lie. I say that it's the kitten's, but Camila's used it as a form of protest. I tell her about the dirty protests by prisoners in Ireland who smeared their prison cells during the Troubles. Every day's a school day. 'The protest tactic was a response to the British government's removal of special category status for paramilitary prisoners. They wouldn't let prisoners wear their own clothes and maintain personal hygiene. It all escalated to include smearing excrement on the walls, mixed with rotting food and urine.'

None of the children knew about this, which makes me realise just how quickly history fades. We get into a discussion about the IRA and what happened in the 70s and 80s with the bombings in England. They really have no idea at all.

'Fear is the greatest weapon and it's much cheaper than weapons of mass destruction.'

This brings the subject round to the war in Gaza. This is their first experience of global conflict in active memory. The war in Ukraine broke out when they were younger and, despite it still going on, it didn't have the same impact at the time.

It turns into a right old history lesson.

They sit down and get their phones out to check dates and names. They are interested in the fact that wars happen all the time. Lloyd is an encyclopaedia on the history of global destruction. One day I think I will need to examine this in more detail to decide if it is entirely healthy, but for now they are all riveted by his knowledge and want to know more.

It's a useful way to distract them from the poo situation. I think I have managed to preserve Camila's dignity. I take myself quietly off upstairs, dragging the heavy feelings of failure with me. By the time I reach the top of the stairs I have an idea. I grab the cleaning stuff from the bathroom then go into Camila's bedroom. Lily still has Mikey and whilst she does I clean up all the poop, kitten and human. I open her window and pull the upstairs Hetty hoover out of the corner of the landing, to suck up all the stray cat litter. I go back downstairs to find my phone.

Hi Cam, I hope you are okay, Mikey is upset and crying. We don't know where you are. He doesn't understand what's going on. What shall I tell him?

I'm not above a little bit of emotional blackmail. I wait a while but there is no reply.

I up the ante. *It's okay, don't worry. He's calmer now. Lily has him.*

I am pretty confident that the idea of Lily bonding with Mikey will inspire some sort of action.

I go back downstairs to the war room and am amazed that the gathering is still in full swing. I make a coffee and don't offer to make drinks for them. I have, after all, been cleaning up poo. Again. I tidy the kitchen area and faff about for a bit. Then the phone pings.

I'm outside.

I don't want to antagonise anything, so I say nothing other than, 'Hello, there,' to Camila, standing at the front door.

She doesn't speak, so I add, 'Didn't you take your key?'

I suspect she did, but she is feeling a bit emotional and probably a bit awkward about the whole situation. I know she is here because she was motivated by the idea of Lily becoming Mikey's kitten-mummy. I have already put Mikey back in Camila's room, as that image has served its purpose.

Cam goes up the stairs with her head lowered, dragging her rucksack behind her. It has stuff in it, clearly, but I suspect a lot of nonsensical items packed in hurry. She bolted because she didn't want to be at her parent's house. But she didn't really want to leave Mikey. Poor girl.

'Have you eaten?' I ask.

'No.'

'Are you hungry?'

'Yeah.'

I suggest that she says hello to her kitten-baby and tops up his food bowl and then comes back down. 'After that I'll take you to town for brunch.'

Cam likes this idea and it all happens swiftly, but gently. We bump into Lily in the kitchen.

'Alright?' Lily asks, warily.

Cam says, 'Yeah,' and that's that.

I'm tempted, briefly, to invite Lily to come with us, but decide on balance that I should do this journey just with Cam. But, as we head towards the backdoor, Cam says, 'Lils, do you want to come for brunch?'

She does. 'Yeah.'

And off we all go. Maybe Camila doesn't want to talk just yet and that's why she's invited Lily. Maybe she's grateful to Lily for looking after Mikey. Maybe she's just suddenly ready to make a connection with Lily. Who knows?

I leave Lloyd to do all the contacting of the various agencies and individuals who need to be told that Cam is back, and we have a nice day. We communicate with each other quietly by text, while the girls aren't looking, so that Cam doesn't have a sense of the drama she caused, as Lloyd stands down the police and the out-of-hours teams.

We end up in a new café-clothes shop in the next town. It's a lovely town and I've noticed over the years that businesses don't actually go away, they move premises. The café and alternative clothes shop have joined forces to create a very New York style cool clothes shop that you can get light lunches in. It's a sort of punk theme.

This is right up Lily's alley, or it was at one time, I can't keep up with her look. The girls look around the clothes section while I order filled nachos x3 for lunch. The lady who runs the café has thick purple hair. She is my age, or perhaps even a little older, and dressed in a post-punk grey/black long dress with purple Dr Martens boots. On a nearby table I notice a load of posters asking customers to sign a petition to the MP to get more support for EHCPs (Educational Health Care Plans). I wander up to the table and pick up a leaflet. I read the posters more carefully and notice that the café-shop we are in is an independent business that supports workers who are neurodivergent. I look over at the girls, who seem very happy looking through the rails, and ask the purple-haired lady more about her campaign. She tells me that she is a lawyer whose son was let down by the education system.

'He was going to be thrown to the wolves, so I stepped back from my career and set up a shop to help him. Then I learnt of more young people who were being failed once they left school so I grew the business to employ over 30 young people – who are all deemed unemployable.'

'Where are the others?' I ask.

'I've set up a small agricultural project that sells its produce in the fruit and veg shop along the road, and eggs.'

After a conversation that lasts less than two minutes, I'm already in awe of this wonderful woman, whose name is Isabelle. I can absolutely relate to her. She does not hear 'no', it seems, and will fight for children. Not just hers, but all children. My kinda gal!

She must sense a kindred spirit, because she sits down with me at the table while we trade experiences of the different departments in the local authority. Between us, we try to work out which one is the worst, then decide it would be easier if we switched to identifying the ones that are okay. It's a depressingly short list. We talk about the injustices to children. We are just on the subject of the accessibility of porn when the girls see the waiter (actually Isabelle's son) bring a tray with our nachos and drinks over. We finish our conversation as the girls sit down.

'Seen anything you like?' I ask them.

They say, 'Yes,' in unison.

'Go and get the items to show me and tell me the price.'

Isabelle and I carry on talking about how dangerous porn is and how it damages children, breaking off again as the girls bring over the items, and I ask Isabelle if we could leave them on the counter while we eat our brunch.

Lily is curious. 'What were you two talking about?'

I tell her that we were discussing Isabelle's campaign, and porn.

'What were you saying about porn?'

'Well, not where to get it!' I laugh.

'Obviously,' Lily says.

I explain again about the damage porn has on the brain and the problems this causes given that so many children are exposed to it so easily on their phones.

She shrugs.

We tuck in and talk about food and life. After lunch I suggest that the girls wash their hands and go and try on their finds. Lily wants a long, net dress thing. I'm not sure exactly what it is, to be honest, but it's only £10 and Cam looks gorgeous in a short lilac dress.

'Will you be wearing that over trousers?' I ask, thinking that it is very short indeed.

Both girls look at me with something approaching pity. I

don't tell them that I wore skirts way shorter than that way back when. I pay for the lunch and items and we walk back to the car. Another reason I like it here is because you can park in this town without paying a fortune, and there are plenty of places where you pay nothing at all. In my town it's 95p per hour, and who carries the change these days to make up 95p? I end up putting in a pound and always resent losing 5p. I don't know why they don't just say £1 and stop people like me feeling annoyed. I often fail to understand the mentality of parish councils.

On the way home, the girls are quiet. It must be the larger portions they ordered making them soporific. I had a 'lighter bite' portion and feel energised. When we get in, both of them go straight up to Cam's room to see Mikey.

The day meanders on and then it's dinner time. No news from anyone. Lloyd dealt with the follow-up call from the out-of-hours team. They asked if we knew where Cam was. He explained that she was out with me and Lily and told them we'd ask Cam where she went later, when she feels settled and calm. That's not the answer they wanted because they want to fill out their little form there and then and sign it off, but they can wait. The whole system is led by insurance and tickboxes rather than people.

After dinner I head upstairs to check on all the children. I knock gently on Cam's door, and carefully push it open. She is sitting on her bed in her pjs, holding her kitten. She looks sad.

'Can I come in?' I ask.

She nods.

'Can I sit down?'

She nods again.

'Are you okay?'

260

She shakes her head slowly.

I sigh. I'm not sure if the sigh is for her or for me. I make myself comfortable because I have a feeling I am going to be here for a while. I'm tired, and the list of all the things I now need to do on Sunday because I lost my day to Camila pops up in my head. Then I tell myself to shut up and remind myself that all those tasks can wait. Cam may at last talk.

I can feel her 'want' to talk.

First, I ask her, very gently where she went this morning.

She looks at Mikey to avoid looking directly at me. 'I went to the park.'

That explains why she was able to be back home inside 10 minutes once she thought Lily was stealing the affections of Mikey. 'When?' I ask.

'I dunno. I think 7-ish.'

That's not so bad. It means she wasn't out all night, which is another relief and also means less explanation to the social workers. Less writing in the logs. I find myself saying out loud, 'Thank God, and thank you, Cam.'

She smiles. She doesn't understand on how many different levels this news is good.

But before we go to where I *think* she wants to go, I want to ask her what she feels about Sarah, her social worker. I have had a feeling all the way through this that they want to put Camila back with her parents. I sense that Cam feels this too, which is why she smears and absconds. I ask her outright.

'She's alright, I suppose.'

'Alright?'

'Well, I can't talk to her. She's just not an easy person to talk to.'

'Why not?'

'She's judgy.'

I ask what she means.

She tells me about several times recently when she has tried to say that she doesn't want to see her parents. 'But Sarah shuts down the conversation. She doesn't want to hear it. So she doesn't listen. I don't think she cares.'

Not listening would lead to not caring, I'm sure.

She carries on talking about all the times Sarah hasn't listened in the past. 'And when I told them how much I wanted to stay with Sian and Gary, she didn't listen then, either. And neither did the manager.'

'Can you tell me more about how you left Sian's?'

'Yes, I know what I did was shit.' She smiles. 'I know I looked like a crazy person, but they weren't listening. Nobody was. And Sian and Gary weren't fighting for me. That hurt.'

I suggest that perhaps they weren't fighting in front of her. 'But I suspect that when you weren't listening they were seriously fighting on your behalf. I've spoken to Sian. I know how much they wanted you to stay with them. But I also suspect, knowing social workers and their managers as I do, those in charge may have felt threatened and annoyed by that and may have punished Sian, Gary and you as a result.'

I actually know from Sian that they wanted a serious case review, but Cam was out of there so quickly that they had no rights. When a manager does not want to listen, sadly, foster carers can't do much about it. Sian and Gary knew that they would face, at best lies, and at worst retaliation, in the form of allegations.

'Would you like a hot drink, Cam?' I ask, when it gets

to 1.15am and she's still talking. I'm shattered and need a pick-me-up.

She asks for a hot chocolate. She must need some comfort.

I head downstairs and put some toast on because I think she might like some with peanut butter. To my surprise, she walks into the kitchen. She has put Mikey in her room and left him.

'Don't worry, the hook and eye are safely secure.'

'Sit down,' I say. 'Your drink is just coming.'

I make toast, spreading peanut butter on several rounds. I have one slice, it smells so good. I sip a cup of tea and begin to wake up a bit. The cats come through the cat flap, hoping for another sachet of food. They're out of luck. Doug is in bed.

I pick up where we left off. We have strayed off the 'real' conversation many times, to things from her old bedroom, which sound lovely, and her old friends, who also sound lovely. Her old life. I can't be in any way offended when she talks so affectionately about her other foster home, especially since I have always had that feeling that she was just passing through. I remember that we never finished talking about Sarah. I am still puzzled by this dynamic because it must feel a bit like betrayal given that Cam has known her so long.

Then out pops the big, and very unexpected, news on Sarah. 'She was alright until she started screwing Mr Forester.'

I must look confused, because Cam explains. 'The headteacher.'

I'm speechless for a moment. I definitely didn't see that one coming. I knew Sarah had a partner and children and she is a social worker. When do people with families and demanding jobs find time for an affair?

I think about the boundaries that have been broken here

and how unprofessional that was. I am now beginning to wonder if Sarah's ineffectiveness is partly to do with the fact that she has a preoccupation that is taking up her limited time. How awful that he is the headteacher of Camila's School. That might go some way towards explaining why the students are creating AI images of the teachers. Perhaps they're annoyed? I certainly get the feeling that Cam is.

I let her know that this is unethical and ask her how she knows.

'She's not very good at hiding it.'

I try to steer the conversation gently back to the issue with her parents, because each time Sarah organises this, Cam is clearly saying, through her actions, that she does not want to go.

I would like the contact visits to stop, at least for now. But to do that, I need a bit more information so I can give a good reason as to why.

Cam shares memories of being at her grandparents' house when her mum and dad had parties.

'You know, the sex parties.'

I let that hang in the air.

'I told you that sex was their business.'

I nod.

Then, like so many times before with children and young people, out it comes, all in a rush, and rolls across the table to me. 'My mum let men hurt me.'

PART THREE

Ten Years Earlier

Zoe

Taz and Zoe head out for the opening night at the new Mexican-fusion restaurant in town. Zoe's mum is happily babysitting Benjamin. The owner of the restaurant, Luc, was once part of their old surf and skate crew, so it isn't a cosy little romantic date for two, but a crowd from the old days, most married or with young children. There is no sign of Robbie or Gabby.

'Anyone seen Rob lately?' someone asks.

'Yeah, quite the family man. Two kids now,' Taz says.

It's explanation enough for why he isn't there. The conversation moves on, but when the customers begin to thin out at the end of the evening, Luc pulls Taz and Zoe to one side.

'You hear about Robbie and Gabby – and the rumours about her latest business?'

'The cakes?' Zoe says. 'Yeah, she's really busy with it. We have the kids quite a bit.'

'Not the cakes.' Luc says.

And what he tells them next sends them reeling.

'Apparently they're into the swingers thing.'

Taz laughs. 'Nah, not Robbie.'

'It's what I heard,' Luc persists. 'It's huge money, apparently. Gabby's all over it as her latest business opportunity.'

'What do you mean?' Zoe asks, shocked.

'There's plenty of the old spondoolies to be made in extra-marital sex. So Gabby and Robbie, yeah, they're running swingers parties. That's what I've heard.'

'Where are these parties supposed to be taking place?' Zoe is alarmed, hoping to goodness that they aren't happening in that house with those lovely kids.

'Well, it's kind of a national thing now. All over the place. People meet up at hotels where whole floors have been booked out. They swap partners and rooms and then end up in a massive orgy. Apparently Gabby's well into it.'

'So they don't – I mean, they don't have any of these parties at home?'

Luc shrugs his shoulders. 'I think they may have done, at least to begin with. I don't know.'

Taz looks as distressed as Zoe feels. He keeps rubbing the back of his head and breathing out loudly. Zoe stays silent. It's all her worst fears imagined. She *knew* there was something up with those kids. Dark thoughts creep into Zoe's mind about what those poor children might have unwittingly been exposed to. Sights they might have witnessed. She can't push them away.

'It's fucked-up, man,' Taz says.

Zoe is beside herself. She cannot be in possession of this information and do nothing about it.

'What the fuck are they up to?' she keeps asking Taz all the way home. 'Who is looking after the children?' Or 'Where are the children when this shit is going on?' She goes round in circles with the same questions.

'Look, we don't know for sure,' Taz says, but he sounds uncertain as he says it. It's not surprising that he feels reluctant to be drawn into what must feel like a threat to the friendship with his best friend.

'You were mates. Like brothers you told me. Would Robbie really do something like that?'

'I don't know. I don't think so. But he's done some strange things for Gabby.'

Over the next few days, Zoe begins to dig deeper into the world of swingers. She checks out online websites and Facebook groups.

'They have the equivalent of Tripadvisor ratings!' Zoe screams, while Taz is watching rugby on the television one Saturday evening.

'What?' Taz gets up from the sofa and walks to where she is in the kitchen.

Zoe turns the laptop so that he can see. 'Look. Their swingers' group is called "Seduction Adventures" and they have a website.'

Taz leans in. 'What the actual fuck?'

Zoe's face is set into a grim line. 'What the fuck is right. Look at this. You can choose.'

She clicks on *Nibbles, Starters and Cocktails*.

The descriptions astound her. The tab explains that this is when couples and singles meet to kiss and feel each other.

Taz draws a deep breath in. 'Is Benji asleep?'

'Yes, of course. Keep looking.' Zoe clicks again and finds another page: *Cum inside or smother me over.* The images of sex are in dark shades of blue with bright red and yellow text accompanying them.

For the givers and receivers, hungry mouths and eager cocks.

Taz's eyes are wide as he spots something in one of the photos.

'Oh my good god, that's Robbie!'

You can't see the man's head, but he points to Robbie's tattoo on his arm, the one he had done in Cornwall. The arm is holding a woman's head as she goes down on him.

'And that's not Gabby!'

They keep scrolling. Zoe clicks on something labelled *F.U.C.K House.* Taz and Zoe screech at the same time.

'That's Gabby's parent's house!'

'Look, there's that painting. And I recognise the stairs.'

'And that's the pool.'

Zoe's mind is drawn back to a party they once attended there, back when she and Taz had first got engaged.

'Hang on, didn't her parents sell that house when they went to Spain?' Zoe tries to think back.

'I thought they had, but evidently not. They can't know it's being used like this, though.'

It's weird seeing a place they know so well on screen in such a different light. They read online page after page of sex, sex, sex. Distorted images of people are draped all over the *F.U.C.K House.* Occasionally they identify either Robbie or Gabby in the photos.

'What the hell do we do?' Zoe says.

Taz is non-committal. 'Look, it's not really any of our

business, is it? It's obviously not illegal. And consenting adults can do whatever they want.' He pauses for a moment. 'I mean, you do.'

Zoe glares at him, knowing that he is referring to the close friendships she shares with a few female friends. Even when they involve intimacy, it's nothing like the stuff they're looking at here. Zoe knows her partner well – Taz will just bury his head in the sand.

'But those kids, Taz. I can't just let this go. At the very least we can make our excuses and not go round there anymore. I don't want Ben exposed to any of this.'

'Yeah.'

Zoe continues her investigations over the next few nights. She waits until Benji is safely tucked up in bed before resuming her searches. In her head, she now calls Gabby 'The Madam'. Taz might say this is between consenting adults, but it feels somehow exploitative to Zoe. She reads in some research pages that *92% of married couples who engage in swingers sex end up in divorce*, and typically it's because one is always more into it than the other.

'It's her. She's the one.'

Taz agrees that it must be Gabby who is behind all this.

'But I'm surprised. I always thought she was so uptight,' Zoe says.

'I dunno. I remember some of the things Robbie used to say about her in the sack.'

Zoe shoots him a warning look. She hates that sort of talk. 'Alright. Controlling then.'

'She definitely wanted to control him alright. And she was always into making lots of cash.'

Zoe books a table at the Mexican restaurant again, hoping to meet more of their friends and learn as much as she can about what Robbie and Gabby are up to.

Taz is reluctant.

'I just don't feel comfortable about being disloyal to my best and oldest friend.'

'I know, but you could be doing him a big favour in the long run. You saw him. He's not in the best shape. He's clearly struggling. His self-esteem is somewhere below the underlay of his thick, expensive carpet.'

At the restaurant, Zoe gets her phone out and shows Luc the website. 'And they have a bunch of reviews. Some of the comments talk about creepy foreign men turning up at hotels!'

'I'm not surprised,' Luc says. 'Gabby always had a sort of weird, sexual wanderlust.'

'Well, what does that mean?' Zoe asks. 'You're going to have to tell us more.'

Luc sighs. 'It was about a year ago, and Gabby and Robbie came over for dinner. It was when I was still with Beth. We all drank too much and there was some coke going around. And, well, Gabby asked us if we wanted to basically have sex with them. If not that night, then another evening.'

'That's a bit much, mate,' Taz says.

'You're telling me. Beth and I split up shortly after that. She thought I was a perv because my friends were. To be honest, I haven't been back in touch with them since. I was busy getting ready to launch the restaurant. But it did disturb me. I mean, I used to think that Gabby was so uptight she squeaked, now she's this fucking sex addict and Robbie looks like he's going along with it. But, man, I reckon his eyes tell a different story.'

Zoe flaps her arm up and down. 'Wait, wait. Jesus, this has just gone up on their news and events page. Look!'

They all squint for a second until Zoe grabs the phone back. 'Give it here. I'll read it.' She clears her throat and reads out the words:

Join us for exciting events at the F.U.C.K House. Please text or WhatsApp letting us know you're ready to join in. Include your name and the date you would like to attend, and we'll send you details of how to book. (A small fee is asked). Whether you're kinky or vanilla, this one night will be perfect for you to explore your fantasies – or just watch them being carried out in this fully equipped play zone. We do not meet away from our parties and we don't chat on here!'

'Seriously?' Luc says.

So much is troubling about all of this. It's not just the fact that it's sex, it's the charging money for it. It feels exploitative. Who do they think they are?

'It's so weird to think of Robbie and Gabby like that,' Taz says. 'I mean, back in the day we were all nice people, weren't we? Robbie was a decent bloke. We all grew up together, surfing, skateboarding, smoking weed and hanging out together, caring about each other.'

'Robbie, maybe,' Zoe says. 'I'm not sure I've ever liked Gabby.'

'Times change. People change,' Luc says.

Zoe continues, 'There's more about the venue. Listen. *Open your eyes to the world of kink and pleasure, filming with permissions. Our venue has a wide variety of equipment to explore with people on hand to show how these are to be used correctly. Dom/Sub scenarios, vanilla playroom, St Andrew's Cross, whipping bench, bed restraints and much more.* I mean, I don't even know what some of this stuff means!'

271

'Do they put the actual address on there?' Taz asks with a frown.

'Not directly. It says: *You can park your car right outside the venue door and the venue itself will be made known to you on receipt of your small fee. Everyone is welcome to our parties, whether you are a newbie or a pro in the swinging and fetish world.*'

'There's loads more.' Zoe hands the phone to Taz who carries on reading.

We put lots of effort into our parties. So book today and 'cum' and try us. Fulfil your fantasies. We've been holding parties for over a year and no one has left disappointed. Just check out our reviews. They have been extremely popular and fun for all because we don't just host, we play too!! Our parties are bi/gay-friendly. There are mixed events for Everyone:- Bi/Straight or Gay, Single or Married, Men, Women And Couples, Tv/Ts.

'Then there's the smallprint, which is a work of art in its own right. Listen:' he reads on.

We do not give out names of guests who are attending. But when you attend we ask you to put up a meet or status on your own profile ahead of the event to state that you are with The Seduction Adventurers.

We have a strict no drug policy at our parties!!!!

Yes, it's an Adult Party however this does not guarantee sex.

Bring your own wine or beer, just please be mindful with any alcohol intake during our events and don't turn up the worse for wear or you will be refused entry.

Any touching without permission is a no-go.

Our main rule: No means No!!!

You will be asked to leave if you break our party rules and will not be invited back.

Book early to avoid disappointment.

Taz looks up. 'Do you think they've turned Gabby's parents' double garage into a dungeon or something?'

Luc chuckles. 'I think that's the understatement of the year, mate.'

'Her parents live in Spain. I bet they never come back.'

'Which means that the house is empty, so I guess they've taken it over. There's loads of parking in the drive. It's the size of a bloody car park anyway. I bet she pays her parents rent and they don't ask any questions.'

'Would they know to ask any questions about this sort of thing?' Zoe says.

'And the drugs thing,' Taz says. *We have a strict no drug policy at our parties.* As if. Robbie and Gabby are doing a lot of coke. They were doing it at a barbecue with the kids there, for fuck's sake. Well, Robbie was, at least. He offered me a line.'

'Exactly. Those kids. That's what I'm really worried about. What happens to them, the children, while they're busy shagging for profit?' Zoe asks, with her usual directness.

'I dunno,' Luc says. 'I guess they're in their rooms. I've never really thought about it.'

Zoe's eyes dart rapidly from left to right as she remembers something from the house. She puts her hand flat on the table. 'Shit! When I went upstairs to the kids' rooms, there were locks and keys on the outside. I never thought anything of it.'

The table goes quiet as her words sink in.

Taz swallows. 'You don't think they lock them in, even when they're not there? When they're at the F.U.C.K. House?'

Now Zoe is more convinced than ever that she has to do something.

At the same time, she knows that no one wants to be the

snitch. No one wants to be the one to say that they're going to phone children's social care and report their concerns. What if they're wrong? But, in her heart of hearts, Zoe knows that they aren't wrong.

No one likes being the grass. Loyalty is a funny thing. But it isn't loyalty. It's fear. And those kids are at risk.

She makes a decision. First thing in the morning, after she drops Benji off at the play group he goes to once a week, she'll be straight on the phone. She doesn't tell the others, though.

What Zoe hasn't banked on is that Taz and Luc are thinking the same thing, too.

Each of them contact children's social care, independently, to express their concerns.

Zoe has been avoiding Gabby, but when it all goes very quiet she is struck by a pang of guilt and, feeling uncomfortable about what she has done, asks Taz to send a friendly message to Robbie.

'Just ask him if he fancies going out.'

Robbie's reply is evasive. *Got a lot on mate, loads happening, thx see you soon.*

Zoe only finds out later that their collective response was enough to trigger a Section 47 enquiry. Outlined in the Children Act 1989, local authorities have a statutory duty to investigate when there is reasonable cause to suspect a child is suffering, or likely to suffer, significant harm.

Gabby

'Just when I *don't* need them,' Gabby snaps.

Her parents have caught a flight home and are arriving any minute, having been contacted by social workers in conjunction with the Section 47 enquiry.

'We thought that the house was being rented out by the pair of you as a *residence*,' John hisses, when he returns to discover that their garage has been converted into a sex chamber, mostly built by Robbie on Gabby's design and orders, and the rest of the house has become party-central.

'Our home has obviously been used for parties,' Marjory says. 'God knows what's been going on in there. That wasn't the deal.'

They are furious, beyond furious, and Gabby is reduced to feeling like a child once again. 'I don't see what you've got to complain about,' she tries to defend herself. 'You've been receiving way above average rental fees and there have been no problems.'

'Until now,' Marjory says.

Life was initially difficult with them gone but, latterly, it has actually been much easier with her parents out of the way. Her mother, she knows, has joined the golf club close to their home in Spain and has made a network of new friends. If this thing with the kids hadn't kicked off then her folks would have carried on enjoying their social lives on the continent and been none the wiser about what was going on in their house.

To her surprise, her father actually calms down when he begins to see the business sense and profit, and can ignore the morality – or lack of it – in the situation. He begins to back away from his initial rage.

'You're a chip off the old block and no mistake,' he says, shaking his head. 'You've always been a hard worker, and can turn your hand to anything, it seems. Sex sells, as they say. Always has done – if you can market it, so be it.'

Gabby is pleased that he manages to calm Marjory down. She's pretty sure they think it's just a venue they rent for other people to use, and that she and Robbie are not taking part themselves.

It means that they will be more on side when they are visited by the social worker. The garage is kept firmly locked. Nirvana, the old campervan, is left to rust and rot outside.

'Whatever investigations and accusations are thrown about, I'm sure it will all blow over with nothing more than a pep talk from some professionals.'

But in the event, Gabby's parents are asked if they would offer kinship care to Camila and Josh. They decline, referencing the fact that they now live abroad and do not have the room for two children. This seems to head things off at the pass.

Until the social worker goes to interview the manager of a regional hotel, where Gabby's Seduction Adventures business booked an entire floor for swinging and an orgy. Again, in itself, this is not a problem. Gabby explains that all participants were consenting adults. Things seem to be going in their favour and Gabby is confident that the interfering social services will soon be off their back.

But the manager of the hotel returns with information from their records that the children were sleeping in the family room through the door to their suite, where the orgy is alleged to have taken place.

'And where do the children stay when you are out at the, ahem, F.U.C.K House?' the social worker asks Gabby and Robbie.

Sheepishly, they are forced to answer that the children stay in the spare room.

'And who looks after Camila and Josh when you are out at other swinger events?'

Gabby explains that they have a babysitter, but is unable to provide a name or contact number.

It is decided that the children will be placed into foster care.

PART FOUR

XXII

Louise

'My mum let men hurt me.'

Cam's words hang in the air. I have been here many times before. I never feel anything other than sheer sadness and fleeting despair.

Social services removed Camila and her brother into care because they were concerned about them being exposed to sex parties. But it is worse. She remembers her mum waking her up, not disturbing her brother and walking her to a bedroom where several men and a few women sat around the edge of the room and asked her to take her nightie off. She was passed around the room as the adults touched her. Camila can't bring herself to say much more.

That is more than enough to contact Kendi first thing on Monday morning and close down contact.

Camila should *never* have to see those people again. She is nearly 15 years old. An age where she is more than capable of choosing what she wants to do.

I get up and walk around to where she is sitting and give her a huge hug. She falls into it, tears coming from those striking blue eyes and mingling with the tears that are coming from me. I crouch down and hold her hand, stroking the hair away from her eyes that are sticky with all the crying.

'Cam, love, you know that I will have to report this. And that means you probably won't be seeing your mum and dad for a while.'

She sniffs and blows out the word, 'Good.'

I reach for the square box of tissues that are on the side and hand them to her. I hold both her hands and tell her that she is brave.

'And I am so grateful that you have told me.' I can see in her face that the effort it has taken to reach this disclosure is exhausting. 'Cam, my sweet, you need to get some sleep. Come on.'

I follow her up the stairs and while she performs her nighttime ablutions I top up Mikey's food, water and litter tray. When she comes back in, her room is much tidier. I always think having a tidy, clean environment helps soothe the soul. I wait for her to get into bed, then I tuck her up and lean in to kiss her on the forehead. I gently tap her nose as I would with a toddler, and she smiles.

I stroke her arm and say, 'It's all going to be fine, Cam, just you see.'

My optimistic nature always believes that a child can feel better, and I want them to feel better as soon as possible.

When I get into bed, sleep eludes me, though I am spent. I

plan my morning. I'll tell Lloyd first, who I know will be sad and angry at the same time, and talk to Kendi.

I leave Camila to sleep in and call Kendi before I email Sarah.

I was right. Lloyd is both angry and sad. He doesn't like the world being this rubbish any more than I do. He hates the fact that people exploit children.

'It's happened since forever and it should have stopped by now,' he says.

'But technology messes with the brain, then add cocaine and you've got a sordid mix.'

The libido and our society's preoccupation with it causes a world of ill. It leads to mistruths and people telling lies to themselves. Worse, getting dragged into doing bad things to children because of it.

'I don't see the animals watching porn and feeling entitled to cause this kind of misery,' I add. 'They might get a bit randy, but no means no!'

'Well, that's not strictly true,' Lloyd begins to say, and I know he's about to launch into some David Attenborough fact about some creature in the animal kingdom.

'I don't care. For the sake of this situation and in my current state of mind, I need to believe that animals are not as bad as humans.'

I've been thinking about all the things that Cam has told me, not just the headlines. After hearing about Sarah's relationship with the headteacher, I'm not sure what to do. I know I have no evidence, not without stalking them, and that would be weird. I decide that I will trust Cam's belief that Sarah is indeed 'pre-occupied' at best. Therefore I feel no issue with contacting

Sian and Gary, whom I believe have greater claim to the title of being the 'parents' of Camila.

I get hold of Kendi and tell him all the news. He pauses before answering, 'This is bad news, Louise. How hard must this have been for Camila? She was just a small child when it happened.'

Like the rest of us, he is genuinely saddened by the news. 'The contact with the parents must stop. It's not appropriate, it's not safe.' He goes on to say that he will speak to Sarah. Good. I'm more than happy to leave him to do that.

I pop up to see Cam, who is, perhaps quite rightly under the circumstances, happy for me to wait on her hand and foot today. She needs lots of love. When I knock on her door, she is lying in bed, awake, but just staring up at the ceiling.

'Hot chocolate and toast?'

She nods.

Mikey is in good form this morning, hanging from the curtain and making little pulls in the thread of the fabric. I'll let him off today. I open the door to go back into the hall, to find Douglas and Mabel sitting outside ready for support duties. Who needs to paint on a horse's backside or hold a guinea pig when we have this furry army of love?

I pop my head back in. 'You have visitors, but do you want them in here with Mikey?'

She gets out of bed and puts Mikey close to her, then says, 'Yes please, can you let them in?'

I open the door and watch Doug and Mabel jump up onto her bed. I quickly lift up the litter tray and Mikey's food before Doug eats it.

'I'll be back in a minute.'

I hear Camila giggle as she tries to control the social gathering of four-legged friends. I find myself eating toast and peanut butter too. I am comfort-eating. Or stress-eating. Or both. Not really paying attention to anything other than staring out of the window until my brain has settled enough for me to think about what's next on the agenda.

Time to get hold of Sian. We need to get Camila back home, where she belongs. I drop off three pieces of toast, two with peanut butter and one with jam, plus a steaming mug of hot chocolate. I go for three, safe in the knowledge that Cam will feed Doug at least one slice. When I go in she is lying down with Doug by her side, Mabel at her feet and little Mikey in the bed. I have saved the NHS and Children's Social Care a fortune.

I put the tray down on the bedside table and ask Cam to sit up for me, to plump up her pillows. She does this in a way that says 'I'm the patient and you are the nurse'. I hope I can be more Florence Nightingale than Nurse Ratched from *One Flew Over the Cuckoo's Nest*, but there's a reason I chose art over nursing as a career.

I close the door but, before I do, I glance at a much happier Camila. I hope that talking about what happened has helped her in some small way.

I message Sian and we decide to chat over the phone. I tell her what's been going on and what Camila told me about her parents, her mum especially.

Sian goes quiet for a moment and then says, 'That explains so much.'

I end up in tears again, and so does she, as we revisit Cam's more recent history of how she was made to leave their home.

'It was awful. There is no other word for it.'

She shares with me that she and Gary had even been to see their MP to try to get her back. 'I didn't tell you before because you sounded nice, and Cam had said nice things about you too, that got back to us via Fred.'

'I'm glad,' I say. 'I've said all the way along that from the day I met Cam I knew that she was only staying a short while. Sometimes you just feel it.'

I ask where she has got to with the MP situation.

'Well, despite his political colour,' she pauses and we share a conspiratorial laugh, 'he does actually seem quite concerned and has written to our children's social care leader. He received a pretty banal reply saying that Camila had been removed and placed in alternative foster care which was in her best interests.'

I sigh, and then hear myself say, 'Same old shit, then.' I apologise, but Sian laughs. 'Still, after these revelations, it's going to be hard for them to argue for Cam to go back to her parents.'

'True. But I know that sometimes social workers can get rather uppity if they don't get what they want.'

We leave the conversation with an air of shared campaign determination. We both want Cam to go back home, but to Sian and Gary, not her parents – not to a woman who used her for sex.

XXIII

Kendi has been busy messaging me while I was on the call to Sian. I call him back.

'Louise, okay, I've spoken to Sarah who has agreed for Cam not to go to her parents whilst there is an ongoing investigation.'

'Good. Cam is fine for now. She seems more relaxed than I have ever seen her. A big burden has been dropped from her shoulders.' And I don't want anything else to replace it, I think to myself.

I say goodbye to Kendi, who I know will be back on the phone soon. I pick up the phone to call the police and ask for a Sexual Assault Referral Centre (SARC). I have a cousin in the police who used to work in Child Protection. She advised me years ago to go to the police first. Let the police interview the children, not the social workers, she used to urge. She also said a few rather disparaging things about the way social workers mess things up by over-asking children questions and playing weird politics.

I get through to a softly-spoken man. His voice suggests he is young, but he seems kind. My opening line is, 'I want to report a case of sexual abuse on behalf of my foster child, a girl aged

14 years. Her mother ran a swingers' business and she used her daughter for sex with her clients on at least one occasion.'

'There are some pretty terrible people out there,' the policeman says. He tells me that a colleague, a woman, will call me back and email me.

Good, I think, because I need the police to talk to Cam before Sarah, or any other social worker, does. Camila wants to go back home, Sian and Gary want her back, and I want her to go. To my mind, it couldn't be simpler to solve this little conundrum, that isn't really a conundrum at all.

I adore Cam, but have refrained from becoming too attached because of the knowledge that she needed to go home. What I am doing now is implementing a strategy. The police report will carry more weight than the social workers, and we need that evidence to give to the MP to keep fighting for Camila. This thing that social workers seem not to like, about children going back to foster carers, seems to have no reasoning. It feels a bit like 'don't open umbrellas indoors'. It can only be superstition because it actually makes no sense. I need to work fast for this plan to work. My years as a union rep at the university have paid off. Often it's about the speed you can work at, not brawn.

The day is spent making frequent trips up and down stairs to check on Cam, who is snoozing a lot. Good, I say to myself, for the umpteenth time of the day. She must be letting go. Sleep is the best medicine. The animals are not leaving her side, so she must need them.

Each time I check on her, I bolt back downstairs to see if there has been any movement. To be on the side of urgent, I get Sian to make an appointment with her MP. I know this can take a while and I suggest she puts URGENT in the subject box. I hear back from the police: a nice lady from a different team who specialises in child sexual abuse. She asks me to tell her the story again. You get used to this as a foster carer. She doesn't like the story either. There is something about a mother selling her daughter for sex, a mother who was financially secure, just greedy, that sits very wrong.

I take the phone upstairs because I have to ask Camila, in front of the policewoman, that she gives her consent to be interviewed. Camila nods her head, frowns and says, 'Yes'. The police officer asks if she can talk to Cam to explain what the interview will be like.

'Are you happy to chat to her?' I ask Camila.

Cam nods again. I hand over my phone and stand by the window, examining the extent of the kitten claw damage while listening.

Cam is open and honest in her responses. Then asks, 'Can you make sure that I don't have to see my parents?'

Without hesitation, the policewoman says, 'No, you don't have to see your parents.' She goes on to explain that she'll be here in the morning, 'if that's okay with you, Camila?'

I make a mental note to call the school first thing and say that she is ill. She has missed so much, another day won't make a difference, and even if the police weren't coming here, I can't imagine she would make it in after all that has taken place in the last 48 hours.

As soon as I walk back downstairs, the phone rings. It's Sarah.

'Hi Sarah, how are you?'

'Fine. But I've spoken to Kendi and I need to come and see Camila today.'

Shit! I need to think on my feet. 'She's sleeping at the moment. It's been rather traumatic for her. I was going to take her out for a drive later. She has said that she doesn't want to see anyone today.'

Sarah is insistent, and this begins to grind my gears. She should respect a child's wishes. When is she going to learn that? I quickly suggest that she can come tomorrow. She says that the only time she has is at 3pm.

'That's great, thank you Sarah, I'll let her know.'

Ha! The policewoman will be long gone by then and her report will be in the system.

I quickly call Sian back. I want to keep her updated. She was just about to call me. She decided to phone the MP's office instead of sending an email. They went into rapid fire and got us an appointment for Thursday!

Here is the real art to fostering, the bit where you behave like an air steward who knows there's a problem in the cockpit but you don't want to alarm the passengers. I have to walk on a tightrope now, balancing Camila's future in my hands. They *say* but do not always *do* 'in the interests of the child', so we shall see. When she is back home, her school life will calm down, it will all calm down, we just need to get her back there and I know that it won't be easy.

I smile and keep everything completely calm. I haven't said a peep about Sian and Gary. I need to manage her expectations. I don't want this poor child feeling any more insecurity. Sending her to stay at her parent's house must have been awful. It makes me feel sick. She must have felt so stressed, which now explains all her behaviour. I'm glad I kept that to an absolute minimum in the logs and emails. If she wants her files when she is older,

I don't want to be the person to make her feel humiliated and ashamed. She did what she did because no one was listening. She was taken away from her family, the ones that she thought of as her family. How would any of us feel in those circumstances?

Instead, I keep things as low key and functional as I can. 'I've called school and said that you're ill,' I explain. 'That way you can talk to the policewoman and then rest.'

I take her up another three pieces of toast and a hot chocolate, we can resume healthy eating once this bit is over. I remind her that the police lady will be here in two hours, plenty of time to get showered and dressed.

She nods but doesn't say a lot. I quickly check the walls in her room – nothing. I think the blend of clearing up animal poo and finally the freedom from that secret has helped her feel better and lessened the need for such compelling self-expression. She certainly seems calmer. The animals have helped, too. They are very relaxed, stretching and smiling as if they are pleased with their work. Almost as if they know they have done a good job.

I go back downstairs to check my emails. Kendi has been busy. He'd like to call a meeting online and that works with me. I wonder what title he is giving this meeting. They all have names to suit a stage in the process, like 'disturbance meeting' or something. This is a 'truth meeting' as far as I'm concerned. I will also suggest, after the police officer has gone, that he renames it as a 'multi-agency' meeting. I have been in meetings before where the police turn up and, I have to say, they carry more gravitas than social workers and usually know their onions – unlike many of the current social workers who tend to rely on the knowledge of experienced foster carers, because they come from their degrees or step-up programmes without the full set of tools or without really ever having their knowledge tested. I do wonder if social work should be more like an apprenticeship and taken away from academia, where it tends to focus on 'pieces of work' rather than frontline activity.

It's a bit like nursing, to my mind. That was a profession that all changed when the universities got hold of it and nurses had to get a degree rather than actual experience. It's one of the reasons the NHS services aren't as good, in my opinion. Mr Blair was all about Education, Education, Education but at what cost? And perhaps, at what profit?

I email Kendi back to thank him. Then I decide to phone him. It goes to answer machine.

'I'll call you this afternoon, after Camila has seen the police lady,' I say, after the beep.

There, it's out. He will be thinking 'Louise?' and shaking his head. Sometimes this kind of 'strategy' is essential in doing the best for the children, despite what the 'process' may dictate. I get the kitchen ready for hot drinks and biscuits and the sitting room ready for confidentiality. I will hang back while they chat, Camila needs to tell her story in safety.

I pop back upstairs to give her a 20-minute heads-up about the arrival of the police.

She will, I know, want to look her best. Like so many I know, including myself, we prefer to tell our stories when we feel and look better. She is busy doing her hair. Unfortunately, in courtrooms, the victims still need to look tired and haggard or the jury might not believe them. But today Cam can celebrate the first day of that poison being out and shared for the greater good. I know I should not judge. We are not supposed to. But Gabrielle is everything that a mother should not be, as far as I am concerned. She doesn't even have the last excuse of poverty. It is clear to see that they are well off; at least looking at their home, cars, clothes and lifestyle. Even if what Cam described happened 'only once', what was she thinking? It sounds like it might have become part of the sex business plan if it had been allowed to continue.

Soon the doorbell goes, and without Dotty to bark, the house no longer has quite the welcome committee that we are used to.

A police officer appears at the appointed time, and I'm pleased to see that she is not in uniform. She looks kind. She is wearing a scarf around her neck that I suspect is her nod to formal attire. I welcome her into the kitchen.

'Cam will be down in a minute,' I say in a low, quiet voice that Cam will not hear. 'I'll call her. I just wanted you to know that I'm keen for Cam to talk to you *before* her social worker.' The emphasis is not lost on her.

She smiles. 'I understand.'

'A meeting has been scheduled which, after today, needs to become a multi-agency meeting.'

She agrees with me. I offer her a drink, switch on the coffee machine, then I call Camila.

She doesn't arrive alone, but flanked by Doug and Mabel and holding onto Mikey. I do wonder how this is going to work, but we'll see what happens. The police officer is straight in with the kitten, which is a good tactic, since both Cam and she seem to connect over the furry, little ball.

When I ask Cam if she wants a drink she asks for a hot chocolate. I walk them into the sitting room, followed by the animals, as if Camila is some kind of Dr Dolittle figure.

'Make yourselves comfortable,' I say. They sit down next to each other on the small sofa, chatting away about cats. The officer has a cat called Bruno who is a big ginger tom, apparently.

'I've had him for five years and I adore him.' Out comes the phone with pictures, lots of ooohs and awws.

'Shall I leave you both alone now?' I ask, now that they seem settled.

Camila looks at me and swallows. 'Can you stay, Louise?'

I look towards the officer.

'Yes, of course, that's absolutely fine,' she says.

I just wish I'd made myself a drink.

I sit down in the armchair facing them, with Douglas on my lap and Mabel sitting on the back of the chair. I can feel her tail flicking across my shoulder. The officer explains why she is here.

'I will be asking questions about the sexual abuse, and if you don't wish to answer, or you want to stop at any point, that's absolutely fine. I'll follow your lead.'

I suspect this won't be necessary, she is clearly an experienced and well-trained professional, who knows exactly how to lead this interview to glean as much as she can about what happened in the past.

I'm interested by her first question. 'Is your father part of this? Is he a concern to you?' I wonder if that's to eliminate him for now to get straight to the issue. Obviously, he will be complicit in some way, but for now he is not the main concern. I'm fascinated by this.

'No, I don't think he knew. I'm not sure. He wasn't there.' She pauses, then says in a rush. 'I don't think he's a bad person, just stupid.'

Well, that clears that up, and it strikes me as very astute from his teenage daughter. Even from meeting him only briefly, I would agree with her analysis. So he will be put on the back burner for now.

I sit and listen as more questions come.

'What can you remember? Take your time.'

There is no danger of confusing this with a therapy session. This is pragmatic, but kind. The police officer, whose name is Jessica, is very good. I actually feel privileged to be here: with the trust of Cam and the opportunity to observe great work. The questions get to the point. Once Jessica is at the point she wants, she is able to skilfully pull out more information.

I sit stroking Doug, learning that Cam was three or four years old when her mum began photographing her naked, then filming Cam in the bath. This is obviously not unheard of, because Jessica asks her if she remembers being asked to pose, or to touch herself. Cam's face becomes a frown, but she shakes her head, not in a way that says no, but as if she can't remember.

Jessica moves on. I suspect she will walk back to that idea. Cam does remember her mum waking her up from her sleep and walking her by her hand to another bedroom in her Grandparents' house. Jessica establishes that the grandparents were in Spain at the time. She remembers a room of people, mostly men but a couple of women too. They were all friendly. Her mum pulled her nightie off her and sat her down on a chair. Cam was only in her pants. She was passed around the adults whilst they stroked her and touched her. Her mum got up and pulled her pants off, then she was told to walk back around the room, this time bending over in front of people.

Cam begins to cry. The crying takes over her whole body, as if it will choke her. I put Doug down quickly and go to sit next to her.

To make room for me she has to shuffle closer to Jessica on the sofa, who compensates by giving her more space. I put my arm around Cam and begin to cry, too, softly, trying hard to keep it all together.

For all her professionalism, Jessica has watery eyes too. Cam's sorrow is palpable, like a heavy cloud in the room. We wait as Cam attempts to collect herself.

'Would you like to stop?' Jessica asks.

'No.' Cam cries her way through talking about how men touched her private parts, she remembers a man licking her bottom. She was told to lie down and open her legs while the adults took pictures and filmed her vagina.

I am finding this so hard to hear, despite having heard similar things before. I think of poor little Stella, and Willow, and other children I have fostered who have horror stories lurking in their history.

I hear Lloyd walk into the kitchen to make himself a coffee. He must be like a cat on a hot tin roof. He has daughters, and has looked after many foster children who have been abused. Perhaps that's statistically unsurprising given that, apparently, one in five girls are sexually abused as children – and that's only the reported cases. I know this makes him so sad, so disheartened, and also uncomfortable, as a man, because normally it's men we hear about as the perpetrators.

This time, it's a woman, and it's shocking. A privileged white woman, calling herself a mother. Our home is a sad place as this story is regaled. But this young woman isn't sad. Yes, she is crying and the process is extremely difficult, but I sense that by doing this, Cam is setting the record straight and taking control of her life. We – Lloyd and I, and Sian and Gary, will do all that we can to help her.

This is enough for now.

I can see that Jessica is gently bringing things to a close, at least for now. I suspect she has enough to do something with, mainly to make sure that Cam does not have to see her mother and father. Cam will know that we can keep her safe now.

Jessica ends the conversation by changing the subject back to kittens. Mikey has been fast asleep on Cam's lap the whole time. Thank the lord for Mikey who, I have no doubt, has made this experience much more bearable for Camila.

I suggest that Cam might need to feed and water and let Mikey have a wee in his litter tray. Jessica thanks Cam for being brave and wonderful. Cam holds Mikey up to her face for comfort, but I see her smile. This is a big day for Cam.

We wait for her to go upstairs, and I don't speak until I hear her door close. Jessica and I walk closer to the front door to talk without being heard.

'Do you think you can get a message to her social worker – and ours – today, to let them know that you have spoken to Cam?'

She nods.

I also tell her that Sarah is planning to come over in the afternoon to talk to Cam.

Jessica smiles. 'She won't, don't worry. I'll send an email and cc you and Lloyd, and then submit my initial report. This is a serious allegation and we'll need to investigate. I would imagine that film footage and photographs of Cam would have been circulated on the dark web among the paedophile groups. We have people who can find them and, once we do, we can arrest her mother. Until then we keep talking and, if Cam thinks of anything else, let me know. She has my card but might not feel comfortable calling me directly.'

It's a 'victory' in a sense, but I don't know how I feel. And, right now, how I feel doesn't matter. I say goodbye to Jessica and pop in to see Lloyd and share what I have learnt. He hangs his head and cries the tears of a kind father, who suffers every time something like this happens, as I'm sure do many good men. With this situation, Cam's father is complicit somehow, even by ignorance. Gabrielle is not going to get away with any of this and I can tell that her daughter will be the one to make sure she doesn't.

The day seems lighter; the atmosphere is cleaner somehow. I know this isn't all over, and there are going to be days that are very challenging for Camila and, I suspect, her brother, too. But for now, there is light.

I look at my phone a little while later and there is a message from Sarah saying she has cancelled this afternoon. Good news. I walk to my laptop and fire it up. There it is, the email I had hoped to see from Jessica to Kendi and Sarah, outlining the gist of her conversation with Cam and detailing what will happen next. Importantly, Camila does not need to see her parents. They are going to be questioned and investigated. Already an image has been found of Camila as a younger child that has raised the threshold of the case. Unfortunately, it was easy to find.

Kendi calls to see how we are. Yes, lovely Kendi genuinely cares.

I sigh. 'We've been here before and will recover. And

we kind of know what to do, although I'm not sure that's a good thing.'

A big part of me wishes that the world was just a better place and we didn't have to be in this position.

'But I'm pleased that Sarah isn't coming,' I tell Kendi.

I don't share with him the strategy Sian and I have cooked up about getting Cam home. Like making art, sometimes it's best not to reveal our secrets. I do take the opportunity to sow the seed and say to Kendi that we think that the best thing that can happen for Camila is to go back to her family, her former foster family.

'I think she's homesick,' I say, 'that's where her heart is.'

I play down everything else. Sometimes we just need to nudge.

'I agree with you, Louise. But how would you feel about Cam leaving you?'

'Nothing would make us happier. And I mean that in the best possible way.'

I phone the school each day to say that Camila isn't coming in. I also ask Sarah cc'ing Kendi and Jessica, to ask her to speak to the school directly about Cam's absence; this really is not Camila's fault.

On Thursday Sian and I arrange to meet in a café near her MP's office. It's in the main town, over an hour's drive away. I park up and put money in the ticket machine, lock the car and try to find Poppins Café. I pull my phone out of my bag to check that Sian is still coming and see a message from her.

Good news, Camila is coming home to us. I'm in the café.

I won't get to meet her MP after all.

Afterword

Mikey, the kitten, went with Camila, before we had a chance to take him to the vets to have his second injection. The vet announced that Mikey is a girl – which was exciting news for Camila. She was thrilled that she had a girl cat. Mikey is now Molly.

We weren't sad to see Camila and Molly go. Far from it. We were excited for her. This was what was meant to happen. She should never have been taken away from Sian and Gary. They would have worked through her behaviour, which was triggered by the urge to reunite her with her parents, if only they had been given the time to do so, and the right support. Which would have meant the social services team being brave and sensible.

It's one of many ways that we currently seem to be failing children in care: the number of apparently safe, happy children in solid placements who seem, from around the age of 12 years upwards, to be making their way back to their birth families, perhaps as part of a cost-cutting exercise. It seems to me to be the ones who are settled and well-adjusted, because the foster carers have shown them love and security. Perhaps they are the ones deemed by the services to be the most resilient.

They are a very different proposition from the children who have been pinged around the system and are likely to cause more problems if they go back and will, in reality, only end up costing more. I have no idea of the statistics nationally, but of late I have encountered too many children to whom this is happening.

We found the 'source' of Cam's behaviour and now know that it was far more serious than the authorities realised years ago, when she and her brother were first taken away from their mother and father. A mother who was using her daughter for profit, and a father who was too brow-beaten and weak to fight for his children, while suffering from cocaine abuse. The drug addiction doesn't excuse anything, but it does explain some of it. Cocaine is, in my view, a large part of what's wrong with the world. New research suggests that cocaine abuse compromises an individual's ability to make moral decisions and impacts how they view right from wrong.

But that is all in the past.

I still don't know quite what happened for Cam's future to fall into place so easily after such a difficult time. I guess that Jessica pulled a few strings, as did Kendi. Perhaps the situation with Sarah changed in part because she didn't want the attention on her to publicly expose her affair. She is still Cam's social worker. Sian and Gary suggested to Cam that perhaps she is better off with 'the devil you know'. Sian tells me that Cam hasn't smeared or head-banged in a long time and that she is sticking out school until she can leave and go to a college to do her A Levels. She won't stay at that school for their sixth form. She needs a fresh start.

Camila hated school so much. And she's not alone.

The more I go on working with young people deemed 'challenging', the more I wonder if we have the schooling system the wrong way round. Over 53% of children are neurodivergent. That's your mainstream, run of the mill neurodivergence, not including the increasing numbers of children born with fetal alcohol and drug damage which is permanent, or the neurodivergence caused by trauma.

For so many children, not just those from care, what they perceive as 'petty' rules detract from the experience of learning. There are a growing number of children who have undiagnosed neurodivergence or Fetal Alcohol Spectrum Disorder (FASD). I've written at length about FASD elsewhere: a group of birth defects caused by a mother's alcohol consumption during pregnancy. FASD is one of the hardest to spot, because it's not just about easy-to-see facial signs, like a slopey ear, or a smooth area between the nose and upper lip, or a smaller than average head size. It has many nuances, many of which are far less obvious, and relate to learning needs. And that's just one example beyond children in care. The sensory needs of all children are so variable. I can't understand why we still insist on putting them in a single room together to learn and expect them all to be 'well-behaved'. It's not possible for them to conform to a neurotypical, adult version of what well-behaved looks like when their brains are doing and saying other things entirely.

There are catch-all terms like 'sensory overload' and so, to address this, there is a school of thought (forgive the pun) that assumes that a silent school will solve the problem.

It won't.

Because so many children with ADHD or FASD need a bit of white noise in the background. That might be one earphone in, listening to music very quietly. It can be hugely beneficial, but it isn't allowed. The ignorance around this subject is failing so many of our children.

Gabrielle and Robbie split up. This was long overdue, I suspect, and Gabrielle faces a prison sentence. Further evidence of child sexual abuse was found. Robbie admitted that he was coked up for most of that time and is now in therapy. He is trying hard to build a relationship with his children, neither of them are rushing towards that. Cam is in weekly therapy. Jessica pulled a few strings there, and somehow Sarah got funding for Cam to go private and avoid CAMHS (because painting a horse's bum was never going to cut it). Josh is able to see much more of his sister and comes to Sian and Gary's for sleepovers. They have a good time together. Slowly the family is knitting itself back together. Josh is in a small residential home that he loves and doesn't want to move. He's getting on well at school and has the option of therapy, too. He doesn't remember much from that time; he was very young, but the support is there if he wants it.

I always felt with Cam that she was on a mission to create some level of justice in the world, and in her own life. She is a pretty wise young woman. I suspect with the love and support of Sian and Gary, she will continue to thrive.

We are so glad that we met Camila. Sometimes things are just meant to be.